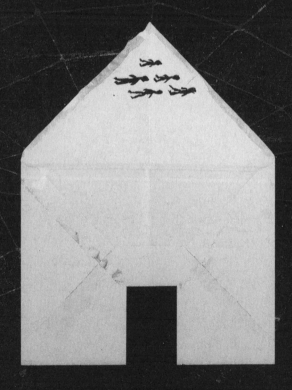

DEY ST.
An Imprint of WILLIAM MORROW

the SPIDER

and the

FLY

A Writer,

a Murderer, and a

Story of Obsession

Claudia Rowe

DEY ST.

HarperCollins books may be purchased for educational, business, or sales pro-
motional use. For information, please email the Special Markets Department at
SPsales@harpercollins.com.

A hardcover edition of this book was published in 2017 by Dey Street Books, an
imprint of William Morrow Publishers.

FIRST DEY STREET BOOKS PAPERBACK EDITION PUBLISHED 2017.

Book design by Paula Russell Szafranski
Title page design by Owen Corrigan
Title page images: © Victor Cea / Alamy Stock Photo (envelope); © Feng Yu /
Alamy Stock Photo (web); © iStock / Getty Images (background)

The Library of Congress has catalogued a previous edition as follows:

Names: Rowe, Claudia, 1966– author.
Title: The spider and the fly : a reporter, a serial killer, and the meaning of a
murder / Claudia Rowe.
Description: First edition. | New York, NY : Dey Street, [2017]
Identifiers: LCCN 2016036818| ISBN 9780062416124 (hardcover) | ISBN
  9780062656599 (are trade pb) | ISBN 9780062497628 (large print) | ISBN
  9780062416131 (trade pb) | ISBN 9780062564139 (audio)
Subjects: LCSH: Francois, Kendall, 1971–2014. | Francois, Kendall,
  1971–2014—Psychology. | Rowe, Claudia, 1966– | Serial murderers—New York
  (State)—Case studies. | Serial murders—New York
  (State)—Poughkeepsie—Case studies.
Classification: LCC HV6248.F664 R69 2017 | DDC 364.152/32092—dc23 LC
record available at https://lccn.loc.gov/2016036818

ISBN 978-0-06-241613-1 (pbk.)

17 18 19 20 21 LSC 10 9 8 7 6 5 4 3 2 1

For my family

Contents

1	The Weight of Paper	1
2	99 Fulton Avenue	7
3	When Night Falls	31
4	Tricks of the Trade	41
5	The Final Insult	59
6	Strange Town	71
7	As If We Were Friends	95
8	Close to Home	115
9	Evidence of Things Not Seen	137
10	Man and Monster	153
11	Solitaire	167
12	U-Turns	191
13	Ghost Story	203
14	A Day in the Life	219
15	One of Our Own	235
16	The Face in the Mirror	247
17	Discharged	259
	Epilogue	271
	Acknowledgments	275
	Author's Note	277

"Will you walk into my parlour?" said the Spider to the Fly,
"'Tis the prettiest little parlour that ever you did spy;
The way into my parlour is up a winding stair,
And I have many curious things to show when you are there."

"Oh no, no," said the little Fly, "To ask me is in vain,
For who goes up your winding stair can ne'er come down again."

Said the cunning Spider to the Fly, "Dear friend, what can I do,
To prove the warm affection I've always felt for you?
I have within my pantry, good store of all that's nice;
I'm sure you're very welcome—will you please to take a slice?"

"Oh no, no," said the little Fly, "Kind sir, that cannot be,
I've heard what's in your pantry, and I do not wish to see!"

"Sweet creature!" said the Spider, "You're witty and you're wise,
How handsome are your gauzy wings, how brilliant are your eyes!
I've a little looking-glass upon my parlour shelf,
If you'll step in one moment, dear, you shall behold yourself."

"I thank you, gentle sir," she said, "For what you're pleased to say,
And bidding you good morning now, I'll call another day."

The Spider turned him round about, and went into his den,
For well he knew the silly Fly would soon come back again:
So he wove a subtle web, in a little corner sly,
And set his table ready, to dine upon the Fly.

—From "The Spider and the Fly" by Mary Howitt (1829)

CHAPTER 1

The Weight of Paper

The door to the Pleasant Valley post office pulled against me as if trying to test my resolve. To swing it wide and begin my dutiful march down the white linoleum floor toward mailbox number 1273 required surprising strength. But I did it, as I had all autumn. I trudged past a wall of small steel doors, each little square a portal to someone's story, identical and indistinct, save for what they held inside: money owed or confessions rendered, forced gestures or pleas unheard, a small universe of private histories locked within those cold metal facings. Boxy and prefab, the post office huddled next to the oldest building in town on a cracked parking lot surrounded by chain supermarkets. Across the street, a feed store and a garage for heavy-equipment repair sat like comfortable old armchairs for the farmers who came into town once a month. But the car dealerships and pizza shops were what blinked loudest to the drivers snaking past in a never-ending line toward somewhere else.

Unpleasant Valley, I liked to call my middle patch of village between the city of Poughkeepsie and Dutchess County's hunt country estates, reminding myself that I was an interloper here. I'd arrived five years before, hired in 1994 as a reporter for the *Poughkeepsie Journal* to hound the teachers union and sift school budgets for waste. I quit after twenty-two months, yet remained in town. I could not say why. To friends, I talked of open fields and the country life. But that was only part of the reason. Something about the city of Poughkeepsie, with its melancholy streets and stubborn boosterism, nagged like a blister.

It was November, and I shivered at the stuffy warmth as I walked toward the back of the building. My mailbox was in the last bank of little locked doors, second row from the bottom. A mural painted on the wall opposite showed bonneted farm wives greeting one another in the market square, baskets clutched in the crook of their elbows, implying that Pleasant Valley had once been a bustling village. I slunk past them in disgrace. The only thing I carried was shame, pounds of shame. I was ashamed to be living here, whiling away my thirties. Ashamed to be sleepwalking through life like I was waiting for a wave to pick me up and rush me to the shores of someplace else. Ashamed to have initiated the quest that brought me to the post office every day in hopes of connecting with a figment, a phantom. Week after week, my box remained empty except for a few free circulars, shoved inside like reprimands.

I wondered if the mail sorters pitied me. I could glimpse them behind the wall, their stout shoulders working like levers to slot each envelope into its assigned bin, fingers capped with pink rubber thimbles. They surely knew no letter ever came for number 1273, though it might be worse if one did. I cringed at the thought of anyone recognizing the return address. There would be no blur of bills and magazines to camouflage my correspondent. I had rented this box for one person alone.

In these final weeks of the twentieth century, mail still carried a discreet sensuality. Another person had touched the page you were now holding, had folded and creased it, then slid the rectangle between thumb and index finger, pushed it into an envelope, and licked the gummy backing. That person had pressed the outside flap down and run his finger along the edge. He had held the envelope in his hands, a whisper of the unknown inside, and determined that it should be sent. For this reason, I'd done my best to avoid the postmistress who jawed with customers when they came by at lunchtime to pick up their packages. But now I was prepared. I'd practiced my pitch, sitting amid the crumpled coffee cups and rotting newspapers in my car. I needed to close my mailbox, cancel my account, and get a refund for the remaining four months of my rental, I'd say. I earned near-poverty wages as a stringer for the *New York Times,* so a hundred wasted dollars hurt. None of these flinty folk were likely to question the need to save money. They drove rusty trucks and salt-pocked American cars, though their family names dotted my county road maps. Whatever the manager said, this would be my last visit to the Pleasant Valley post office. I was worn out writing to someone who never wrote back.

At the beginning I'd been almost jaunty about this project, as if it were a game I knew I'd win. As if all I had to do was swing by and collect my prize. That vain assumption dissolved into confusion after a second letter met with continued silence. Now the feeling verged on humiliation. My chest was hollow with the ache of ridiculousness as I slid my key into the lock for one last look. I would pull out a final round of inky coupons, dump them in the overflowing garbage can, and be done.

But no. Lying inside the narrow steel slot was a single cream-colored envelope, the paper stock textured and substantial. I paused, staring at my name and address scrawled in rounded cursive across the front. Shaking just a bit, I tore it open.

Mrs. (Ms.) Claudia Rowe

Greetings, I would like to thank you for your letter, but you know as well as I do that you don't want to be my friend. You want a story. I'm feeling generous, so if your on the ball this may be your lucky day. I don't need to make friends with some one that will later betray me. So here is the deal.

I want to know everything about you, everything. For every ten pages (typed) I will answer ANY four questions you have for me, completely and honestly. So twenty pages gets you eight questions, but nineteen only gets you four.

I will answer your questions with the completeness and honesty you answer me. I want to know about your hometown, childhood house, elementary school and high school up through college, your first car, your first kiss, the dress you wore under your graduation gown, I want to know the first time (if ever) you gave a guy a blow job, the first time you had intercourse, the last time, people you hate at work, affairs, when (if ever) you dyed your hair, the types of computers you have/use. Remember the more details the better.

This isn't an article for a newspaper so don't write it like it is. It should have some heart, a spark. If it is cold and indifferent I may think you're lying. If I think it is a lie there will be no response.

Good evening!
Kendall Francois

The two pages of legal-sized paper were covered top to bottom, from the left margin all the way to the edge of the opposite side. The handwriting was concentrated, childlike, but each word had been carefully formed and there were no cross-outs or squeezed-in afterthoughts. It suggested someone working with great determination and control. I read the letter once standing in the back of the post office, then drove home, shoved it under a stack of books, and did not touch it again for two weeks.

CHAPTER 2

99 Fulton Avenue

T he first rule of reporting is that the writer is never the story, so my tale, by definition, is not journalism. But that is where it began. The desk where I stashed Kendall's letter was an old office table with steel legs and a polyurethane top made to look like wood. My landlord had hauled it out of his garage as a loaner. I lived above the garage, in a tree-house apartment with my boyfriend, Derrick, the person from whom I was hiding this envelope. A curious deception, as Derrick had been the one to goad me into covering this story to begin with. Every night he came home from reporting environmental news at the *Journal,* grousing about the paper's refusal to run anything longer than a brief after two women had vanished. Then three. Then four, and still hardly a word. I had left the newsroom by then, and I saw their inky faces on missing-person flyers taped to storefronts and lampposts, smudged by weather and time, their gazes defiant, distant, drugged. But not until the summer of 1998, after seven women had disappeared, did I pick up the phone.

My first call went to Marguerite Marsh because, of all the missing women, her daughter looked the most approachable. Marguerite's voice was thin and weary as she spoke to me from her home in Schenectady, an hour's drive north, but she answered all of my indelicate questions about Catherine—her hobbies and sports teams, favorite songs and unrealized promise. I nudged toward the relationship between mother and daughter, street life and addiction. Being a reporter allowed you to do such things, to barge into strangers' lives with authority, as if you had the right. This always felt like fraud to me, but victims bowed to it every time. Most were already accustomed to intrusion—from social service agencies and court personnel, hospitals and police—and if not exactly comfortable with the process, they acquiesced. After Marguerite, I called Pat Barone, mother of Gina, and James DeSalvo, brother of Kathleen Hurley. I called boyfriends and detectives and finally, I called an editor at the *Times*.

"What's going on up there?" he asked amiably. I'd just finished nine months of babysitting a libel trial notable for one lawyer who demonstrated part of his argument by lying on the courtroom floor, writhing. After that came a domestic violence case that spurred our district attorney to seek the death penalty. My next story concerned a religious cult in the mountains above Woodstock. I was becoming a reliable source of country quirk for the Metro desk. They were always happy to hear from me.

"I'm not sure. I mean, I'm not sure there's a story. Women keep being reported missing in Poughkeepsie—a lot of women. I've made a few calls. But it's been going on for a couple of years."

"Keep digging," said the editor. "And check back with me when you've got more."

I BECAME A reporter because I thought it would teach me to write. Journalism would instill discipline, which I lacked. It would force me to structure my rambling attempts to make sense of the world. It would help me develop focus and clarity, pin down what was real. In that area, I had problems. Everything felt meaningful, the intuited even more than the proven, the rumored as much as the visible. And I cared too much about all of it. Possessed of a lacerating anger that attached itself to every story, I never tried to untangle the genesis of this sensitivity. Instead, I told myself the fire would lend power and energy to my work. Which it had. In my first newspaper job I arrived at my desk by six A.M., and spent weekends off tracking delinquents. I ran down a teenager who'd scrawled swastikas outside a string of Jewish businesses in the Bronx and came up with a portrait of a metal-head dropout that crowned me the New York Press Association's Rookie Reporter of 1992. I talked my way into legal archives where I had no business, and uncovered the dissolute past of a city school board member who'd been the getaway driver for a failed teacher-assassination plot. All of it chasing answers to the question I never spoke aloud. "You want to know what makes people do the things they do? You want to understand motivation?" said my first editor, cutting to the heart of the matter. "Cover schools."

No pitch could have hit harder. Whether they were in classrooms or jail cells, or standing on street corners, I ran down the misbegotten and reviled to measure the distance between us and find my way toward comprehension, if not forgiveness. I was not much good at forgiving. But journalism at least allowed me to interview and dissect my fears, flattening human mystery into twenty inches of type.

* * *

THE INSTANT I stepped off the train in Poughkeepsie's sooty old railroad station to start my second newspaper job, I knew I'd made a mistake. The *Poughkeepsie Journal* had hired me as its education writer, and at the time, being wanted meant more than who was asking, so I'd ignored the tight flutter of foreboding in my throat, boxed up my dishes and furniture, and joined a dozen other would-be writers in a grimy newsroom where rainwater leaked from the ceiling. We pecked at our keyboards, churning out stubbornly cheery tales from the center of a dead-end town and focused the bulk of our coverage on the suburbs. Crime reports came on press releases faxed by the police department. We maintained a list of blacks to quote so the *Journal* might appear representative of all its readers. And we tiptoed around scandal. Few with money appeared in our pages against their wishes. Nor did the questionable practices of any government official. Not until the city's personnel manager was gunned down in her church parking lot and the tax assessor was found floating in the Hudson River did the *Journal* run a few stories indicating that life in Poughkeepsie might not be precisely as we'd suggested. Even then, you had to read between the lines. The *Journal* managed to sanitize a municipal assassination and attempted suicide, a federal investigation, rampant drug addiction, and the endless drip of low-level corruption.

This polite approach suited Dutchess County, which surrounds the city of Poughkeepsie like a wreath and rates among the most picturesque landscapes in America. In autumn, when scarlet oak leaves rustled in the golden light, it was difficult to argue the presence of a divine plan. Here was a land of horse farms and gracious estates, of winding roads and old stone walls that skirted gently sloping fields. The Vanderbilts and Roosevelts had built their family estates just north of town, and it seemed perfectly reasonable—if you averted your gaze—to believe evil was a universe away. Far be it for the newspaper to say different. Once a year the country gentry of Dutchess might steel themselves to visit the city for a Christmastime benefit at the old vaudeville theater, but they otherwise avoided Poughkeepsie as you would a dead animal lying in the road. Who could blame them? The place was a pockmark, a blotch of stale-smelling bars and bulk-discount stores where broken-down homes crowded together like bad teeth. Main Street was all but deserted, even on the sunniest afternoons, because every thoroughfare had been built to whisk drivers away, toward the gleaming mall just south or the Catskill Mountains beyond. But young men still slouched along the arterial, hands jammed into pants pockets, chins jutting forward.

A WEEK AFTER phoning Marguerite Marsh about her daughter I was sitting in Poughkeepsie's police station, ready to interview the chief of detectives about the lingering mystery of Poughkeepsie's missing women. But as soon as I walked into his office, Lieutenant Bill Siegrist shrugged and told me it was all over.

"What do you mean over?"

"Solved. Last night," Siegrist said, sounding more exhausted than satisfied. He reached for the hotel bell perched on the corner of his desk and dinged it eight times for eight cases, now closed. "Investigation complete. Guy we arrested is called Kendall Francois." It was an exotic name for Poughkeepsie, and Siegrist uttered it with a mocking lilt.

At the bright little noise, Detective Skip Mannain popped in, snapping a wad of chewing gum and grinning like he'd just won a Super Bowl bet. His eyes gave me a cool up-and-down. "Talk to you when you're done here," he said to the lieutenant.

Poughkeepsie's chief investigator exuded none of Mannain's swagger. At fifty, Siegrist's skin retained the pinkish look of a schoolboy scrubbed clean. He preferred early mornings to night duty, Lipton tea over coffee, and his greatest professional gratification came not from recounting heroic arrests but recalling particulars from cases solved long before he'd joined the police force. The Human Encyclopedia, his men snickered. When the district attorney dumped out cartons of old crime scene photos, Siegrist spent an afternoon fishing through the garbage bin, retrieving hundreds to restore at his own expense. They hung in tidy frames around the office, vintage black-and-whites showing a busy Main Street that no longer existed. Siegrist was milder than any cop I'd ever encountered. He was also the first to note my resemblance to Kendall's victims.

"Ninety-nine Fulton Avenue," he said, scribbling the address on a scrap of paper and ushering me out the door.

I hurried into the morning sunshine, dialing the *Times* Metro desk as I tore across town. My destination was a surprise, within sight of Vassar College on a quiet, tree-lined street. I'd passed through this neighborhood many times. Two blocks away skinny women darted between cars, selling ten-dollar blow jobs. But Fulton Avenue felt far from their tawdry commerce. Residents here were professionals, doctors and academics living above well-trimmed lawns crowned with generous porches. The Francois home, however, looked nothing like its neighbors. A sickly mint green, it sat back from the sidewalk atop a few cracked steps, its windows opaque with dirt. An enormous oak had grown into one of the side walls, and even crawling with investigators the house exuded a sense of isolation, as if trying to recede from view. It was easy, perhaps preferable, to ignore.

That was impossible now. Police had roped off the entire block from traffic. Media thronged driveways up and down the street. Teachers accustomed to using Fulton Avenue as a cut-through to their jobs at the elementary school were forced to detour. But mothers ferrying children to the pediatrician across the street were hastily waved along, kids twisting toward us in their car seats. We surged toward the Francois family's crumbling stoop like blood cells coagulating at the site of a wound.

I knew how a house could both absorb and exude pain, how memories seeped into floorboards and hung from the rafters over a bed. But describing such impressions was the furthest thing from my job. Journalism channeled every energy toward what was concrete. The psychological had little purchase. As print report-ers we'd all been warned about waning newspaper readership; our only hope for survival, said an army of consultants, was to provide the "context and analysis" that television could not. Yet journal-ism in Poughkeepsie remained primarily an exercise in dictation, stitching together opposing quotes from warring parties with deft transitional phrases. All of my time at the *Journal* I'd been loath to acknowledge this factory work. I wrote earnest stories that made forgotten people feel noticed for a day, and thought I'd done something that mattered, despite my boyfriend's observation that the newspaper's only value was in supermarket coupon delivery. Reporters were not real writers, he frequently reminded me. We were hacks, drones, information bulldozers. But staring up at the Francoises' front porch that sultry September morning, blood in my veins turning to ice water, I knew I was looking at a story that would prove Derrick wrong. It felt as if every mistake in my life had been pushing me toward this moment.

Skin and skulls and old clothes, résumés and feces and broken dishes—all of it came tumbling out of the Francoises' drab colonial. Children's pajama bottoms intertwined with old brassieres had to be peeled off a floor sticky with rot. Ripped panty hose lay among used condoms. Decayed food, torn insulation, and broken baby furniture crowded attic steps in a stairwell where the wallpaper was tacky with grime. Chicken bones were scattered everywhere. In the upstairs bathroom, a tube of toothpaste balanced on the edge of a sink overflowing with maggots. Their shells clogged the toilet. The police kept track of everything, a jumble of evidence tangled in cat hair and filth, but there was no sense to any of it and their records, like the home itself, made an unsettling collage. Schoolbooks and soiled underwear in the kitchen. Handwritten love letters next to rape counseling pamphlets. Syringes and a tear gas canister nestled alongside family photos.

Kendall's father, McKinley, used an oily sofa in the living room as his bed. There he reclined, staring at a mantel still hung with Christmas stockings, though it was late summer. On an end table near his head lay a letter addressed to Kendall's mother, Paulette, written by a woman who described being raped and beaten by the couple's son. McKinley spent hours in the basement at night, where a washer-dryer stood along one wall and a child's bike leaned against a mountain of old boxes. A metal chair had been placed beneath a crawl space for easy access, and inside that dim tomb, Kendall placed his sixth, seventh, and eighth victims. Sandra French lay with her feet wrapped in plastic baggies, knees open as if giving birth, next to Audrey Pugliese, who still wore her Support Can Be Beautiful bra. Audrey was heavier than the others, and she'd fought harder. Kendall had to stomp her throat to end it. Exhausted afterward, he'd left her slumped in a corner for hours. Later, he pushed Audrey into the hole next to Sandy, and a week afterward slid tiny Catina Newmaster on top.

Upstairs in the kitchen, where a bare bulb gave off a bit of light, towers of crusted dishware leaned against pots wriggling with bugs. Unconnected wires hung from the ceiling like vines. Kendall's younger sister, Kierstyn, slept nearby, in a back room littered with pornographic magazines, men's underwear, condom wrappers, rubber gloves, and a roll of duct tape. Her mattress—where Kendall raped, but did not kill, a series of women—sat on the floor amid hair scrunchies and maggot casings that rained down from the ceiling. Police said later that at night while she lay awake, Kierstyn thought it looked like the walls were alive.

On the second floor, Kendall might be listening to educational tapes ("How to Study Better and Faster") or reading *Star Wars* books or watching his stack of porn videos. It was only him and his mother up there now, and Kendall did most of his sleeping down the hall in his younger brother Aubrey's vacated bed. His childhood room was where Kendall murdered women. He left Sandra French—at fifty-one, just a year younger than Paulette—lying dead on his Mickey Mouse comforter as he dressed for school and softly closed the door behind him.

IN THE WEE hours of September 2, 1998, as I lay sleeping next to Derrick, Kendall had been flipping through a stapled-together sheaf of mug shots. He knew them all, these cheating faithless women, and he tore off several pictures: Wendy Meyers, Gina Barone, Catherine Marsh, and Sandra French. He pushed them into a neat pile and placed his hand on top. "I killed them. I did it," he said, sounding like the matter was really quite tedious, like taking out the garbage or gassing up your car. The other photos he set aside. He'd get to them later. State Police investigator Art Boyko offered a second notebook, this one filled with pictures of black women, but Kendall shook his head. "I don't need that. There's nobody in there."

"Now, when I first came in," said Assistant District Attorney Marjorie Smith, narrating her last seven hours with Kendall for the spinning tape, "what was the first thing you asked to see? You wanted to see some pictures?"

"Yeah, pictures of prostitutes."

"Okay," said Smith, ticking off the names of the women Kendall had selected. "How do you know them?"

"I killed them."

This prosecutor Smith seemed nervous as hell, he thought. But at least she was polite, sort of like a bank teller. He liked that. Nice manners, never acted displeased with anything he said. Though by the time he pronounced his name for her tape recorder—repeating his story for what seemed like the sixth time that night—he'd grown irritable and bored, spelling out the words letter by letter, like Smith and that square-jawed investigator next to her didn't already know who he was. They were such dopes, the cops. It was a wonder anyone stayed safe. They'd made him reiterate the same dull sequence all afternoon and through the evening and now, into the early morning hours of the following day. He never changed his tale, never asked for a lawyer. Officially, he didn't need to tell them any of this. But he knew he had to take charge now. It was time.

After killing someone, there was no thunderbolt that shot through you. No sense that God had seen and would rain down his punishment, as he'd always supposed. Killing wasn't like that at all. There were details to be handled, bones that wouldn't fit into bins, bodies that needed to be cut and folded, mess to be contained. But that was just manual labor, like shoveling snow.

"What's her name?" the prosecutor said sharply, tapping her nails on the photo of a woman with large liquid eyes and a heart-shaped face. Smith knew her from a half-dozen street busts and from prosecuting her boyfriend. She'd watched as Wendy lost custody of her son, and she would make Kendall say this woman's name out loud. She would make him remember every one.

"Wendy Meyers. I killed her."

She was one of the first he'd been with after returning from the army. Enlisting was such a stupid decision, though it made sense at the time, a way to escape 99 Fulton Avenue and earn money for college. He'd made friends on the base like he always did, delighting the white boys with his *Star Trek* impressions, his skill at games.

"What kind of discharge did you get, Kendall?" asked Smith.

"Honorable," he sighed.

Army brass picked on him from the day one, sneering as he stepped onto their scales, grimacing as the technicians spread their calipers to measure his fat. Failure. Always failure. The red flags screaming "overweight" clung to his record month after month until they'd finally booted him. "Obesity," the discharge papers said. Then it was back to Poughkeepsie and his parents' house, with just a few thousand dollars. No college, no job. Though he did have ideas.

He met Wendy on Main Street. She was pretty, with that long brown hair, and reliable, always working so she could get high with her boyfriend later in the motel where they lived across the river. Kendall marveled at all the people his army earnings went to support—hundreds of dollars a week he was doling out. And what did these women do with his hard-earned money, his hopes for love? Stole from him, ran from him, bought drugs to do in hotel rooms while lying in bed with other men.

Anything remarkable about Wendy? the prosecutor was asking, and now he was going to have to tell how she'd humiliated him like all the rest.

"She ripped me off," Kendall whispered. He chose not to mention that he'd been diagnosed with HIV shortly after their first time together.

Wendy was one in a long series of women who'd shamed him, he told Smith. They'd promise sex, he'd hand over cash, and the women would skitter away. Wendy did it twice. He tried to chase her, wheezing down Main Street as the other whores pointed and laughed. The last time, Wendy was sitting in his bedroom yapping that she had to leave for some appointment with probation, like he was stupid, a fool for her, a buffoon. It was always this way, he thought, women whining to get something from him, then lying to get away.

"Why, Kendall?" Smith asked.

"Why?"

"Why did you want to kill Wendy Meyers?"

How could he explain—why should he? He wasn't even sure he knew, not in any way that made horse sense, as his grandmother might say. His mind was wandering all over the place, to memories and blankness, to nights in his attic and the death chamber that would surely follow after today. Anywhere but this little gray room.

"I didn't originally," he stammered. "I guess I got mad about it and started choking her—I didn't want to get ripped off again—and once it had gone to that point I figured there was no turning back."

Wendy fought hard. He wasn't even sure he'd finished her when the upstairs bathroom occurred to him. It was the only one where the water still worked. He laid her in the tub and turned on the faucets, staring down as Wendy's leg twitched.

"Then you put her in the attic?" the prosecutor said, leading him. It was better that way, when she asked the questions and he could simply answer yes or no.

"Yes," he said.

"Where is she now, Kendall?"

"She's in the attic."

He was such a lump. Smith could see why all these women had hated him as a customer. She kept thinking of that fat Professor Klump from the Eddie Murphy movies. A 350-pound slob, crushing women who might go days without a meal. If her life had gone according to plan, she wouldn't be talking to this grotesque man at all. Hell, she'd studied business in school, planned to become a labor lawyer, worked summers in a bank. She was no investigator. Yet here she sat, interviewing a guy who talked about watching women die in his bathtub.

"Why'd you keep at it, Kendall?"

"I don't know, it seemed easier than getting into a relationship."

The secret to talking with killers, Smith knew, was believing in the fundamental commonality of all people. Of course you weren't the same. You'd come from different places, made different choices. But Smith could usually fool herself long enough to bridge the gap and get what she needed. She was probing for such a bond with Kendall—they'd grown up in the same county, attended the same high school and college—but it wasn't going well. She could not keep herself focused. Could not get past this enormous man confessing to these enormous crimes like they were no more significant than a trip to the grocery store. And she knew she'd be judged. Years later, when law students and criminologists listened to her interviewing this murderer, Smith knew she'd be found wanting.

Kendall had picked up Gina Barone one cold autumn night on the arterial highway that cut through town past old warehouses and abandoned buildings. He had seen her out there for years. But she was ugly, often rude, too high most of the time to be much use. Gina was other things as well—a mother, a Poughkeepsie High School dropout, a girl who'd met her father only once, after searching all over Yonkers to find him—but all Kendall knew was that Gina stood out there, night after night, waiting for partyers from Confetti's nightclub to stumble past. She saw him, waved toward a vacant lot, and hopped into the backseat of Kendall's red Subaru, pulling off her pants as he climbed in behind. Immediately, she began to complain. Kendall was too heavy. He took too long to climax, and she wanted to get high. Bitch, bitch, bitch—and he was paying her! Stupid whore in her dirty sweater, finding fault with his performance—like *she* was the boss.

"How'd that make you feel, Kendall?"

Again, these questions he couldn't answer. Most of the time he hardly knew what he'd felt—forget about describing it for this white woman.

"I was kind of upset because I didn't like her anyway," he said.

"So how come you picked her up that night?"

"She was working."

"What happened next?"

"I started choking her."

It hadn't taken long, two or three minutes, until Gina passed out. Then he could get on top and bang away without listening to her mouth. That worked for a while, until Gina woke up.

"And what happened when she woke up, Kendall?"

"I choked her," he said, matter-of-factly. This time, he acknowledged, it took much longer—five or six minutes—before Gina went limp.

"What ended it?" Smith was asking. "Why did you stop?"

"She stopped moving."

With Gina half-clothed and collapsed across his backseat, Kendall drove to his parents' home. In their driveway, he pulled Gina from the car, heaved her into the trunk, and quietly closed the lid. She lay inside as Kendall ferried his mother to work early the next morning, then returned to pick up his sister and bring her to school. That night, he dragged Gina's body out and flung it into a corner of the garage, pulling an old mattress down on top. Fall turned to winter, Thanksgiving slid into Christmas, and Gina remained curled on the Francoises' floor. In April, as the trees began to unfurl lacy leaves, a snowstorm hit. There was one nearly every spring in Dutchess County, always something to push you back into the cold and remind you nothing came easy. The snow lay so heavy on those baby leaves that branches crashed to the ground all over Poughkeepsie. At 99 Fulton Avenue, an entire tree fell onto the Francoises' garage and lay on the roof for months, like an arrow pointing the way. By early summer, Kendall's parents began to talk about repairing the damage, so he hauled Gina's stiff corpse from the building and carried it upstairs, dumping her in the attic like broken furniture. Wendy Meyers and Catherine Marsh were already there.

"When—" Smith fumbled. "How were you feeling when— What were you thinking about— What were you feeling when you had your hands around Gina's neck?" There, she'd finally said it.

"I wasn't thinking anything," Kendall answered.

"Happy? Sad? Mad?"

No psychologist, Smith was nonetheless interested in the ways a mind worked. It mattered little to her courtroom strategy, but Kendall had asked to speak with a prosecutor, which made her a witness, so she wouldn't be trying this case anyway, and she was curious about what went on inside his head.

"How did you feel?" Smith asked again.

"Mad."

"What were you mad at?"

"Her."

"Do you remember what you did that day? Was there anything about it that was remarkable?"

"No."

"You were just mad at her."

"Yeah."

Kendall pushed his chair back to stretch. Smith could hardly blame him, this huge man sitting for hours on a little steel chair. She didn't know where to go from here. The guy was no idiot, just unreachable. He showed nothing—neither bluster nor remorse, barely any range of emotion at all. She slid the picture of Gina to the bottom of Kendall's pile and moved on to Catherine Marsh.

"Do you have any idea why you killed her, Kendall?"

That same damn question, Kendall thought. This woman kept repeating the same damn question.

"I was angry at being ripped off so much."

He could have said more. Could have told Smith what he thought of women in general—always acting like they knew more than you—and about hookers, in particular. Worthless trash. The black girls were worst of all, always so much attitude. Why did this prosecutor even pretend to care about them? But he stayed quiet. Unlike the others, Cathy Marsh had barely fought. She lay there like she'd expected this. He remembered meeting her in the morning at Soldiers Fountain, outside the office where people went to pay their cable bills. He'd handed her twenty dollars, puzzled that she settled for so little when he gladly paid other girls more. They went straight home and upstairs to his old bedroom. Dutifully, Cathy removed her clothes, but that was all he could recall. He knew her face—blue eyes, dimple, gap-toothed smile—and he knew the room where he'd killed her. But whatever had set him off was gone. "I was probably pissed off at someone else," he said. "She was just in the wrong place at the wrong time."

"Do you have any remembrance of whether Catherine Marsh ever ripped you off?"

"Not 'pecifically."

All he could remember was the way she lay there. It bothered him. Afterward, he carried her into the bathroom to place her facedown in the tub, already filled with water, like he'd done with Wendy. He poked at Cathy as you might a tangle of wash left to soak, making sure she was fully submerged. Then he hauled her out, drenched and dripping, kicked aside some cardboard boxes and old blankets clogging the attic stairs, and, holding her aloft, proceeded upward, step by step. No one in his family went into the attic anymore. Only Kendall, bearing his mangled trophies. He laid Cathy on the floor next to Wendy, prodded them both, and muttered that it was their fault.

But here was the prosecutor again, trying to slow him down, reminding him that earlier he'd remarked, "Killing people is harder than I thought."

"What did you mean by that?" Smith asked.

"I don't know. It's not like the movies, where they die in a minute or two."

Smith paused to explain that investigators would need to drive to Kendall's home and confirm what he'd told them. Was there anything he wanted in the meantime?

"I could really use a doughnut," he said.

IN FRONT OF 99 Fulton Avenue a few hours later, I watched crime scene investigators in hazmat suits holding bags of evidence at arm's length. I interviewed bystanders, taking down names and ages, saw their mouths form tight little Os of shock at what they were learning. A nurse at the edge of the crowd trembled as she told me she'd considered Kendall's mother a friend. They worked together at the psychiatric hospital. She'd known one of Kendall's victims, too, years ago, in the IBM clean rooms where they stood side by side making computer chips on a high-tech assembly line. Now that girl was being carried out of Paulette's house in a garbage bin. I could hardly miss the reporter's gold mine standing before me, the threads of a small-city life knotted in the frame of this frail woman. But she shook her head when I pressed, walking away from me with stiff, tentative steps, as if favoring an injury.

For a week journalists swarmed Poughkeepsie's crumbling sidewalks. We were looking for anything—a shred of rumor, a snippet of memory—that might explain the truth about this city now torn open on display. We fanned across Main Street, interviewing prostitutes who resented our interest, yet grabbed for the attention like children at a candy buffet. They knew we'd move on the minute we gathered our quotes and anecdotes, but they kept talking. Most had known Kendall for years and claimed they'd reported him to police for rape and assault month after month. There were whispers about Kendall taking a polygraph at Siegrist's request; suggestions that a detective had walked into Kendall's home, and out again, five corpses lying a few feet from where he stepped. But this was gossip, dangled by drug addicts and hustlers, so we hammered officials with requests for information, waited for whatever they saw fit to dole out, and gulped it down like fast food.

District Attorney Bill Grady convened regular news conferences to keep us sated. The first took place a few days after Kendall's arrest, in a training room at the Town of Poughkeepsie Police Station. A janitor had arranged six rows of folding chairs, and the linoleum floors gleamed. Outside, James DeSalvo, brother of Kendall's fourth victim, Kathleen Hurley, stood in the parking lot and watched us stream in. I had spoken to DeSalvo while gathering background on the missing women a week earlier, before Kendall confessed, and he'd greeted my questions not with the resignation I'd come to expect but a knowing superiority that made me wonder. I had imagined the pompous schoolteacher as the killer, thrilling at the families' tears and pain. But when I met DeSalvo outside the police barracks, he was just a nervous man lost in a swarm of reporters, trying to appear well spoken and stumbling over his words.

Inside, Dutchess County's chief law officer was preparing his remarks. A slight, balding man with pale hair and watery eyes, Grady's low-key style camouflaged canny political instincts. A son of the county's longest-serving district attorney, Grady had worked in the office all of his adult life, and held the distinction of being New York's only sitting district attorney who'd never passed the bar (an allowance made for service in Vietnam). Whenever I found myself in his chambers asking questions, whether about a death penalty case or courtroom protocols, Grady would pull a weighty tome from the bookshelf behind his desk and flip to the appropriate statute. He was uncomfortable around the national media, which had lately found increasing reason to descend on Dutchess County, but had come to enjoy bantering with those reporters he considered friendly.

Always unhurried, he waited while we settled ourselves, then announced the name of the latest woman to be pulled from 99 Fulton Avenue.

"She is Audrey Pugliese—"

"I know her!" shrieked the man next to me. "Oh my God, I did her hair!"

On his opposite side, a heavyset black woman stared straight ahead, immobile as a statue.

At news conferences I often sat near people who were not journalists, partly because the frantic scribbling of other reporters made me nervous, and partly because anyone who was not taking notes usually had some other, more interesting reason to be there. The shrieking man had been flapping around 99 Fulton Avenue for days, trilling his outrage like a drag queen on ether, and now he identified himself as Kendall's cousin. Mon-Ray Francois was not, in fact, related by blood or marriage, but he had grown up with the Francois children, slipping on their family name like a well-worn overcoat.

Grady continued. It now appeared that all eight of Francois's victims were white women. But despite the obvious racial divide, race was not a motive. Reporters raised their eyebrows. Grady went on. Investigators had expected to find eight victims inside the home because eight women, in total, had been reported missing. But the bodies at 99 Fulton Avenue were not precisely those police anticipated. A woman they'd never heard of lay in the heap, and Michelle Eason, the only African American they had hoped to find, was nowhere. All identifications were now complete. The Francois family, Grady added, had known nothing of Kendall's crimes and would not be charged.

IT TOOK A month to clear the Francois crime scene, cataloging bits of human skin alongside snack wrappers and old bedding. State Police investigator Art Boyko ruined two pairs of boots walking through the rot strewn across their floors. Each night after work he crept back into his own home through the basement, where he stripped off his clothes and tied them in trash bags before stepping naked into his wife's clean kitchen.

Boyko had smelled decaying flesh a thousand times, the same cloud of stomach-churning rot that blanketed most murder scenes and suicides left too long before discovery. But in the basement of 99 Fulton Avenue he'd staggered backward at the weight of this stench. It hung about the place like billows of smoke, choking everyone who entered. People who'd never even seen a dead body knew the meaning of that smell. His wife had pulled away from him, eyes wide, as soon as he stepped through the kitchen door. Boyko had his methods for handling this: a scalding shower with deodorant soap scrubbed into his skin until it was tender-pink, then a walk to clear his mind. In the predawn hours after clearing bodies from the Francoises', he wandered his development, triggering motion sensors that spotlighted the homes of his sleeping neighbors against a violet sky. The compound was so new its asphalt lanes still felt spongy beneath his feet. Boyko trudged up a hill to look west toward Poughkeepsie's lights twinkling low on the horizon. He couldn't erase what he had seen there—a woman's body dissolved in a garbage bin; a pile of skulls; a bit of rope with an eyebolt attached, tied to a skeleton's arm—but at least he could breathe now, release a huge sigh in the suburban night and feel cleansed of things he could not discuss. Boyko sucked in cool fresh air, anticipating the tickle of mown grass, the sharp scent of his own shower. Instead, he retched. The corpses were all over him, their decay and sadness—in the grooves of his thumbprints, the back of his throat. It was impossible. A trick of the mind, the investigator told himself, rolling his neck, shaking his head. He was standing on a hillcrest ten miles away. He had washed, he had scrubbed. But now Boyko could not stop searching for it—sniffing, testing, and there it was again. The reek of indictment, of evil and loss, creeping out of memory and back into life.

AS KENDALL CONFESSED, describing each woman and, with significant editing, what he had done to her, he drew little maps. He made a cross with a circle in it to show the streets intersecting at Reservoir Square where he'd met Catherine Marsh. He wrote *Cable* in the top right corner for the nearby Cablevision office and *Catharine* beneath it, then sketched two lines showing where the arterial highway cut through a block away. It was a sloppy scrawl, replete with misspellings, and Smith joshed about his handwriting, making fun of the way he'd scribbled *arterial*. People could do that, Kendall marveled, jab at you with the rudest questions and smile like it was okay.

"That's your spelling of the arterial?" the prosecutor asked.

"Yes."

"We would agree that spelling is not your strong suit, Kendall?" she said.

"Absolutely. That's why they invented spell-check."

"That's, well—that's a good point."

His remark reminded Smith to inquire about Kendall's computer. Had he written anything on it to keep track of all these women? "How many, altogether, did you kill?"

"Eight," he said, clear and strong.

At first he laid their bodies on a small sheet of plastic, then moved them to a larger piece after more piled up. When the corpses of Catherine, Gina, and Kathleen Hurley began to leak, he sawed them into pieces, shoving some parts into a plastic bag, folding others into a zippered suitcase. The skulls he dumped into Kierstyn's old kiddie pool and pulled a garbage bag over it.

"A garbage bag," Smith repeated.

There was silence as she stared at him and the tape spun.

"Now, you've been living in the same house with your mom and your dad and a sister over this period of time, right?"

"Yes," said Kendall, in a strangely helpless tone of voice.

"And when you think back to growing up with your mom and your dad and sisters and brother, what are your thoughts? What impressions did you have of your parents?"

"I thought we were average."

"Average. Did you like your parents?"

"Yes," Kendall said.

"Did you ever see them— Did they fight, or did they have a normal marriage? What about their— What about your household? What do you remember about growing up?"

"I guess we were a pretty normal home."

"But all this time you've had dead people in your attic?"

"Yes."

"Has it smelled or had you noticed anything about that?"

"Sometimes the smell would seep out, but I told them there was a dead raccoon upstairs and I couldn't find it."

"So there had been complaints about the smell?" Smith pressed.

"A few times."

"Who had complained about it, Kendall?"

So sadly he could barely form the words, Kendall said, "My mother."

CHAPTER 3

When Night Falls

I was walking in the woods behind my home when the idea of writing to Kendall took shape in my mind. He was always a first name to me, always that familiar. This was late in the summer of 1999, and I'd mulled the squalid facts of his case, the holes in his life story and the way it nonetheless gripped me, almost daily since his arrest eleven months before. I thought about Kendall as I churned out lifestyle features about new restaurants and resident movie stars. I pictured him hunched over his jailhouse dinner tray while I made apple pies for Derrick. I saw Kendall everywhere—in the silhouettes of hulking men on line at the supermarket, filling their cars at gas stations—and I stared, unable to keep from imagining what it might have been like to grow up huge, black, and awkward in a white-bread backwater like Dutchess County. By the time Kendall hit the front pages, the place had been crushing my hopes for years. It was only ninety minutes from Manhattan, but remained rural at heart, conservative in both politics and manner.

With my L.L.Bean boots and white skin, I could at least blend in. How lonely had it been for shambling, oafish Kendall?

I interviewed anyone who would talk to me about him, hoarding bits of information like Cracker Jack prizes: he'd been educated in the same red-brick buildings where I'd covered school board meetings at night; his aunt was the mail carrier on my road; he'd browsed the same bookstore I favored; ate burgers at the Wendy's I passed on my way home. These minutiae I gathered like shells from a beach, brooding over my collection, as if by looking long enough I might discover the roots of his rage.

I'd had only one actual sighting of my quarry, at the court appearance where he was arraigned and pleaded not guilty. Judge Thomas Dolan often opened his jury box to reporters for pretrial proceedings, and I'd taken a seat in the front row, close enough to touch the back of Kendall's sleeve. I wanted to feel the air around him to see if it was different, somehow. Kendall stood with his hands clasped at his waist, eyes downcast, and his voice was so soft the stenographer asked him to repeat every word. I pictured my fingers reaching toward his elbow.

But the idea of writing to him was mortifying. I was paralyzed, strangely, by the prospect of offending.

> *Dear Mr. Francois,*
>
> *I have never written to anyone in jail before so please forgive me if this letter is kind of awkward. I've seen you in court and in the newspapers, and I've spoken with a few people who know you. I keep hearing that you were a pretty good student at Arlington and a very good chess player, interested in history and political science, but I would much rather hear more about you from you, yourself.*

I covered the first part of your case for the New York Times
as a freelancer because I live here, and whenever something hap-
pens they call me and I get the information, though someone else
in New York usually writes it up. But I am not writing this letter
for the Times.

I told Kendall that I felt bad for his mother, father, and teenage
sister, forced to abandon their home, reviled for his crimes. This
overstated my feelings, though I could summon a certain pity for
feeling like a refugee in your own town. They were living with relatives now, unable even to whisper their last name. I asked Kendall what he'd wished for and if he'd ever felt sad. I said I wanted
to understand what had brought him to this wretched point in
life, and I offered to send books. Then I appended the words that
festered in Kendall's mind as I'd never anticipated, and warped
our correspondence ever after: "Your story seems somehow important to understand. That's why I am writing to you. I am interested in you, as a person. I want you to know there is someone
out here who is concerned about you." The same trope countless
reporters have used to score a jailhouse interview. But that didn't
mean it was a lie.

Could I be concerned about a man who had crushed the necks
of eight women? I wanted to be. I wanted a tale of abuse, a litany
of signs ignored and pleas unheard. This was what I listened for at
every media briefing and expected to read in someone else's coverage. But unless you counted the cognitive dissonance of the Francois home—a tumult of family photos and rot among the corpses—
such explicit answers never came. Could I possibly be concerned
about a man who giggled in court as the women's families wept?

"Your time's gonna come, Fat Boy!" an uncle of Kendall's eighth victim bellowed during the arraignment, a T-shirt stretched tight over his gut.

"You got to face God!" shrieked the frazzle-haired mother of his first, staggering to her feet as Kendall chuckled, his shoulders shaking beneath his blue dress shirt.

His lawyer told me I was wrong—Kendall had been terrified, he said—but I was sitting in the jury box three feet away, and I heard him laugh. It was a tiny sound, tremulous and inadvertent, like a child caught breaking the rules.

IN LATE AUGUST 1999, I typed my letter, sealed it in a business envelope, and handed it to an administrator at the county jail. You couldn't miss the thoughts flickering behind his pale eyes: *A stupid woman doing a stupid thing. Women always did this shit, chasing after these filthy criminals when the right thing to do was let them rot.* We were sitting in the sheriff's office, surrounded by photographs of Dutchess County's top cop posing with James Earl Jones and a half-dozen other movie stars who lived on country estates east of Poughkeepsie. The crowning shot showed Sheriff Butch Anderson in Washington, D.C., shaking hands with Ronald Reagan at the White House.

I rented box 1273 at the Pleasant Valley post office so the serial killer I'd contacted wouldn't be sending mail directly to my home, and sat back to wait for what I assumed would be his quick response. There was nothing. After a month without reply, the first pinpricks of humiliation began to crackle across my skin, a sensation that sharpened daily as I slipped past the women in the mural. They made me think of the mothers of Kendall's victims, tough women with iron-gray hair who'd endured decades of disappointment and still apologized if their eyes watered when they spoke to me. I'd let Pat Barone and Marguerite Marsh hug me as they remembered daughters my own age, girls who'd become walking phantoms during a dozen trips through rehab, a hundred earnest promises broken. Pat's granddaughter twirled around us in a tutu while the woman she'd come to know as Mama spoke in a voice flat as a dial tone, describing the day she took out a life insurance policy on Gina. She was preparing for an eventual overdose. The mothers tried to speak evenly about children who'd brought more pain than joy, and here was I, only the latest agent of betrayal. I jammed my key into the narrow postal lock, the mothers' faces before me. I could not stand to think what they might say. Kendall's last victim, a birdlike addict named Catina, grew up twenty steps from the post office door.

When October came without a word, I began driving to Kendall's old home. It had been relinquished by his parents and purchased for fifteen thousand dollars by a developer who stripped it to the studs, changed the siding, and sold it to a new family. I sat in my car across the street, watching crows swoop overhead and waiting for something to happen. I drove home and studied dead animals disintegrating by the side of my road. A deer, a possum, a mangled bird. Each day their carcasses changed. Nighttime creatures pawed them. Chill air slowly dried the convulsive stench. I'd walk past and inhale, searching. Over time, the skin fell away and bones emerged. The skull. The spine. The rib cage, becoming cleaner, clearer, delicate and almost pretty now that the flesh was gone. It seemed natural to discuss this with Kendall, if only in my head.

I went by your house today. It barely looks like the place where you used to live. It's white now, not that weird creepy green you had, and there are red shutters on the windows. Your old door on the side is gone. The new people are going to use the main one out front. It has glass panes down the middle and potted plants on either side. Your porch is a real porch, with columns that make a formal entranceway. But your attic looks the same, like the builders were afraid to touch it. The window's still dusty and the sash is cracked. A woman drove by, letting her car slide all over the road while she stared, and a man walked past with his head pulled down into his coat, though he kept peeking up to look. Did you ever climb that big oak tree out front? There was a huge maple at the country house my family had when I was a kid, and when I made it to the top I felt like the toughest, bravest girl. Then I was too petrified to come down. What do you think about when the lights go out at night?

AT THE END of the month, I sent a second note. I was working on a magazine profile of Fred Rogers, the children's television host, and I wrote to Kendall about it, asking if he'd ever felt drawn to that Neighborhood of Make-Believe. Rogers told me that black children in particular loved his show, and he believed this was because they might be uniquely sensitive to a white adult communicating respect. Still no response.

The irony of soliciting a serial killer while interviewing the gentlest man on earth was not lost on me, and I wondered if Kendall would notice, too. By now, I was beginning to worry about my shameful obsession. Derrick was disgusted. But other than him, I had told no one. Academia briefly provided me a fig leaf of excuses, sociologists who hypothesized that serial murderers serve as proxies, fantasy outlets for our most inadmissible desires. Some suggested that those alienated from the chirpy flow of life delighted to see fellow sufferers tearing at mainstream complacency. I thought of an aunt who'd locked herself in a room at the Plaza Hotel and shredded the curtains, smashed the furniture, clawed the walls. "We hope you'll be feeling so much better soon," said the card with a bouquet that management sent her afterward.

All the theories were intriguing. None of them fit me. My interest in compulsive violence, a preoccupation long before I'd ever heard of Kendall Francois, felt somehow linked to a persistent fear of the dark. This was my most stubborn terror, rising up even in daylight if my back was bent over a sink, eyes clenched against the sting of soapy water. I'd whirl around half-blind trying to catch this thing, confront the shadow I could not keep from imagining in every corner. Alone in my bedroom, I'd fling open the closet and stare at the clothes and boxes inside, then force myself to do it again, and once more. But the fear clung. It chased me through girlhood into adolescence and lingered still as a blanket of melancholy that descended every day at dusk. I loathed that gloaming. I pulled my curtains shut at four o'clock to hide from nightfall. Yet I'd been the kid who raced for the haunted house at every amusement park, who plowed through murder mysteries and devoured horror movies. Adults thought me plucky, daring, bold, when in fact I was powerless against the compulsive draw of my fear.

I was eleven during David Berkowitz's killing spree, and it made no difference to me that he was going after women twice my age, sitting with their dates inside parked cars. The Son of Sam slipped into my mind and stuck there, a seed of dread that grew into certainty: security was an illusion, solid as the skim of ice over a lake. Berkowitz was a symbol to me more than a man, and he haunted my nightmares when I stayed home from school, sick in a damp, rumpled bed.

The bed sat in an apartment overlooking Central Park West, with high ceilings and parquet floors that made my blood curdle when they creaked. Affluence conferred no sense of safety. It was a costume concealing the truth of my family: a volatile, unhappy mother lashed to a meek but cutting man. Any sound might rouse them from their books into a squall of judgment and shame. I began to peer into darkness because it matched something I knew.

Still, I cringed at the stories about women who were "into" serial murderers. It had become fashionable by the time I graduated college in the late 1980s to know your killers and recall their transgressions encyclopedically, like baseball stats. I kept up to speed. When the Jeffrey Dahmer story broke I could not get enough. I consumed more than read these articles, gorging on crime. I collected European case studies and statistical analyses, ghoulish paperbacks and psychiatric tomes. Quite a library, I amassed. But would I ever meet one of these men? Could you even do that? They were like celebrities in their remove from the rest of us, superstar criminals who granted interviews only to those as rarefied as they. And if I ever did sit face-to-face with one, would I finally crumble before a reality I could not withstand, or would virtue be my shield? This was my true agenda: to test myself against seething evil and emerge unscathed.

BY LATE OCTOBER, I stopped visiting my mailbox every day. I had been playing a silly, stupid game, and Kendall recognized it. He understood that I would exploit his confidence, publicize his failures. How could I not? I was a journalist now, and it was time to give up juvenile fantasies. But at night Kendall's world entered my dreams. His family whispered from broken homes where beams hung from the ceiling and the walls were transparent. Sometimes he was there, telling me what I needed to know. Sometimes I watched, mute, as hundreds of other reporters won his secrets, his story. I'd awake frenzied, and spend the rest of the day debating whether to visit the post office again. But now, just as I'd given up and resolved to devote myself to menu-planning for Thanksgiving, here he was, lying under a stack of books on my desk.

The rules, as he laid them out, were simple and clear: my pages should be single-spaced with one-inch margins, all my questions at the end. And I was to include a photo, full body and semi-revealing. "I don't really care what you look like, but I do want to know just how serious you are," Kendall wrote, saying he would answer my questions with the same honesty and fullness with which I addressed his.

The problem was not that I had nothing to say—just the opposite. I found myself fighting *not* to tell him things, reining in a bewildering desire to lay myself bare and offer every sad secret, every humiliation and regret. I wanted to tell Kendall about the mother who'd framed my childhood in fear and the father who let it happen; about men who hurt and used me, and how I'd fled it all to hide in the woods of Dutchess County. I wanted to tell him about media hypocrisies that made me rage and the feeling of being an impostor in my life. But in the end, I ignored all of his directives, including no photograph or personal detail other than a sentence saying I was from New York City and had fit in neither in my hometown nor in his. Then I added a few remarks about how hard it must be to grow up black in America and, sick to my stomach, pushed the letter into a mailbox.

Three days later, Kendall phoned my home. No one was there to pick up—Derrick and I were out chopping down a Christmas tree that afternoon—and the answering machine said only that I'd had a collect call. It did not mention the name Francois or the Dutchess County Jail, but I knew it was him. An itchy sweat spread across my back as an electronic operator's voice crackled through the speaker.

CHAPTER 4

Tricks of the Trade

Bill Grady had vowed to seek the death penalty, but just before Christmas 1998, Kendall's lawyers offered the district attorney a better deal: Kendall would plead guilty to every charge—eight counts of first-degree murder, plus rape and assault—as long as Grady spared him a trial. That was Kendall's only goal.

For Dutchess County, it was a tidy arrangement. There would be no public testimony about the Poughkeepsie detectives who had shown Kendall's picture to streetwalkers and warned them to stay away a year before his arrest. No mention of the investigator who had interviewed Kendall, bought him lunch, walked into his corpse-packed home and out again with a shrug. No talk of Catina Newmaster, who'd worn a wire to help police solve the case and was now dead at Kendall's hands. No testimony from the prostitutes, Catina among them, who had reported Kendall themselves, telling police about the smell in his home, the things he'd said while raping them. No details about their broken lives at the center of Dutchess County nor about the suburbanites who supported Main Street's sad economy. None of that.

The media packed up, and Poughkeepsie withdrew into a bruised, defensive silence. Kendall's siblings moved out of state, his family canceled the mail, and his father died of heart failure while Kendall spent the next two years in the county jail, awaiting Grady's decision. Only Paulette remained, living quietly with friends so she could finish out her thirty years at the psychiatric hospital and retire with a full pension. In June 2000, after Grady decided that a death penalty trial presented more risk than reward and finally accepted Kendall's guilty plea, Paulette released her sole public statement:

> We wish to finally express our sentiments publicly regarding this tragedy that has befallen so many people. First, to the family members of the women whose lives were lost, we continue to feel the greatest sympathy. These events have taken a terrible toll upon them. We know their sorrow firsthand as this ordeal has caused us to lose our beloved McKinley, husband and father, whose broken heart finally yielded. We have also lost Kendall, our brother and son, to imprisonment among strangers until the day he dies, and made worse from the horrible disease which will take him.
>
> We wish to express our gratitude to Mr. William Grady in not seeking the death penalty and to those families of the victims who agreed with that decision. While there are probably many reasons for this, we ourselves have always believed that death followed by more death is not a solution and never will be. Only by society acting humanely will individuals ever learn to behave humanely.

To those people, some of whom were strangers, that helped us with clothes, food and lodging when we found ourselves homeless and desperate, we want them to know that their kindness and generosity will never be forgotten.

We also express our thanks to the press which, in large part, respected our family's privacy when we asked for it.

I read her words standing on the courthouse steps, impressed by Paulette's eloquence, moved by her loss. But my admiration soon soured. The lines that at first had sounded gracious also conveyed a puzzling distance, as if describing a story already faded to legend, and the most deeply felt sections concerned Paulette's own family—it was they who had suffered most. They who should be pitied.

No one talked much about Kendall's reasons for wanting to avoid court. The possibility of a death sentence was the least of it. To reporters, his attorneys claimed that their polite, well-behaved client wanted to spare the victims' families more misery. But Kendall and I had been writing for seven months by this point, and the longer we corresponded the more clearly I saw that shielding himself from further humiliation was the real motive. More urgent still was the need to protect his family. The idea that their secrets could be arrayed before crowds of gawking strangers he found unbearable. I'd written to Kendall's mother shortly before she made her statement, inviting Paulette to share her feelings, and in response received two pages of furious scrawl from the Dutchess County Jail.

I have chosen to write with you and I accept that responsibility, but because I have doesn't mean that the few people that I care

about are now fair game.... If you continue along this path, I will
consider it a personal attack against the people I care about and
therefore a personal attack against me. If you have any doubt
about a person's relationship with me you should ask me before
you write them (or otherwise contact them). This isn't a warning
it is a last chance.

Kendall told me that Paulette had read him my letter during one of their twenty-minute phone calls. I'd interpreted this as a good sign initially, thinking it meant she was considering an interview— her lawyer suggested Paulette might be amenable if I paid—and I guessed that Kendall was commanding her to withdraw the offer. But as the months passed I began to wonder if it was the other way around: Paulette demanding that her boy take care of this pest, this reporter. Either way, mother and son wielded vise-grip control over their story. Every family member I contacted duly reported me to Paulette, who promptly relayed this information to Kendall, and within days I would receive another blistering set of pages from within a locked cell.

Around this time, a publisher of true-crime paperbacks, hearing of my newspaper coverage, rushed a book contract to my home. I stared at it for hours, knowing that what I wanted from Kendall Francois would not be so easily packaged for sale. The letter writing that had stemmed from curiosity was solidifying into a harder shape. I couldn't trace its contours yet, but I knew his story was intertwined somehow with my own. "Why should I help you?" Kendall shot back. "I am a paycheck to you and let's not pretend I am anything else." But he wanted me to pretend. He wanted me to protest my innocence and prove it by being his friend. I told him his story was important to understand. I told him I would try to hear without judgment. I used all the tricks that writers do to flatter a subject into submission. Kendall knew the routine. He'd practiced it on dozens of broken women, listening, understanding, drawing them closer.

Toward his relatives, I had been forthright in every overture. I told them Kendall and I were writing. But even this simple statement became twisted and warped as it moved from person to person, like a dream-game of telephone in which words changed meaning and nothing was what it seemed. "I'm amazed that you would tell people that you have me under control, in the palm of your hand, wrapped around your finger," Kendall wrote, quoting phrases I'd never used. It was like trying to defend myself against a jury of ghosts, people I never saw and never spoke to, but who judged and damned me, whispering lies. In every letter, he demanded to know who I was interviewing, slinging insults when I mentioned former teachers or school acquaintances, as if trying to flood the void with venom before anyone else might do the same. Yet everyone I spoke to remembered Kendall fondly; they were dumbfounded by his crimes. When I asked him to suggest sources, Kendall pointed me, again and again, toward the women on Main Street. "Talk to Cheryl," he said. "Call Christine."

Alone at my desk, I stared at newspaper photos of his round face. I bored into his almond-shaped eyes and tried to fathom the brain inside, embroidering intricate pasts that might explain his impenetrable gaze. Was there anything we shared, any point on the spectrum of human emotion where once we might have met? I took the wounds of my own childhood and laid them over Kendall like a shroud, hoping to find an outline I could trace. I thought of the things people had told me about Paulette, how sweet tempered and cheerful she was—teaching Bible classes to children, attending every parents night at Arlington Elementary School—and felt myself drowning in contradiction. The newsprint piled up in my living room, a bulwark of clippings, notes, and psychology books that loomed behind Derrick and me as we watched television.

Friends peered at my growing collection of Kendall memorabilia, but only a few asked questions. For that, I was grateful. I could not have admitted that whenever they told a story from their lives, my mind spun back to him, calculating where Kendall would have been at the same moments—playing kickball at his grandmother's home or eavesdropping on Vassar students; trolling Main Street or wondering when the police would come. Each detail I learned of his history, I plotted on a timeline of my own. Kendall's teachers told me of the quiet, introverted fifth-grader he'd been, and I thought of myself that same year: a high school sophomore branded *slut* and *druggie,* walking through the hallways with my head angled down. I imagined Kendall on the Arlington High School football field, chugging galumphing laps around the goalposts as I stumbled through my first writing jobs in New York City. By the time I landed in Poughkeepsie—moving backward, everyone said—Kendall would have been back, too, tossed from the army for being overweight and searching, like me, for a way to start new. He had just enrolled in community college, thinking he might try to become a science teacher.

Dutchess County was not especially friendly to aspiration. Nor to difficult topics. The final straw for me at the *Journal* came in the form of "clarifications" two reporters were forced to write after their sources complained about the way they appeared in print. One of those reporters was me. A woman I'd quoted on the changing demographics of her school district thought she sounded like a racist. Another writer had to backpedal after she wrote about a teenage boy discussing venereal disease. No one claimed our words were wrong, only that they caused unnecessary discomfort. I resigned with righteous indignation and no idea what to do next. The other reporter became a bartender at Club Med.

Derrick seemed like an answer, or at least a plausible way to delay the question. He appeared painfully innocent—twenty-five years old and still living at home. He'd had only one previous girlfriend, but I found this attractive. I thought it made him safe. The two of us were lying in a friend's backyard, looking up at the stars, when we decided to pack up my Volkswagen and tour the country in search of somewhere else to live. For hundreds of miles, he played poker on a handheld Game Boy while I drove. In Las Vegas he sat at the roulette tables, a little boy on a tall stool trying to keep up with the professionals. He won two hundred dollars in ten minutes, then lost it all and more. We'd planned to loop the Grand Canyon and drive east in time to reach New Orleans by Halloween. (It was Derrick's favorite holiday.) But deflated after Vegas, we had little will to do anything more than slink back to Poughkeepsie, poorer, angrier, and more confused than ever. Derrick returned to his job interviewing environmental scientists for the *Journal*. And I, disgusted with the compromises of reporting, took a job at a bakery near Vassar College. I'd open the shop at dawn, pushing muffin tins into the oven while Kendall was strangling women a hundred yards away.

MY DISAVOWAL OF journalism lasted all of six months, and I returned with blazing ambition. Editors at the *Times* were glad to have someone north of the city willing to chase news oddities that cropped up with regularity in the Hudson Valley. I wrote about Renaissance reenactors and nineteenth-century paupers' bones popping up from the earth around a public swimming pool. Editors kept patting my head, and I kept swallowing the flattery. Against this backdrop, Kendall's opening letters posed a number of problems. He'd dangled the prize that a dozen reporters wanted and told me how to get it: to gain what I sought, I'd have to allow his scrutiny. Drop the notebook and open up my past. Slowly, stiffly, we began a conversation.

"I've never met you, so imagining that we could be friends right off the bat is maybe a bit hasty. But I'll tell you right now, I do not want to betray you," I wrote. "For this to work, we both have to feel comfortable. We have to trust each other. So here's a start: I grew up in New York City, where I went to private schools and didn't fit in. But I liked the freedom and the independence of the city. I liked riding the subways and walking through Central Park and looking at all the different types of people. It's hard for me to explain why I have trouble getting along with bosses and parents and people I know well, yet feel so much for those I've never met."

Kendall was intrigued, but not swayed. And he saw immediately how carefully I doled out my confidences.

Well, well, Claudia. Can I call you Claudia? I'll have to give it to you, when confronted at least you're honest, as honest as any reporter. You're also prompt, as a good reporter should be, but you still write like a reporter. You're not showing any heart or passion. Details, details, details. You letters are an okay outline, but not what I'm asking for. Stop treating me like I'm stupid. I may be a lot of things but I'm not stupid. You want to go into the depths of my mind and into my past. I want a peek into yours. It is only fair, isn't it?

He sneered at the rote quality of news writing, the lack of risk in my words, and I winced in recognition. He was the most unlikely editor I would ever have. He said he wanted to confide in me but kept pulling back for fear of "a negative outcome lurking in the shadows." He wanted to believe my intentions were good but saw "misleading motives" in every paragraph, though he understood they weren't necessarily there. At his most lucid and controlled, Kendall could be exceptionally polite, addressing me as "Ms. Rowe" and apologizing for earlier letters that had been "tactless." He set rules and deadlines, most of which I failed to meet, and he tested me constantly: My letters should be written longhand. They should come every week, and a money order slipped inside would be nice, too. ("We live in America so things work that way.") Never did he stop insisting that I send a photograph. He asked what I thought of him. "Not my case, not how it all went wrong, or fits together," he said. "Just me."

I told him that he was frightening. He said I was lying. I told him he was powerful. He said that made no sense.

I am physically strong, this is true, but powerful I'm not. If I was psychically powerful, as you suggest, I wouldn't be here. I have much more reason to fear you. While I am far more complex than most people, you are also complex, in your own way. If you truly fear me that much, when I'm so far from you, maybe we shouldn't continue to correspond. I don't want to cause you any trauma. If giving me a picture of yourself causes so much pain, receiving letters from me must be quite chilling and hard for you. Something doesn't feel quite right, as if everything is only a lie. Don't dance around, just explain.

Those friends who did ask about my mounting pile of pictures and news clippings got only vague answers. I was considering a bigger project, I said, something about Poughkeepsie and how this cloistered community had spawned a killer. Those things were true. But the deeper reasons—that brutality tantalized me; that I was fascinated by the mystery of Kendall and flattered by his interest—were impossible to admit. No one wanted to hear that. Derrick suspected, though, and the longer Kendall and I corresponded, the more furious he became. It was sick to willingly become the obsession of a killer, he said. Disgusting. Someone who had done the things Kendall had did not deserve attention from anyone, let alone me. He sounded almost jealous. I'd confessed the letter writing one evening when he came home from work, affecting a casual tone, though I was frightened by what I'd fallen into. I hoped Derrick might help me, or at least praise my courage. He looked nauseated. We were standing in our pine-paneled living room, under the low peaked ceiling. It was cozy and warm, our tree house tucked away in the forest, but could quickly become claustrophobic.

"It's just like *In Cold Blood*," Derrick said, unimaginatively, about the book that had inspired so many reporters. "Those two guys killed a family because of something they heard from some scumbag in prison—because of a mistake. He could do that, too, you know. He could send someone here."

It always surprised me when Derrick leaned toward the dramatic, because he had such a mild affect. Beautiful doe eyes with long lashes, a quiet voice, heart-tightening smile. He pictured Kendall as I had at first—a bloodthirsty beast, not the blithering pile of insecurity, bravado, infantile anger, and thudding sadness I'd begun to sense. Anyway, if Kendall ever thought about killing me, he'd want to do it himself. A proxy would never satisfy.

"It's nothing like *In Cold Blood*," I said.

Derrick's words streamed past me like rushing water; I recognized the sound of logic, but drew no meaning from it. Rationality, morality—those things only kept me from my goal. I watched his cold, pinched face, ashamed to confess I was more interested in Kendall's past than in the new homes and babies of our friends; more intrigued by the import behind Kendall's words than by Derrick's litany of complaints about the newsroom. I could not help it and did not want to.

AFTER I REFUSED to send money or pictures or answer questions about my sex life, Kendall wrote that this had impressed him. I was not a reporter who would do anything for a story, he said. I had integrity. But there was so little inside Kendall that was solid, one day's fleeting affirmation of worth counted for nothing. It was just another way for him to tempt me forward and criticize every step. But I took the bait every time, showing more of myself with each page. I told him my father had worked in advertising and my mother was a literature professor—rigid, strict, controlling. This description I extended as an invitation, a door opening onto a warm parlor where Kendall might unburden himself. He responded by asking my opinion of Shakespeare and volunteering that his favorite play was *Macbeth*. I confessed that tears poured down my face whenever I watched footage of civil rights marches; that I winced when welcomed into hotels where I had no reservations, knowing my treatment would be different if I was black. None of this got me any deeper into Kendall's life or heart or past, despite his demand for the information. Anything I unveiled served only as evidence of his superiority, textbook behavior from every description of a psychopath I'd ever read, yet I was blind to it. My need for connection with a monster, and my desperation to prove he was more, were so great that all the signposts slipped by, unnoticed.

For several months, I tried to reach him through subjects that had nothing do to with his crimes or background. I wrote about the changing seasons and a group of Tibetan monks who'd come to Vassar to make a mandala of colored sand, thinking Kendall might appreciate their patience and precision.

> *Do you know about these sand paintings? It takes the monks years of training, and the Vassar kids kept saying the mandala looked like a computer graphic but I thought it was more like a beautiful tapestry. Then, after their whole week of work, the monks blessed the sand, smushed all the colors into Dixie cups and dumped it into the Hudson. They said it symbolized the impermanence of life and earthly things.*

I wondered what Kendall, hoarder of dead bodies and old candy wrappers, would think of creating beauty like that and releasing it to the wind.

WE HAD BEEN writing for almost half a year when he suggested a phone call. Our correspondence, as far as I could tell, was getting me nowhere. I had neither gained Kendall's trust nor uncovered any reason for what he'd done. Each exchange merely entangled me deeper in a bruising contest. But I agreed to the call. It was scheduled for 3:00 P.M. on a late spring afternoon, and the phone rang at 2:57. A recorded voice asked if I would accept collect charges from a correctional institution.

"Hi," I said brightly.

"Uh, hi," Kendall answered softly. "So what do you want to talk about?"

I had prepared a list of questions on a legal pad—the basics about his family, his youth in Poughkeepsie, and his thoughts about the future, none of which he'd yet shared. But with the phone in my hand, I went blind. My heart pounded the way it had with boys in high school, my mind flying through the silences, every sentence a dark obstacle course. The notes I'd made turned to blue scrawls in a language I no longer understood, and I was adrift, talking to a murderer with nothing to shield me but a telephone cord. I made jokes. I tried to be charming. I shied from asking anything of substance. Evidently, Kendall was nervous, too, because the lacerating letter writer was gone. Here, he was a mumbler who swallowed his words, a man whose voice I could barely hear. When I brought up his family name, an unusual one for Poughkeepsie, he coughed, "It's French."

"French Haitian? I've been to Haiti, actually. I spent a month there, traveling."

"My condolences."

His father had been raised in central Louisiana, one of nine children born to a rural farming family that grew corn, sugarcane, and fig trees. There was a whole community of Francoises out there, a huge clan living on humid fields devoid of shade. They had cows, chickens, miles of land.

"Sounds nice," I said. "Did you visit a lot?"

"When I was a kid. But I hated those trips."

"Why?"

I wished I could see Kendall's eyes.

"The heat—I hate the heat. Of course," he chuckled, "I hate the cold, too."

Jail was always too hot or too cold, and though permitted an hour in the rec yard every day, Kendall rarely stepped outside. He preferred to remain in his cell, writing or reading. The one time Kendall broke this habit had been to save a boy, a skinny teen who'd angered other inmates on the basketball court. The older players puffed out their chests, shoving the boy backward into a corner. Until Kendall walked over. "Be cool," he said, raising his hand. A model prisoner, he told me with pride. Kendall loved order. He drew comfort from rules. Right, wrong—at least you knew which side of the line you were on. He rose with the sun when a thin shaft of light speared the darkness in his cell. Breakfast came on a tray at seven A.M., and by nine A.M. all the inmates were herded into a common room where they could read or write or watch TV. Then it was back to the locked cell for a few more hours and later, another trip to the television. A series of lock-ins and lock-outs that shaped every day.

"What about the army?" I asked. "How was that? I heard you were stationed in Hawaii."

"They sent me to Oklahoma first, fixing radios. Then Washington State. Then Hawaii."

Derrick and I had spent a week in Washington during our cross-country quest, camping at the base of Mount Baker under a pink-and-peach sky, our lungs raw with the thin air atop a mountain range that made us imagine being in Tibet. When we headed west toward the ocean Derrick insisted I close my eyes so my first view of the Pacific would be one enormous expanse of blue, unmarred by billboards or mileposts.

"Washington's a beautiful state," I said to Kendall.

"When it's not raining. The Pacific Ocean gets on my nerves."

I fumbled for a response.

"Is there anything I can do to help you be productive while you're in there?" I asked, imagining myself as some sort of confessor-nun.

"I'm not sure what you mean. It's hard to be productive when you're in jail."

"Maybe I could bring you a book?"

Kendall was quiet for a few moments, just breathing.

"I'd like something called the *Star Wars Encyclopedia,*" he said.

"Okay," I agreed, irritated at myself because I didn't actually want to buy him anything. "How do the other inmates treat you?"

I knew he was hated. Many of the men in there had known his victims for years.

"Pretty well," he said, brightening. "A couple of guards even asked for my autograph!"

Plainly thrilled by the attention, Kendall nevertheless denied these requests. He professed disgust with people who bought or sold criminals' artwork and through all the years of our correspondence would maintain an extraordinary sensitivity to being used. "I don't even like them calling me a serial killer," he said. "Not that it's wrong—I just don't think it's anything to celebrate."

Overall, he struck me as depressed. Kendall Francois was the most notorious criminal ever to sleep in the Dutchess County Jail, but he sighed every time I asked a question, as if bone weary and doing me a great favor by summoning the strength to answer. Experts would interpret this as evidence of his screaming narcissism. But all I could hear was the river of sadness beneath it. Kendall's official sentencing date was still months away, though the punishment—eight life terms—had been determined. I wanted to know how he'd felt before, when facing the prospect of death at the state's hand.

"Honestly, I didn't care. I never believed in the death penalty, and my feelings haven't changed. But it's not up to me anymore."

"What do you think a fair punishment would be?"

"One of those old chain gangs where they take convicts and work 'em till they drop."

Imagining his upcoming court appearance meant thinking about who might be there—friends from college, poseurs like Mon-Ray, and of course, Paulette. Kendall's weary affectation vanished the moment I asked about her.

"My mother will never walk into that courthouse," he said, nearly growling. "I'll make sure of it. There's no reason for her to be there."

I dangled my bait.

"But wouldn't she want to stand by her son?"

"I'm still her son, whether she's there or not, and I don't want her there. It's going to be nothing but pain and lies. No one has any reason to be there except my lawyers and the district attorney and the victims' families. I know the macabre seekers and bloodsucking media— Sorry," he caught himself.

"That's okay. I'm sorry all of this—writing and talking with me—makes you so angry—"

"I never get angry in my letters. Never."

"Aggravated?"

"I guess. You're always changing your story. Sometimes you sound like a nice person, sometimes you sound like a bitch-reporter. Your letters don't match."

"I'm the same person every time, but some days I'm tired or having trouble with work, or just in a bad mood."

"I understand that," Kendall said. "I understand bad moods."

He was right, of course. I was lying to him. Trying to sound confident when I was flailing. Clinging to the fact that my writing appeared in the most important newspaper in the country when I was, in fact, utterly disposable to the *Times*. Any sane person would tell me I had every right to shield myself from a psychopath. Nevertheless, by the terms I'd advertised for our relationship—sincerity, bravery—I was in the wrong. I was never going to tell him how Derrick glared, walking into our living room to see me poring over the letters, taking furious notes. I asked, instead, about writing. Investigators had discovered that Kendall was a prolific scribe, filling dozens of notebooks with stories, poems, diaries, and essays. He spoke of wanting to create a work of art with words.

"Are you working on anything now?" I asked. "I'd love to see some of your stuff."

"Just fiction—nothing based on anything real. My life is pretty boring to me."

We spoke about journalism and fantasy, writing and lies. The local paper was rife with them, Kendall said, and not only concerning his case. I knew well how the *Journal* glossed reality with innocuous headlines and four-color graphics, but I tried to explain that reporters did not deliberately set out to tell untruths. They made mistakes all the time, yes, but these were inaccuracies, not lies. To Kendall, the distinction was meaningless. "A mistake is still untrue, which means it's a lie, and lies have ruined my life."

Our twenty-minute phone allowance was nearly up. I could hear shouting in the background, and Kendall's voice turned leaden with boredom. He was surrounded by dozens of perverts and idiots with nothing to do. Their noise drove him crazy. No one used their time for anything constructive, and he was smarter than them all. It was a trial. Life itself was a trial. Then, suddenly humble, he asked if we might have another conversation.

"That is, if you want to," he said. "I didn't know if this was a one-shot deal."

To my surprise, I was reluctant to hang up. I liked talking with Kendall Francois. I thought about what this might mean for him, twenty-eight years old and trapped forever by what he'd done, with the chance to talk to someone outside of it. He'd thought I might cut him off after the call, knew I was likely chasing one prize—My Interview with a Serial Killer—and having won that, would move on. But I'd had only the barest glimpse of what I wanted from Kendall Francois. I was nowhere near closing the door.

CHAPTER 5

The Final Insult

We spoke again in August of 2000, the night before Kendall's final appearance in court, when his sentence of eight life terms would be officially pronounced. I wanted to know if he planned to make a statement. This was the true point of the proceeding. The parents and children of his victims would have a chance to revile him in public, and Kendall, the long-silent cipher, could respond. But with less than twenty-four hours to go he still hadn't decided whether to speak.

"Better to remain silent and be thought a fool than open your mouth and remove all doubt," he muttered. "My grandmother used to say that."

I told him that if he scanned the courtroom looking for me, I would try to catch his eye.

"You'll be the only one," he said with a hard little laugh.

Five months had passed since our first phone conversation, with several more in between, but Kendall didn't know how to recognize me because I refused to send a picture and he refused to put me on his visitors list at the jail. Tucking a shiny print into an envelope would mean crossing a line. But my reluctance to do so was motivated only partly by self-protection. The truth was, I owned almost no photographs and dreaded looking at those I had. While Kendall treasured the family album he'd been allowed to keep in jail, my personal archive sat in an old plastic bag at the back of my closet. Pictures to me meant fraud, a whiff of happiness, now escaped. I kept no visual record of my life because snapshots showed only loss. They were reminders of how different life looked when viewed in reverse. They were all the people who had come and gone, mementos of grief. Yet this was what Kendall clung to, artifacts of all he had destroyed.

I said it made me uncomfortable to give a picture of myself to someone like him. His response left me squirming.

> I understand how you feel, and luckily I don't feel the same way about you possessing a part of me . . . your picture is only what you look like. Writing is part of me (anyone). These letters, my stories, and especially my poetry is part of what I think, what I feel, my heart and my soul. It is part of who I am (beyond my flesh and bones).

Others, apparently, shared none of my misgivings. A pretty blonde from Court TV had mailed Kendall three separate head shots, he said. But I recoiled, thinking of the driver's licenses and methadone treatment cards he'd collected, his wallet-sized gallery of victims. Rather haughtily, I explained that I was not in the habit of handing out portraits to people I wrote about. This, Kendall found insulting. He hated being lumped in with the rest.

How many of the other people you write about send you hand-made cards? How many of these people do you care about? And don't try to tell me you don't care because I know you do.

When I pointed out that some of those whose photos he'd kept were now dead, Kendall bore down so hard that his pen ripped a hole in the paper.

It's true that some of the people in my photo album are now dead, like my father, and grandmother, but everybody in every photo ever taken will die someday. You can't blame that on me. I'm guessing that you were referring to other people in my past, and that is such bullshit. I can't believe you even wrote such a lie as a reason. I had one photo from anyone in that life that I kept purposely. It was given to me by the woman in a heart shaped frame, and she was very much alive the last time I saw her. The only thing that you could possibly be talking about is a driver's license that slipped under a small TV I had. If I had remembered it, it would be gone too.

Though we had been writing for nearly a year by this point, Kendall's fears whipped up constantly. I was "skilled in the art of manipulation," he wrote. "A good person with impure motives," a user, a seller of pain on paper. Someone who would suck out all the information she could and leave him to rot, his family in ruin. Kendall knew he'd been nothing but a dupe to women, and I was merely the latest in a long line. I'd lied to every person in his household and church, he said. Everything I knew about him I'd learned dishonestly. Whoever had told me about the Francois homestead in Louisiana was a traitor—as soon as he discovered their identity, he'd make sure the rest of his family steered clear. But my source had been Kendall himself.

> *I am not a project that needs to get done, and you say you under-*
> *stand that, but talk is cheap. Your actions say otherwise. I don't*
> *want to insult you by comparing you to some of the "working*
> *girls" I knew, but it was all just manipulation (getting as much*
> *as they can for as little in return). I have an uneasy feeling and*
> *for once I'm going to trust my feelings.*

It must have stunned him, sitting in jail, when out of nowhere came this faceless correspondent, this woman who loaded so much into every paragraph and demanded that he show his heart, this reporter whose letters revealed an urgency that had no place in any newsroom. What Kendall wanted was a friend to toy with, not an amateur archeologist stumbling through the wreckage. In almost every letter he said there were things he wished he could tell, secrets he wanted to confide. His next would list all the ways I had failed to deserve this. In the following, he'd apologize for being cold or hard or mean, and the cycle would begin all over again. Kendall's brand of humiliation was like drinking seawater when parched; it never quite sent me running, only tempted me forward to gulp down more.

The hairs on my arm prickled each time I reached into my long cool mailbox, knowing by touch if there was a letter inside from him. The envelopes were usually ribbed paper, formal and heavy. I'd trace their width, weigh each in my hand to determine if the note inside would be rambling or curt, and steel myself. But it was useless. I tore each one open and read standing at the post office counter.

I was important to him in some way. That much I knew. Whatever the facts might be about psychopaths and their incapacity for feeling, the faceless figure whom Kendall called "Ms. Rowe" or, more and more often, "Claudia," meant something to him. That he had walked a similar path with dozens of women—and that those stormy sagas of betrayal had almost nothing to do with the women themselves—was a humbling realization that came much later. At first, the feeling of mattering was like a drug, and I could not get enough. I held on like a dog with its jaws clamped round a piece of rotten meat. Never did I take the next step and consider what it meant that a man who had murdered eight women was focusing his attention on me.

Derrick had by now retreated into icy silence. He did not want to know about the phone calls from jail and did not care what I was learning. So we spoke no more about it. I plunged ahead, alternately terrified and thrilled, while Derrick watched the Weather Channel, his mouth pursed in a tight little line. This was a change. When we'd met in the newsroom, Derrick appeared to be the most openhearted man I'd ever known. He loved mountain hikes, drank only microbrews but, given the choice, would opt for a peanut butter sandwich over beer. On his second visit to my apartment he'd pulled from his knapsack a box of tinfoil and a packet of lightbulbs filched from his parents' supply closet, placing them on my wooden floors like an offering. Irritation twitched within me—surely he didn't think I was unable to buy these things for myself? The discomfort squirmed again when I went to collect some old books from an ex-boyfriend and four hours later found Derrick, near tears, waiting on my front stoop. Where had I been? he demanded, though I'd already explained my errand. I checked my voice mail, stomach tightening at his increasingly panicked messages. By the last, he sounded almost menacing. But this, too, I waved aside. On the summer morning we set off for our cross-country drive, he'd grinned at my blurted apologies for arriving late to his front door. "Hey, it's all right, it's all right," said my gentle Deadhead.

I wept as we drove, barely thirty but exhausted by my youth. *So much mileage,* I whispered, thinking of men who jerked off while whistling from bushes in the park; bouncers who'd ushered me into Studio 54, at fourteen, as bait. When we got to California, Derrick shyly unknotted an old bandanna to reveal a diamond ring nestled inside. "It was my grandmother's," he said. "I thought you might wear it someday." I was running on a treadmill at a drop-in gym as he presented this, thundering down a four-foot conveyor belt, and I did not stop.

With his fleece pullovers and hockey skates, Derrick looked like every prep-school boyfriend I'd never had, the easygoing jocks I'd pined for. He would never cheat or cloister himself in the bathroom with stacks of pornography like other men I'd known. He seemed purer, his desire proof that I was no longer the weird girl, the different one. A son of suburbia loved me, a boy who looked like America, and I was grateful. Derrick knew about the waif I'd been before. He knew about the boys who'd pulled me into dark closets, forcing my head down onto their skinny penises. I told him because he demanded it—fixating on those grubby high school sex scenes, making me tell and retell—reassuring him, always, that he was different.

I'd anticipated his disapproval about writing to Kendall, but it still hurt. Derrick knew who I was. He'd smiled with bitter understanding when I ranted about *Journal* editors forcing reporters to sand down the sharp edges of a quote, rather than allow readers to face their town's racism in print. My refusal to go along had charmed him. *"Devolve,* I love that word," he'd said one night outside a Poughkeepsie bar, using my latest jottings about school board dysfunction as a pickup line. But now there was no more talk about creative vocabulary or engagement rings, just daily barbs making clear Derrick's total rejection of my quest to unravel the mystery of Kendall Francois.

AS IT TURNED out, Kendall made eye contact with no one when he entered Judge Dolan's courtroom. He was silent, lumbering through the pews, and Catina Newmaster's mother whimpered as he passed. Other than that, there was no sound. Midday sunlight streamed in, silhouetting a row of police officers who stood along the back wall, legs apart, hands clasped in front of their crotches, whispering among themselves by tilting their small square heads to the left and right. Assistant District Attorney Margie Smith sat with the victims' families. Her small, sharp eyes darted everywhere.

All of the families clutched handwritten statements. Each of these had been edited by the District Attorney's staff, then turned over to Kendall's lawyers so their client might prepare himself. But few of the families knew that he'd been briefed. They came hungry for confrontation. They imagined goring Kendall with their hatred, and they wanted to watch his face as they did it. But the speaker's lectern had been placed behind Kendall's chair, forcing them to spit their curses at the back of his head. A final insult, Marguerite Marsh said.

From my seat in the jury box, I saw Pat Barone and remembered her five-year-old granddaughter spinning around for me in a tutu. That girl knew Pat as Mama now, stories of her real mother

fading by the day. I nodded at Kathleen Hurley's brother, thinking about Kathleen introducing him to the writing of Jack Kerouac
when no one in Poughkeepsie read the beat poets. I watched Heidi
Cramer, twenty-nine-year-old daughter of Sandy French, glower-
ing at Kendall from her seat in the front row. And now I prayed
that he would not seek me out.

Heidi had grabbed a moment of celebrity when the story broke,
leading reporters from the crime scene to the courthouse like an
actress trailing paparazzi. Sometimes she smiled and flirted with
us. Sometimes she shrieked and spat like a drowning cat. Every
day, she brought her infant daughter to 99 Fulton Avenue, resting
her pointy chin on the baby's head as photographers snapped. Yet
when I'd approached Heidi outside the Office of Child Protection,
she was aghast, as if there were rules for operating inside a media
storm and by ambushing her I had broken them. To make amends,
I attended Sandy's wake. Heidi greeted me at the door like a professional hostess, wanly extending her hand. Media offered a certain
celebrity, which included a first-class ticket to Los Angeles, where
Heidi spoke about her mother's murder on *The Montel Williams
Show*. And though she understood that pity and gossip colored her
fame, Heidi clung to it, hugging me like an old friend outside the
courthouse while the cameras rolled. On the day of Kendall's sentencing, she wore a floral sundress and flounced into court, tossing
her hair.

As long as Heidi could remember, her mother had been addicted
to drugs. But the prostitution was a surprise. Each morning, Sandy
French kissed her boyfriend good-bye and headed out the door
toward what she claimed was a horse-grooming job at one of the
gentleman farms in Pawling, near Martha Stewart's estate. Then
she turned and drove forty-five minutes in the opposite direction.

She made a few hundred dollars blowing IBMers in Poughkeep-sie, en route to their own work, and arrived home by early after-noon to knit booties for Heidi's infant on the way. It was Heidi, eight months pregnant, who went to the police when her mother's daily check-in calls stopped. Heidi who kept insisting they look in Poughkeepsie. Heidi who finally went herself and found Sandy's blue Camaro parked on Main Street. Plenty of people whispered about the Frenches—how Sandy wasn't above stealing from her daughters when she needed to; how she lived near Oniontown, an unincorporated settlement of trailers and corrugated tin shacks less than two hours from downtown Manhattan, where carpets covered dirt floors, and some families still used outhouses. County social workers hated making trips out there—any stranger was at risk of being pelted with rocks—and state police officers shook their heads just thinking about it. Appalachia within sight of hunt country, they said. A place that had shut its doors to the twentieth century and did not exist on any map. Oniontown didn't even have an address. Residents were allotted postal boxes in nearby Dover, and everyone knew what a PO number meant. Hillbilly hovels. Rural American wreckage. Despite this, Sandy French had been a proud woman. I could see it in the portrait set on her casket, the way she threw her auburn hair back, high cheekbones gleaming. In that frozen moment, Sandy French looked like a woman who had never known fear.

Heidi inherited none of her mother's features. A wispy blond stick figure, she stood at the lectern during Kendall's sentenc-ing and begged him to face her. He did not so much as shift in his chair. Heidi's pleas stretched into screams. "You fat nigger!" she screeched.

"Order!" shouted Judge Dolan.

"He is not a person!" cried Catina Newmaster's sister, rising to point a bony finger at Kendall's head. "He is a monster, incapable of human emotion."

"Order!" yelled the judge.

Wendy Meyers's aged aunt staggered to her feet. "When you choked Wendy, did it make you feel like a man?" she bellowed. "Francois, you have no light or love to give to anyone."

Kendall looked nervous. He had spent weeks thinking about this day, filling spiral notebooks with frantic scribblings about the things he wanted to say, how he'd been wronged, too, tricked and deceived. How he was sorry, but angry, an incoherent tangle. Instead, he sat motionless and mute, eyes focused on nothing. None of his family were present.

When the room quieted, Kendall's last victim walked to the lectern. Christine Sala had escaped his car with thumbprints embedded in her neck, and she sat trembling in the courtroom for half an hour before the proceeding started. "I will probably never understand why you have done this," Christine began. Once, she told the court, she'd considered Kendall a friend. She spoke of conversations that meandered through warm summer nights, of hopes confided and secrets shared. And though her face was tight with disgust, in Christine's voice I heard the realization of a girl who knew she'd been used. Judge Dolan looked uncomfortable, as if he'd stumbled onto an unexpectedly intimate conversation. "Good-bye, Kendall," Christine finally spat. "I hope they kill you in prison."

The judge invited him to respond, but one of Kendall's lawyers stood instead. Glenda Grace said her client deeply regretted what he'd done but would remain silent, fearing any words he might utter could be "misconstrued."

Dolan, a bearish ex-marine, gazed down at the lumpy man shackled before him. "Kendall Francois, a person would have to have a heart of stone not to feel the pain in this courtroom. You have changed the way we think about our community. You changed the way we think about ourselves."

He reiterated the sentence of eight life terms, rapped his gavel once, and watched as a quartet of guards escorted Kendall from the room.

Outside the courthouse I waited in the parking lot near a phalanx of television cameras, wondering if Kendall would look for me now. I wanted him to. I wanted him to meet my gaze and know I'd been the one listening, hovering close, all this time. He stepped into the searing August sunshine and strode toward the sheriff's van. For an instant, he glanced my way, then muttered something angrily to himself, ducked inside, and was locked away forever.

When I got back to Pleasant Valley, his latest letter was waiting.

I think about what the women's families are going to say, and what I'm going to say, if anything. It is a lose/lose situation all the way around. If I say something and just say it (as I would) I would be cold and heartless, but if I show any sort of emotion it is just an act. I could never convey my regret or remorse sufficiently in any case. . . . I'm sure that these women had another side to them, one I never saw. Just like I have a side they can't see.

In closing, he thanked me. It had been helpful, he said, to write it all down.

CHAPTER 6

Strange Town

I could never convince Kendall to tell me what had led his family to settle in Poughkeepsie. His maternal grandparents, Mittie and Roy Blackwell, were Virginians who'd arrived in 1954, part of the Great Migration of blacks moving north in search of jobs. Later, Kendall would rhapsodize about the meals he remembered eating at their home, heaping plates of okra and black-eyed peas cooked by Grandma Blackwell, "a good, religious, southern woman," he said. At their place fifteen minutes away in the town of Hyde Park, the Francois children rode their bikes through the woods, launching into the air over mounds of earth and landing just shy of a dried-out streambed in his grandmother's backyard. Only weeks before his arrest, Kendall had wandered back to gaze at the spot. "I can't believe we used to do that—so dangerous!" he told me over the phone from jail.

Kendall's mother was eight when her family arrived in upstate New York to find themselves roundly shunned for their farm country ways. But the Blackwells never saw any need to assimilate. Instead of driving into Poughkeepsie to worship in a dignified stone building with one of city's established black congregations, they became members at Central Baptist Church, housed in an old barn well outside of town. Paulette and her younger brother enrolled at Traver Road Elementary, where they were among the only blacks in the building, and Mittie and Roy found jobs in food service at the Hudson River State Hospital for the Insane. By the time she was twenty, Paulette was on staff, too.

Because Kendall had forbidden me to contact his mother, I hung around the Victorian Gothic hospital, dreaming up newspaper stories to write so I could get closer to her. Roger Christenfeld, second in command, was eager to show me around. An administrator there since the 1970s, Dr. Christenfeld wore a bow tie and his wiry hair stood almost vertical, as if trying to swoop away from his head. He unlocked creaky doors with a six-inch key while narrating the history of his thousand-acre campus, as if the place were a dear old family manse. We walked carpeted hallways, Christenfeld pointing out limited edition prints along the walls and nearly weeping at the ways government downsizing had forced his staff to relinquish their oak-paneled offices for cubicles.

When Kendall's grandparents worked there, the sprawling psychiatric hospital was a world unto itself, a haven for staff as much as patients. Its nursing school, where Paulette trained, was a regular speaking stop for Eleanor Roosevelt, whose family had donated the grounds. There were private churches and a morgue; farm fields and a butcher, baker, milliner, and cobbler; a bowling alley, indoor swimming pool, and golf course, all perched on a hill overlooking the Hudson. Patients hated to leave. Retirement parties were planned months in advance, attended by hundreds. Cooks and nurses might spend their entire working lives walking those hushed hallways, and it was standard for parents and children, like the Blackwells, to work side by side for years. Often, a single family had three generations on the payroll.

With a glint in his eye, Dr. Christenfeld asked if I'd ever been inside a mental hospital before. I shook my head.

"Capital!" he clapped. "We'll take you to see the borderlines!"

We drove the single block from his warm woody office to the sole remaining ward on the campus. Cheney Pavilion, a ten-story tower of steel and glass, looked nothing like the manor homes dotting the rest of the property. A guard at the entrance gave me a quizzical look before buzzing us through the outer door and into a small holding pen, where we waited, in suspension, for the inside gate to slide open.

A sleek marble lobby greeted me, its walls lined with patient artwork (large purple flowers, detailed dream scenes), and as we boarded an elevator to the fourth floor, Dr. Christenfeld's eyes burned with anticipation. A woman with long gray hair stood before us as the door slid open, her neck arched and craning downward like a bird's.

"They're building the new place on bones," she said, peering at me from behind her curtain of hair.

"Hello, Diane, how are you feeling today?" Dr. Christenfeld responded.

"On bones. Old body parts is how they're making the new building."

"Really? I don't think so, but I'll look into it. Have you had your medicine today? How are you feeling?"

He took my elbow and steered me toward the next room, where five fat women sat around a television. I could feel Diane staring at my back, still muttering about a hospital built of bones. Dr. Christenfeld ignored her, introducing me to the other patients as he made his rounds. The chattiest of the group was Jane, in her early twenties. She inquired about my work and told Dr. Christenfeld that she was feeling better than she had in a long time. She cracked a few jokes and mentioned how eager she was for her family's next visit. Compared to Diane, she appeared completely functional. Back in the elevator, Dr. Christenfeld smiled wanly at my assessment. Jane was the most dangerous woman on the ward, he said. She needed to be restrained almost every day.

Paulette's mentor at the hospital, director James Regan, had long been uncomfortable with such tactics. The notion of straitjackets made him wince. Dr. Christenfeld left me with his boss just as a loudspeaker squawked "Code Red." Regan's jaw tightened. But he relaxed when touring me through the top floor of the old asylum, a garret crowded with faceless mannequins and chairs where patients once sat with their heads encased in steel boxes. I saw the rocking bed where they'd been chained, the bathtubs where they were soothed with ice water.

A foxlike man with a trim red beard, Regan had spent decades training nurses at the hospital, but he'd never forgotten Paulette Francois. From the moment he spied her sitting in the front row of his abnormal psychology class, Regan had been drawn to the lively woman with moles spattered across her chubby face. She struck him as eager to please. True, she sometimes wore the same dress for days and perhaps had not showered, but there was nothing that could have prepared Regan for what he read in the newspaper years later. He was flabbergasted to learn that Paulette had been unaware of eight corpses stuffed inside her home. He'd known her more than twenty years. "She was hard to miss," he said. "Bubbly, enthusiastic. Maybe she wasn't a genius, but she certainly was not stupid."

The same gap-toothed smile that initially charmed Regan remained as Paulette was shuttled from ward jobs to office work, and he moved up the ranks to become her boss. She was a cheerleader, in Regan's view, valued for her unflagging, positive attitude, a boon to kids entering the hospital's apprenticeship program. And when Paulette was transferred off campus to handle paperwork for the mentally ill living in city projects, she found acceptance again. Regan considered her a motivator, an optimist. "We were lucky to have her," he said.

We spoke in his fifth-floor office, a former ward where the hospital director served his secretary fresh-brewed Starbucks from a plug-in coffeepot and Beethoven blasted from computer speakers. The question of Paulette's mental health hung over every comment, running in the shadows behind Regan's eyes as he peered out windows threaded with restraining wire.

"I imagine," he began, recalling Paulette's aptitude as a student, her diligence and general functionality, "that you're wondering how this squares with what the police have said, and I don't understand it at all. She was your basic bubbly person. No one could have detected psychopathology in Paulette."

"But if that's true, if she was sane, how could she be oblivious to her son keeping dead women in their home?"

Regan sighed. His path and hers had diverged over the years, but he considered Paulette a friend. Their children had gone to school together, and he felt bound to protect her, even now. So instead of answering directly, he told a story: Once, there had been a patient at the hospital who sincerely believed herself to be the queen of England. She was lobbying for release and, aside from this fantasy, appeared perfectly sane. A sympathetic doctor made a suggestion: "Keep your royal lineage a secret," he told her. "Don't let the evaluators know anything about it." Which is exactly what she did. The woman spoke well, convincing the experts of her mental health, and went on to live a relatively normal life—all the while believing herself the unrecognized queen. That was delusion, Regan said, full-blown mental illness.

Denial was different, a desperate and elaborate defense erected to block out the intolerable. It could allow a mother to live with a son who hoarded dead bodies. It could enable an educated woman to sit in a car littered with used condoms and strangers' jewelry, and avoid asking questions. But when forced to confront the truth, a life built on denial would crumble like sand castles at the beach. This, in Regan's opinion, was what had happened to Paulette. She'd been shattered by Kendall's crimes. She showed up for work but walked through her days as if shell-shocked. She attended a mental health conference in Albany, wandering the convention center hallways in a daze, a wig covering hair gone white, her hearty frame shrunken, as if half of her had withered away. Paulette's good manners, however, remained. She chatted lightly and said she'd moved to Connecticut. "You look great, Paulette," colleagues whispered kindly. But no one gathered for her retirement party. After thirty years at the hospital, Kendall's mother cleaned out her desk without fanfare one Friday afternoon and vanished.

What happens when delusion is shoved down your throat, when you are forced to confront reality? "If it's real mental illness, it continues," Regan said. "If it's denial, you get hit over the head."

Kendall's mother had never been crazy. Her devastation was proof, Regan believed. But a merciful person might wish she had lost her mind.

DESPITE ITS DEEP-ROOTED African American population and strong church community, Dutchess County had never been much of a haven for blacks. By the 1920s, the Ku Klux Klan was holding rallies there that drew thousands. As late as 1994, during my first weekend in the *Journal* newsroom, I picked up the phone to hear an elderly African American woman shrieking about a cross burning on her lawn. She had already alerted the paper twice and been told that someone would get back to her. But the police had come and gone, and Dorothy Williams, aged seventy-four, sat in her living room as dusk fell, looking at an ugly stake hole in front of her house. No reporter had even called. "What is wrong with you people!" she screamed in my ear. Days later, when an editor finally sent someone out, Williams said, "When you're in the South, you already know what the whole situation is about. Here in New York, it's supposed to be different. But it's only quietly different."

The cross burners had attended Arlington High School a few years behind Kendall, though he never knew them. When I mentioned the incident, his only comment was that far more happened in Dutchess County than the newspaper ever told.

If tension between whites and blacks had long existed there, residents of all colors had just as long been reluctant to admit it. The nation's first black woman judge, Jane Bolin Mizelle, grew up in Poughkeepsie and returned in 1944 to lambaste her community for their complacency. It was ludicrous to talk of interracial brotherhood when there were no blacks in the district attorney's office, police, or fire departments (only slightly better progress today). Mizelle was no bomb thrower. Her ancestors had founded the Ebenezer Baptist and AME Zion churches downtown. They participated in politics and held their heads high. But they did not welcome newcomers. "They talked bad about them," said Walter Patrice, himself a son of the old guard who remembered how his parents had sneered at the southerners' cornbread-and-collards diets, laughing at their country ways.

Even urban blacks received a chilly welcome. Rupert and Marie Tarver, community organizers from Chicago, arrived in 1956 to discover that the home they'd been promised disappeared when the owner learned they were black. It took another six years for the Tarvers to find someone willing to sell to them. "It was a mixed bag—that's the best I can say," Marie would tell me four decades later. She had been born in Louisiana and fought her way through segregated schools to a graduate-level education, but still lived in the same modest colonial wedged between two abandoned buildings on Mansion Street, where broken glass tangled with weeds on the sidewalk.

Like most in that small city, Marie Tarver and Paulette Francois had crossed paths. They were mothers, and churchgoers, and transplanted southerners, any of which might have forged a connection, but the federal government's urban renewal program brought them together. Marie ran the local branch, known as Model Cities, and was responsible for doling out millions in aid to community groups. Paulette supervised one of them, a youth-employment office based at the psychiatric center.

"Kendall looks just like his mother," said Marie as I sat in her immaculate living room. "I cried when I saw his picture in the paper. I thought, Oh, that's Paulette!"

Model Cities sought to involve the poor in "reclaiming" their communities, and Poughkeepsie became well known in Washington, D.C., as a recipient of public largesse—forty million dollars, all told, making it one of the nation's largest per-capita recipients of federal aid at the time. With government money came government plans to overhaul the old river city and plow highways through small-town lanes. Main Street would become an auto-free promenade where passersby might rest on benches and gaze at the flower beds as they shopped. That the new arterial highway accompanying this pedestrian paradise would funnel cars straight through town and away from the shops somehow escaped notice. Throughout the 1970s, federal dollars flowed and Poughkeepsians spent them blithely, bulldozing their city in the name of progress. In less than a decade, downtown was all but deserted.

MY ATTEMPTS TO share this history with Kendall were met with scorn. But it continued to fascinate me. After emancipation, hundreds of former slaves had moved from the surrounding farm country into Poughkeepsie proper, and lower Main Street became a hub of black social life, with black-owned bars and brothels, a formidable-looking First Baptist Church, and regal Ebenezer Baptist a few blocks away. A century later, the founders' descendants remained faithful still, the women attending every Sunday in colorful hats and matching shoes, the men in somber suits. Vassar students sped past toward the hippie town of New Paltz across the river, staring at beings from another world.

To an outsider, distinctions between the city of Poughkeepsie businesses and those in the surrounding town would have been all but invisible. But to locals this divide was as important as the Mason-Dixon Line. Despite sharing a name, the two municipalities ran under separate governments, school systems, and police departments. Kendall, living on the town side, often told me that before turning eighteen he'd never crossed the boundary between them. The city's blight appalled him, Main Street most of all. He heard classmates from Arlington mocking the addicts and bums, and he couldn't fault them. Black slang made him cringe. Kendall had no interest in learning, especially from me, about the proud history of African Americans in his hometown; it was too humiliating to reconcile with what came later. So I never told him about the city's pre–Civil War abolition meetings; nor the threats, in reaction, to burn Poughkeepsie's black churches. And we never discussed the slave descendants who'd moved from working Dutchess County farms to become some of the city's most prominent citizens. Any attempt to explore these stories was silenced. American history was lies, all lies, Kendall said, too full of hypocrisy to absorb.

Paulette and McKinley aspired to a life beyond Poughkeepsie's limits from the first. Shortly after marrying in 1969, they moved into Vassar Gardens, a dank apartment complex a few feet past the city line. Across the street, stately maples framed wide lawns of sweet-smelling grass on the Vassar College campus, where students dozed or kissed or read French philosophy. But you couldn't see any of that from their apartment. Tenants at Vassar Gardens curtained their windows with bedsheets and left old barbecue grills to rust outside. After a few years, the Francoises packed up and decamped, temporarily, to a trailer on Paulette's brother's property in the country, waiting until McKinley could buy them a place of their own. It was a small colonial with a backyard too tight for anything larger than a kiddie pool. They moved in when Kendall was ten and his younger brother eight. The boys' older sister, Raquelle, remained with relatives, but there was a new child now, baby Kierstyn, who clung to her big brother Ken's hand as they wandered through the wrought-iron college gates to gaze at all that space.

Sitting a few hundred yards from downtown Poughkeepsie, 99 Fulton Avenue teetered between these two worlds, close enough to the edge that after Kendall's arrest, police officers from the town squabbled with their colleagues in the city over who had responsibility. No one wanted to sort through all that mess.

It was like this in Poughkeepsie, where class differences were calculated down to the inch. Anyone could see why. The city schools, nearly all black, had the highest dropout rates in Dutchess County; while just two miles south, Spackenkill, which Derrick had attended, was, though public, essentially a prep academy. To the north lay rural Hyde Park, which sometimes recruited Poughkeepsie boys for sports, and stretching east into former farm fields, mostly-white Arlington, where Kendall was educated.

Arlington families reviled the city. They lived in ranch-style homes dotting dairy-land-turned-developments, and made firm distinctions between the worn city storefronts of Poughkeepsie and their sprawling suburban town of the same name. Their elementary school, with its stone staircase and pansy-ringed flagpole, had been built in the 1930s, a WPA project for citizens who believed themselves worthy of proud, permanent edifices. The ceilings were high, the classrooms airy. The hallways smelled of construction paper and apple juice. Principal Art May walked them for thirty years.

May was descended from one of Poughkeepsie's oldest black families. His skin was toffee-colored; his suits always pressed. At school board meetings where red-faced men fumed over property-tax increases, May in his bow tie remained circumspect. He handled every crisis with the same calm dispatch, the same polite, if distant, smile. Even after he'd retired, the former principal never appeared in anything other than impeccable professional wear. He had watched thousands of children stream through Arlington Elementary by the time Kendall's picture hit the papers but recalled his former student instantly. Not that there had been anything remarkable about Kendall's personality. It was his size. He was simply the biggest kid anyone had ever seen, as tall as his teachers by the time he was ten, and it unnerved them to see that pudgy child's face on top of a man's body. Freakishly large, they thought, and so very quiet.

Aside from his size and race, little else about Kendall stood out. Few students sought his friendship—the Francois kids spent most of their time together, anyway—and even if some boy or girl had been drawn to the oddly reserved youth, there would have been no playdates. Kendall's parents forbade their children from bringing anyone home.

When Kendall enrolled as a fifth grader in 1982, the family appeared typical enough. The kids had entered midyear, which was unusual, but their mother came to every meeting and was among the school's more involved parents. She inquired about her children's progress and embraced teachers' suggestions for improvement. She acted just as a mother should. It had to be hard for the Francoises, blending into a nearly all-white district, but Paulette never complained.

If Kendall's mother was a familiar presence at Arlington Elementary, his father was an enigma. McKinley left early for work and arrived home late. The rare times he showed up at school McKinley sat silent as a stone. Neighbors saw him only when they happened to meet on the well-traveled path that cut behind the playing field. Principal May spotted him there in the evenings, a large man moving quickly, his head down. He muttered a terse hello in an accent May could never place, and kept moving. I reiterated this sketch for Kendall, and he agreed with most of it. "Yeah, my father was a big man. I can attest to that personally," he said through gritted teeth. His only argument was with my assertion that McKinley had walked the footpath at all. "My father never took a shortcut to do anything in his life," he said.

In the afternoons, Kendall could have ambled home from school on streets that glowed golden in the autumn sun. He could have gazed at brick edifices brushed with ochre or pink dogwoods silhouetted against the steely Hudson sky. He could have wandered Grand Avenue, with its weathered stone walls and bursting gardens, or looked up at filigreed cornices hidden atop the old rooftops of Main Street. But Kendall's preferred route was the back way. The trail cut through a parking lot at Vassar Gardens and led straight into his yard. Everyone knew about the shortcut—it was quick and private—though it offered little to look at beyond weeds and garbage.

As far as his teachers could tell, the transfer into Arlington did not bother ten-year-old Kendall. A polite student with thick glasses and deferential manners, he seemed only to want reassurance that the midyear changeover from Hyde Park would not delay his passage into sixth grade. An odd concern for such a young kid, thought his homeroom teacher, Ralph Forsythe, but Kendall was clearly intelligent. He spoke well and at first caused no problems. Forsythe assured the boy he should make it into middle school without a hitch.

Similar worries would plague Kendall throughout his academic career. At twenty-five, he panicked at the thought of failing community college algebra, quaking to imagine his father's response. Imprisoned at Attica, he remained furious at the middle school guidance counselor who'd deemed his math skills too weak for a Regents program and tracked him instead into consumer arithmetic. "They taught us how to balance a checkbook," Kendall growled. The decision had wrecked any chance of getting into college as a science major, he believed, and was yet another example of the ways life had been derailed by forces beyond his control.

The truth cuts deeper. Kendall was bright. Plenty of people recognized that. He was quick with words and possessed of laserlike focus, but lab coats and research grants were never going to frame his world. Teachers nodded kindly at his labored concentration as Kendall spent months carving a chess set in shop class. High school athletes marveled at the will that would keep him returning to football practice, wheezing and humiliated, year after year. Yet the discipline to commit to a larger vision, to vault himself away from home and toward a bigger life, required grit that Kendall lacked. He dreamed in colorful detail. But when unrealized, these yearnings did not dissipate. They spun into fury. Affirmation, in turn, was narcotic. When Kendall got an A on a college ethics paper, he leaped around the classroom like a crazy bird, waving the essay overhead and whooping in ecstasy.

Ralph Forsythe, standing at the blackboard in Kendall's fifth-grade classroom, could never have anticipated such enthusiasm, for despite the boy's tremulous inquiry about getting into sixth grade, good marks seemed the least of his concerns. He sat stoically at his desk all spring, refusing to pick up a pencil. When other children opened their schoolbooks, Kendall remained frozen. He would neither acknowledge his teacher nor read aloud when called on. He did no homework at all. Kendall simply sat, immobile and impenetrable, waiting for summer to come. Seventeen years later, when the families of his victims wailed in court, pleading for a flicker of insight, he maintained the same impassive silence, staring straight ahead, hands at his sides.

Despite this obstinacy, Forsythe did not consider Kendall a mean-spirited kid. There were no tantrums or overt signs of anger. He did not hurt other students. He was simply the most unmotivated child Forsythe had ever seen. When the teacher asked what was wrong, Kendall shrugged. When he inquired if there was something else the boy would rather be doing, Kendall shook his head. Desperate to provoke a reaction, Forsythe took his schoolbooks away. Kendall did not protest. He curled deeper into his mind, and the books remained stacked on a shelf until June. "As a teacher, you kind of feel that a kid in your class would have all the feelings and morals you passed down, so I feel badly, I really do," said Forsythe years later. He was one of the few in Poughkeepsie to admit a sense of failure or personal responsibility for what had happened to the Francoises.

At recess, Kendall stood off to one side of the play yard, drawing pictures. These were concentrated pieces, visions from a child who displayed unusual dexterity and articulated his imagination with careful control. Yet Kendall took no joy in his artwork. He considered it unimportant. Teachers praised his skill, and Kendall shrugged. That nonchalance lasted into adulthood, Kendall wrapping his thick hands around slim colored pencils, lightly shading vines and flowers, affecting utter boredom when complimented. Before holidays, during the years we corresponded, I could always expect a hand-drawn card with "nightling," his signature, on the back. On the front, he'd sketch sunflowers, daisies, peaceful country scenes. But Kendall had a strange relationship to nature. He told me that he'd wanted to become a marine biologist, yet he could not tolerate the smell of the ocean. The scent of natural decay nauseated him—an amazing admission, considering how he'd lived. He despised bugs—spiders, in particular—with a vicious, angry fear, leaping onto his jailhouse cot and cowering in the corner when one crawled into his cell. Yet spiders appeared frequently on the cards he drew me, dangling from capital letters, waving from cartoon-perfect webs.

One summer I told him that I'd gone strawberry picking, and the next week received a letter saying, "I think strawberries are the MOST DISGUSTING food in the whole planet, but I used to enjoy picking them. My grandmother used to take my cousins, siblings and me strawberry picking almost every year when we were young."

I could picture Mittie Blackwell leading a trail of kids through the fields, Kendall lumbering along behind the others, bending to pick a fruit that he hated and twisting inside.

I TELL MYSELF that if Kendall were a fifth grader today someone would step in and try to figure out why a bright, capable boy refused to speak. But in the spring of 1982, with two months to go before summer vacation, perhaps it seemed pointless to arrange the necessary meetings. Kendall would be passed as promised into sixth grade, and if there were indeed a serious problem, surely teachers at the next red-brick building would catch it. No one knew that Kendall walked home to rooms where feces littered the floor. How could they? None of the Francois children came to school looking bruised, and on class-picture days they were immaculate. Kendall wore a white button-down and V-neck sweater when other kids showed up in T-shirts.

There was one final hint about Kendall's life outside of Arlington Elementary, though it, too, went mostly unnoticed. When students presented their report cards to parents during the last week of school, Kendall's was switched accidentally with another boy's. That child's mother, staring down at a miserable string of fifth-grade failures, called Forsythe immediately to correct the mistake. But Paulette and McKinley never said a word. Their son's pathetic record lay exposed and unclaimed in the school's front office all summer long, a stark column of Fs next to the name KENDALL FRANCOIS. Ducking in to prepare his classroom for the fall, Forsythe saw the card and wondered how the boy's parents could leave such shame open to the world, lying there for anyone to see. But the Francoises were different. They had dark skin and an exotic last name, and no polite teacher was going to pry too deeply. You could hardly blame a family for simply wanting to get along. Criticizing their odd behavior just seemed cruel. Maybe it made you look like a racist.

If the Francoises had lived just a few yards west, Kendall would have attended Poughkeepsie High School with Donte Turner. Instead, the two met several years later, at community college, after Donte took pity on the hulking loner playing solitaire in the cafeteria. He recognized the guy from American Government, reason enough to invite him to join the crew who met weekly for tournaments of Magic: The Gathering in Donte's living room. For hours they binged on fantasy role-playing in a game where wizards bested warriors and sorcerers beat witches. Afterward Donte would drive Kendall home to Fulton Avenue, where he received a polite thank-you but was never invited inside.

A year after Kendall's arrest, Donte still could not comprehend how he had repeatedly opened his home to a multiple murderer.

The guy was so timid, slumping through those Monday-afternoon games, refusing to assert himself with so much as a request for toppings when they ordered out for pizza. He lost every hand. But Kendall knew he possessed a secret that made him more powerful than anyone in the room. They thought he was a nobody. But he'd touched limits they never would. Power like that could make you dizzy. You were at Donte's, playing cards with the guys, but your mind was up in the attic with Wendy and the others.

In retrospect, it was this duality that most infuriated Donte, who was proud of the way he'd pulled himself up from the street, living on his own since sixteen. He'd been a high school dropout and small-time dope dealer, but the kind of kid that teachers love— canny and charming, brimming with potential. When we met at the Italian bakery near his home, he'd clawed his way from a GED program into candidacy for graduate-level courses in international relations. But Donte could not stop mulling the divide embodied by Kendall. "I just feel so stupid!" he said, slamming his cappuccino on the marble table between us.

He lived with his girlfriend and baby daughter in Poughkeepsie's Little Italy, a tangle of nineteenth-century homes clustered near the railroad tracks, where sinewy old men sat outside the bakery, marking the hours by watching commuters come and go. In the city's tic-tac-toe of neighborhood division, Little Italy was predominantly white, but Donte—handsome, athletic, and black— had always been able to move easily between castes. Even dealing dime bags on Main Street, he knew he was meant for more. Community college would lead to the state university and eventually to a Ph.D. program somewhere far away. Donte planned it all while mixing drinks at Outback Steakhouse in the mall. Sometimes he imagined returning in triumph. Maybe he'd run for mayor. But more often, Donte told anyone who would listen that once out, he'd never return. Kendall was never going to have that choice. He saw it the moment they met. Kendall wasn't going anywhere. "You just got the feeling nothing ever went his way," Donte said. "I definitely could never imagine a girl going out with him."

Despite their obvious differences, Donte and Kendall shared important traits. Both chafed at what it meant to be African American in Poughkeepsie. Both had struggled to find a foothold in parallel worlds. As a teen, Donte would leave his shabby North Side home to sail through Advanced Placement classes with the handful of white kids enrolled in Poughkeepsie High School, then follow them home to cavernous South Side living rooms. When their parents arrived from work, Donte knew he would not be invited to dinner. "There was a line, definitely," he said. "You'd see the look on their faces and know you were black." As the sky darkened, Donte loped back up Academy, passing one gingerbread-trim mansion after the next before crossing Main Street and the arterial that cleaved Poughkeepsie in two. Then he was on the North Side again, where he'd sell a few dime bags and go home.

For all his finesse at navigating these social divides, Donte found them maddening. Living in Poughkeepsie felt like being stranded on the bank of a river as the rest of life rushed past, he said. People simply languished. Donte saw women who used to babysit him still working the same dull day jobs fifteen years later, still spending their nights in the same dingy bars. He'd run into them on the street and notice they'd grown older, with looser skin and sagging breasts, but their expressions, the curve of their backs, the rhythm in their labored strides remained the same. "It's like this city just wants to forget," he said. "What kind of environment are we where eight women can disappear and no one does anything for two years?"

The arterial was still relatively new when Donte was crossing over it during the mid-1980s. Beforehand, Poughkeepsie's racial divides had been somewhat less obvious. But now motorists had a long snaking highway cutting a fifty-mile-an-hour swath straight from Arlington's farm fields through town to the stone courthouse, where hundreds of county residents arriving for jury duty listened to a sordid litany of tales—the guy who kept boxes of pubic hair under his bed and sent it to society ladies in envelopes sealed with semen; the man who checked himself into emergency rooms complaining of urinary pain because he wanted to be catheterized. Jurors left shaking their heads. "I just didn't have a clue what was going on," they told Assistant District Attorney Margie Smith, who agreed that Dutchess County did produce some particularly bizarre crime.

Many of her classmates had fled after high school, but Margie Smith remained. She'd seen no reason to turn up her nose at community college. From there, Margie transferred to the state university with plans to become a labor lawyer. A summer stint in the district attorney's office was only temporary, a stepping-stone, she told her parents. At first she'd been the only woman on staff, a starry-eyed twenty-two-year-old, shy when police asked if she'd like to tag along while they interviewed a man who'd hacked his wife to death. But Margie would not flinch. Everyone knew the Smiths, and she would not tarnish their good name by wilting at a crime scene. Within a year Margie was listening to a middle school history teacher confess to luring a Spackenkill football star into his home so he could kill the boy and eat his testicles. Not long after, she found herself questioning a black girl who described a gang rape by white cops. They'd covered her with dog shit, scratched NIGGER on her legs, and dumped her in a garbage bag on the hard

November ground, Tawana Brawley said. Television reporters from around the world flocked to Poughkeepsie for this one—but Margie had a bad feeling about Brawley's claims from the start, and she never found a shred of evidence to support the teenager's account. Not a bruise or stray hair, or even a willingness to discuss the incident. A decade later, after the charges had been investigated and finally dropped, Margie was left to wonder what kind of life would drive a girl to smear herself with feces and lie down in a garbage bag to begin with. It was almost as troubling as the tale itself.

Despite these disquieting interludes, lifelong residents insisted that theirs was a beautiful town. They pointed to its Victorian mansions and college campuses. "Remember *It's a Wonderful Life?* Well, that was Poughkeepsie," said Marco Caviglia, the lawyer who represented Kendall's family as police ransacked their home for human remains.

Social tensions aside, the place had boomed during the 1940s and '50s. IBM moved its world headquarters to Poughkeepsie's suburbs, and engineers flocked from around the country. The new money spawned housing developments, country clubs, and the entire Spackenkill School District. Main Street was a busy boulevard in those days, and Marie Tarver, stepping out to buy a new pair of shoes, marveled at the throngs. Margie Smith, then a snub-nosed kid from Pleasant Valley, would ride in with her family on Thursday nights, when all the stores were open late. She followed her mother through the wide hallways at Luckey, Platt & Company and waited as her father burrowed through the racks at Shwartz's. Afterward the Smiths, who owned a prosperous auction house, might take their daughter to Effron's for a new party dress. As a teen, Margie would sit on the benches at Reservoir Square, gloating over her purchases. A few blocks away, opera singers and presidential candidates made regular visits, pleased to spend an evening in one of the mansions lining Raymond Avenue so bedecked with cupolas, balconies, and trim that each seemed to be making a statement about the place Poughkeepsie ought to hold in American history.

THIRTY YEARS LATER, IBM tanked. The region's great benefactor began laying off engineers by the score. Derrick's father hung on to a job, but two-thirds of his colleagues lost theirs, and when I arrived in 1994, fewer than one hundred local families earned more than $150,000. By 1995, taxes, suicide, and domestic violence had spiked measurably, while the city's population plummeted. Suburbanites, even those who had been raised in Poughkeepsie, drove in only when compelled by jury duty or overwhelming nostalgia.

There was something different about her town, Margie Smith often told friends from other places, something that seemed to generate particularly desperate behavior. It got to the point where she dreaded calling colleagues in other jurisdictions. "Oh, it's Margie, from Poughkeepsie," she imagined them thinking. "What god-awful story has she got this time?" Still, what good did it do to dwell on that? Margie could have gone anywhere after Arlington High, but, for better or worse, she had chosen to stay, which is how the forty-two-year-old divorced prosecutor found herself sitting in a police station at one A.M., taking notes while Kendall Francois explained how he'd lived for two years with a growing pile of women's corpses.

For all of Margie's long experience, the interview with Kendall was more than she could handle. He talked about strangling Catina

Newmaster, and Margie felt the air go out of her stomach. Catina had been such a tiny person, a shred of a girl, with wispy blond hair and a squeaky voice. "Innocuous" was the first word that came to Margie's mind. They all knew each other, the cops and criminals, the prosecutors and defense attorneys, faces on a wheel that spun round and round. Year in, year out, she saw them walking to and from the courthouse. Sometimes they landed on her desk in a rape victim file, sometimes as child abusers. Whoever they were, Margie with her good country breeding would offer a firm handshake and quick smile. She prided herself on being able to find a bond with each, some way to empathize. A woman let her boyfriend have sex with the children? Well, Margie could try to understand that, even if she was going to put both adults in jail—love, need, these things were complicated. Another woman tortured her kids? She'd probably been beaten half to death herself. You had to take these things into account. Even when Margie sent someone to prison, it didn't mean she couldn't feel for them.

Kendall Francois was different. Margie probed, but she could find nothing to help her comprehend what he had done. In college, when a professor asked her to argue in favor of the death penalty, Margie had balked. She'd have to be ready to stick the needle into someone's arm herself, she said, and she was never going to hate anyone enough to do that. Kendall Francois was the first. The only defendant Assistant District Attorney Margie Smith had ever encountered for whom she could feel nothing. After his nine-hour confession, she stepped out of the interview room and fell, sobbing, into a detective's arms.

Driving home through the predawn dark, Margie felt ill. She was thinking how much she despised this man, how he'd pushed her into emotions that were not entirely professional. Yet when the interview was over Margie stuck out her hand, and Kendall shook it. They were still two humans, and Margie Smith was damned if he'd keep her from acknowledging that. Afterward, she wouldn't leave her house for days. But before Margie collapsed into sleep, she called her mother. She wanted Mrs. Smith to hear it all from her, not the morning news.

"You touched him?" Margie's mother gasped.

"Yes, Mom. I touched him."

As If We Were Friends

The idea that I had been sitting in court for his sentencing, watching yet unknown to him, frustrated Kendall enough that he phoned immediately upon returning to jail to propose that we meet in person. I had suggested this before, but Kendall always demurred. It made no sense, he'd say. If I was so leery of his gaze that I refused to send a photograph, how could I be comfortable sitting close enough to talk? Reasoning was useless. It was like trying to make yourself heard in a cave of echoes. Kendall couldn't see how a face-to-face conversation might feel safer to me than knowing he held my picture in his hands. Control was the sticking point for both of us. I refused to relinquish it by allowing him to view me whenever he chose, running his fingers over my image, creasing the paper across my face, thinking thoughts I didn't want to know, and he was demanding the right to do exactly that. But to hear Kendall tell it, my image on a piece of paper meant nothing much. He said he rarely glanced at the photo album of family and friends he'd been allowed to keep in his cell, though he liked knowing they were close.

All of that prior back-and-forth now gave way to Kendall's curiosity. He told me to visit in two days, and to arrive at 7:45 A.M.

"You're sure about this?" I said. "Don't make me wake up that early if you're just going to have me turn around and go back home."

Kendall chuckled. He was always up to see the dawn.

Bright and modern, the Hamilton Street jail had recently been renovated, with an air-conditioning system so powerful that visitors hugged themselves in the lobby, though it was August. Besides a serial killer, the building held approximately one hundred prostitutes, drug dealers, and pedophiles—most of them barely literate, Kendall complained. He sometimes helped a Jamaican murderer sound out the words in a children's book of Bible stories. Compared to everyone else in there, Kendall believed himself calmer and saner. Meant for better things, he'd say.

I wrote down the name of the inmate I'd come to see and presented my driver's license to a guard. He immediately shook his head. No, Kendall Francois was not accepting visitors. But I'd been invited, I told him, Kendall was expecting me. The guard stalked off to confer with an administrator. He was still shaking his head when he returned. Across the icy room a fat teenager began to wail, barred from using an out-of-state ID to visit her brother. She was blotchy and bloated, her hair ratty. Her shrieks grew louder as the guards marched back and forth, trying to handle my request. The sobbing turned hysterical, then abusive. Next to her, I sounded reasonable—just a young woman waiting to visit with a serial murderer, all her papers in order. They let me in.

I was shown to a stuffy cubicle with cinder-block walls painted dull mustard. Inside, a filthy armchair had been pulled up to the narrow shelf where you were supposed to lean your elbows, speak into a handset, and stare at your loved one through Plexiglas. The chair was low and saggy. In it, I sat only high enough to rest my chin on the ledge. "One hour," said the guard, locking me inside. A moment later he cracked the door open and scanned my face.

"If you don't mind my asking, how'd you get hooked up to see this guy?"

I told him I was a reporter who wanted to write about the case, and that Kendall and I had been corresponding for a year. He nodded.

"You know, a lot of them looked like you—the victims."

Yes, I knew that.

He shut the door again. Seconds passed, thick, slow, suffocating. The fabric of my shirt clung to my shoulders, bunching up at the pockets across my chest. I'd thought so carefully about what to wear. Something that would make me look approachable and pleasant. Something that would say I was there neither to punish nor to judge. I wore jeans, flat shoes, no makeup. I wanted to look like a friend, in no way a flirt.

On the other side of the glass I heard keys turning inside a lock, the sound of an unchangeable moment. I couldn't quite believe this was happening. Until now, corresponding with Kendall had felt like a dare I set myself, almost a game, something separate from real life. Our letters, no matter how tortuous, provided a certain distance. They allowed me to craft the person Kendall saw. I could be the authoritarian interviewer or show sensitive vulnerability, whatever I thought might draw him out. Phone calls were harder. It felt like Kendall could hear my heart pounding through the silences. Still, there had been the safety of my home, the knowledge that he couldn't see me biting my lip, scribbling questions. Now we would be looking into each other's eyes.

I froze as the door swung open, paralyzed like a mouse beneath the claws of a descending owl.

Kendall stared down at me. He filled the entire frame. Three guards worked to unlock his restraints as he waited patiently, his face brushed with the trace of a smile. When they left, his mouth broke open into a grin, greedy and expectant, like I was a Sunday dinner he was sitting down to eat. His lips and teeth were huge. He picked up the handset but could not get control of himself long enough to speak. He gaped and guffawed, turning his big head away and swiveling back in awe. "You're tiny!" he gasped.

Just an illusion, I told him. Merely the result of my low-slung chair. I jumped up and sat on its hard steel arm to demonstrate. But that left me oddly exposed, and Kendall was laughing again, shaking his head in disbelief. I slid back down onto the moldy cushion.

"Most of the people on this planet look small to me," he offered.

I cast about for the right introduction, something that would put us both at ease. But a decade's worth of chatty interviewer tricks turned to stones in my mouth, useless as a pen without ink. I asked Kendall when he would be transferred to state prison and if he knew where they were sending him. He did not. I asked what it had been like growing up in Poughkeepsie and how he felt about leaving.

"This feels like I'm being interviewed by the high school paper!"

So I began there, inquiring about his days on the football team and wrestling squad, his friends and favorite teachers. Kendall had little to say about any of that. He wanted to talk music and movies. At one time I'd imagined him alone in his bedroom, listening to the blues and soul, the music I liked. But almost all of my early assumptions turned out to be wrong. What Kendall liked was white pop.

"Queen is the best rock group. Billy Joel is probably the best songwriter," he said, perfectly parroting the "favorites" listed by his graduating class in the 1989 Arlington High School yearbook.

I swallowed my disappointment. I had enjoyed thinking of Kendall as complex and independent. He was, instead, a mimic. He reeled off several favorite films, most of them cartoons and sci-fi fantasy. But one stood out.

"*Regarding Henry*, I think it's great," he said of the Harrison Ford vehicle in which a ruthless and self-centered lawyer, shot during a street mugging, falls into a coma and emerges from it purified, with no memory of the horrible things he has done. Kendall considered it a masterpiece.

As we spoke he blinked often, eyelids fluttering rapidly, as if flustered or confused by my questions. Had we met two years earlier, before he was wearing an orange Department of Corrections jumpsuit, I might have considered Kendall a bit off but harmless. He seemed like a goof, a silly, low-commitment pal. His teammates had loved him for that, for being big and gentle, constant and unthreatening, holding court with his *Star Trek* impressions. Guys like Donte thought nothing of leaving him alone with their girlfriends, and the girlfriends barely remembered him at all.

"I think a lot of people were friends with me because I'm a good listener. People always mistake kindness for weakness," Kendall said.

How many times had I heard this? Kendall repeated it like a mantra. He had an idea of himself that he was determined to impress on me, though in fact Kendall was a terrible listener. He heard people speak without registering any of the emotion behind their words. His recall, however, was amazing. Kendall could quote back every comment he'd ever heard me make. He told me

I reminded him of a friend from kindergarten, a bubbly redhead named Rachel. She was one among dozens of people he'd cataloged over the course of his life, ruminating over remarks they'd made, determining that these were slights and announcing that he did not wish to discuss them any longer. "I hold grudges," he said. "I noticed every tiny thing anyone ever did against me." These memories he'd collected like bits of kindling, splinters ignited by the Francois family secrets, and fueling the bonfire like an accelerant was Poughkeepsie itself, a hard, dirty place surrounded by wealth and natural beauty that Kendall would never touch. Anger about high school had sparked the whole murderous cycle, he said, but Poughkeepsie itself was really to blame. "The gateway to hell is somewhere in this town," he pronounced with great finality. "I've been saying that for years."

He reminded me that as a child he had never crossed the line separating Poughkeepsie's suburbs from its urban core. Other black kids might be destined for some sad life on those broken streets, but Kendall never considered himself one of them. He disdained the place as dirty, immoral, and complained bitterly about the *Journal*'s portrayal of it as a quaint country town.

It certainly was not that, I agreed. But what was it?

"I told you," he said. "The gateway to hell. It's not like I was killing saints."

"Are you telling me those women deserved to die?"

"I'm not saying that," he mumbled, rubbing his hands over his face.

"Did you like killing them?"

Kendall looked puzzled, almost pained.

"Why would you ask something like that?" he said.

"It seems like an obvious question."

"Move on to something else."

I asked him again about the army. "Worst mistake of my life," he said. While he'd been stationed in Hawaii, several local prostitutes had disappeared. Kendall insisted he knew nothing about that. His few trips off the base revolved around playing video games at the nearest bar and keeping a low profile. "Hawaii is full of the most racist people on earth. They hate everyone—black, white, anyone who's not Hawaiian," he said. "Of course, pretty much everyone hates white people, though that's not 'pecifically your fault."

I often wondered at his curious style of speech—officiousness punctuated with such childlike phrasing. He said "lie-berry" for library. Made pronouncements from on high, a booming authority who then scurried to apologize, curry favor, soften the edges. I stared at his hands, so pudgy and clean. The police, who often asked what I was learning from their cipher, remarked constantly on the size and power of Kendall's paws, likening them to baseball mitts or the head of an ax. But all I saw was the baby fat puffing his wrists.

"Was there anyone in the army you remember fondly?" I asked. "Anyone who became a friend?"

"I don't think I've ever had a real friend in my life."

When he was discharged for obesity, Kendall came home. But he refused to talk about this, saying only that he should never have come back to Poughkeepsie. The memory of returning to his parents, a failed soldier with few prospects, made him wince.

"What did you do when you got here? Did you look for work?"

"I don't want to talk about that time," he whispered.

I barreled ahead anyway. Kendall had been discharged in 1992, but as far as anyone knew his crimes didn't begin until 1996. What had happened during the intervening years? He was shaking his head before the question was out of my mouth, muttering about public assistance and saying he'd hoped to study zoology at Dutchess Community College. He liked animals. He'd wanted to become a science teacher.

"High school science?"

"No, high school kids aren't very nice. I wanted to teach middle school."

He got only as far as cleaning the hallways. It must have been hard to come home aimless and broke, I suggested, kicked out of the army and hired to sweep floors at Arlington Middle, a place you'd left eight years before. Kendall rubbed his face again and said he didn't want to talk about that, either.

"Did you ever get any sort of help or counseling?"

"No."

Kendall had trudged through twenty-seven years, massive but unseen, all signs of his rage ignored. In the winter of 1998, seven months before confessing to murder, he'd stood stoop-shouldered in front of a county judge, suggesting that he might need therapy for anger management. He was responding to sexual assault charges against Catina Newmaster, whom he knew well enough to call "Tina." But it was not his first time through Poughkeepsie's legal system. Kendall was a regular on Main Street, a known quantity, arrested the previous year for solicitation and frequently reported by prostitutes for his attacks. One said he'd thrown her down the stairs. The judge sentenced him to a few weeks of jail time and group therapy for sexual deviants. By then, five corpses were decomposing in his attic.

"Did you ever want to talk to someone when you were a kid?" I asked. "Do you think it would have made any difference?"

Kendall was quiet for a long time before answering.

"Looking back from what I know now, yes."

DERRICK CAME HOME late that night. He had left the *Journal* and taken a new job doing public relations for a fancy liberal arts college. He knew about my jailhouse visit but did not ask any questions. I thought dangling a few details might change his mind.

"Kendall told me his favorite movies. You won't believe—"

Derrick stared at me, wordless.

"He said *Star Wars* and *Star Trek*. I know, I know—standard geek-weirdo stuff—but he also said *Regarding Henry*! And he loves *The Lion King*!"

I'd found this revelation fascinating because the film struck a chord in me, too. Derrick and I had watched it together, talking for hours about the underlying themes—overcoming loss, the journey from shame to self-acceptance—and now I wanted him to help me pick it apart, analyze every element. But Derrick was already clicking through channels on our enormous television set. He'd surprised me with it several months before, heaving it up our narrow staircase though I rarely watched.

Our dog began to whine and paw at the rug.

"Did you take Moses out today?" Derrick said.

"Before I left for the jail, and then a quick walk when I came back."

I knew our mutt needed more time outside. I knew he needed to run. But I'd been exhausted after Kendall. I'd hoped Derrick would help.

"C'mon, Moses," he said, flinging himself off the couch.

When they returned twenty minutes later, I was making dinner. Spaghetti, because I'd been too tired to shop. I served it to

Derrick in front of the TV, and we ate in silence. A half hour later, Moses was whining again.

It was Derrick who'd insisted we get a dog. He'd been searching for something to glue us together, though three years in the same house had made plain how incompatible we were. I knew a puppy was the wrong decision. But masochism was among the few traits Derrick and I shared, both of us happier to load the rickety cart of our relationship with more weight, rather than admit it was only good for scrap. He combed the newspaper for pet ads, while I remained silent. I preferred to be seen as a brawler, a fighter for truth. I hated admitting anything as weak as uncertainty or fear. Anyway, I loved dogs.

Within two weeks, Derrick heard about a box of puppies dumped in nearby Kingston. It was early December, and I pictured the little balls of fur squirming together for warmth. Kingston was similar to Poughkeepsie, with haunted old buildings and streets that sighed of age. Thinking of a tiny creature left alone in that rough darkness made my chest ache. We raced to City Hall like expectant parents as soon as Derrick got off work, and waited outside the assessor's office where secretaries had been peeking in at the pups all day. These foundlings looked like Newfoundlands, the dog catcher told us, and we imagined raising a big shaggy beast, slobbery and sweet tempered. A gentle giant. Derrick reeled off possible names while we sat on a wooden bench in the empty building, preparing for our surrogate child. "Hudson. Kingston. Moses." That was it, Moses. We decided before we chose him, and it was a relief to agree on something finally, to find one place in our mounting mutual anger where Derrick and I could meet. We crept in to claim our little one and saw that he was the last dog left. The one no one wanted. The runt. He huddled into a corner and would not lift his head.

That first night, Moses cried without ceasing. We set up a pen for him in the living room, and the moment we'd drifted off to sleep his pitiful yelps would start. I stumbled toward our baby in the darkness, soothed him for a few moments, and returned to Derrick, who was burrowed hard into dreams, his face turned toward the wall. An hour later, Moses was bleating again.

Whatever terrors our puppy had endured during his first weeks of life never left him. He was distrustful from the start, so weak he couldn't chew a dog biscuit. A bluish film covered his eyes. But it quickly became clear that Moses was no Newfie. Within a year, he was ninety pounds of snarling aggression, standoffish with any adult other than Derrick or me. Children were the only humans Moses would tolerate. But friends with kids soon stopped visiting, Derrick gave up hosting outdoor barbecues, and I began apologizing to pregnant women startled by the growls emanating from our car in supermarket parking lots. The longer we kept Moses, the more isolated we became. His loyalty toward us, however, was total. Moses might despise the world and everyone in it, but we were his saviors, the sole happy fact of his life, and I loved him the way a mother might a psychotic child. He walked with me in the mornings after Derrick left for work and slept under my desk while I wrote to Kendall in the afternoons. We were similar, I felt, for I knew what it was to fear everything and trust no one. I knew Moses wanted to please but somehow could not. I forgave him anything.

Derrick was different. Everything Moses did either shocked or enraged him. Our dog barked too much. He whined for attention, begged for food. A veterinarian suggested that we grab him by the scruff of the neck to show dominance, as his natural mother would, and Derrick adopted this advice with desperate zeal. But the more he did, the more ferocious Moses became. By two years old, he was a ball of crazed muscle with bared teeth and blaming eyes that incited in Derrick qualities I'd never seen before. Pale helplessness would cross my boyfriend's face, then frustration, then fury, as he leaped upon our dog, shaking him by the throat while Moses's downy head cracked against the floorboards. Perhaps I squeaked a little, made a tiny sound of protest, because Derrick would stare at me sometimes, his hands digging into Moses's fur. I returned his gaze, mute, as if in a nightmare where you walk through terror yet remain apart, drifting through scenes you feel but cannot touch.

KENDALL'S DEFENSE TEAM had hired the eminent forensic psychiatrist Michael Stone to analyze his behavior and, had the case gone to trial, to suggest to a jury that the middle school custodian was too deranged to qualify for a death sentence. But Kendall's plea deal preempted this, and for that reason Dr. Stone had never interviewed his subject. He flipped through reports from Kendall's lawyers, glanced at a stack of statements made by women who'd survived their experiences at 99 Fulton Avenue, and felt he'd collected enough information to include Kendall on a chart he was making about "gradations of evil." Now that the case was resolved, with Kendall sentenced and the records sealed, officials in Dutchess County trotted out their theory of the case: Kendall, unable to climax during sex, became enraged at this humiliation. Beyond that, they had little else to say. But Dr. Stone seemed amenable to talking, especially when he learned that by this point, in the fall of 2000, I had a year's worth of correspondence from Kendall and might be willing to show him some.

I took the train south, staring bleakly at the Hudson River as it slid past in a dull gray line. Kendall, after peering at me in the county jail, had announced in his next letter that he was going to call me "Elf," which I interpreted as a good sign, believing it meant he saw me as magical or mischievous like a character from Magic: The Gathering, certainly not a threat. On the other hand, Kendall said, meeting me in person had been "the worst thing that could have happened."

> *I built an image in my mind based on what I felt fit your voice and what I know of you. In short, that person wasn't in the booth (pictured you taller, longer hair, a medium build and look in your mid-thirties). Worse yet (and it does get worse) until that point, you were just a reporter, now you are also a woman. A woman I can't stop thinking about. . . . I don't want to think of you in any way that is the least bit sexual.*

I did not bring this letter to show Dr. Stone.

Kendall had written it from the inmate reception center at Elmira state prison, where he was sent the day after our meeting and remained for three weeks, simmering in loneliness. For years he'd done nothing but excoriate Dutchess County, as if it were somehow responsible for what he'd done. He said he couldn't wait to get as far from Poughkeepsie as possible. But the fact was, Kendall found comfort in the local jail, where everyone knew him and displayed a certain awe. Watching a guard slowly suffocate a mouse in a jar, he'd felt confident enough to quip, "Wow, and they say I'm cruel!" But at Elmira, he spent cold days in an echoing complex where no one was interested in his jokes. No one even spoke to him. He had none of his books or papers and no idea where he was headed. He was so frantic he didn't try to hide it, firing off notes to family, friends, lawyers—anyone who might write back. I got two during this period, filled with the usual rants about my failures as a letter writer and human being. "I've tried to call you the last two Sundays but didn't get through," he wrote. "I can't seem to get through to anyone." Then he asked if I knew any women with red hair and freckles who wouldn't mind corresponding with a confessed killer and being his friend.

That was the whole problem with me, as far as Kendall was concerned. I sounded like a good person whose interest implied friendship, but I wanted something from him and this was not friendship at all. Every time I asked a reporter's question, I transgressed. Kendall did not want to think of me as a journalist he had allowed into his life, because that would mean ceding control. He was equally afraid to see me as a woman. The more comfortable he felt, the more frantic he became.

> *Elf,*
>
> *I don't want to think of you as just a reporter, and I try not to, but you make it hard. . . . If you want to know something about me, I have let myself be taken advantage of many, many times almost always by women. . . . I let them for different reasons, none of them all that good. I'm not saying that you are even trying anything like that, but that is one of the reasons I am more careful.*

DR. STONE'S OFFICE WAS on Central Park West, a few blocks from where I grew up, and he opened the door to me as if roused from a dream. I followed him through dim hallways lined with Oriental carpets and parlors walled in tapestry. Heavy velvet drapes shaded every window. Stooped and elderly, the psychiatrist wore a shapeless charcoal blazer that hung from his shoulders like vulture wings. He led me to his study, seated himself behind an antique desk, and immediately turned back to the spreadsheet of murderers he'd been working on, pecking demographic information into a computer with quick, sharp strokes. I plopped into a velvet chair and waited. Without a word, the doctor pushed a book at me—his own—and I opened to a bookmarked column of psychopathic character traits, a menu of descriptions by which Kendall might be dissected and categorized: glibness, egocentricity, craving for stimulation, pathological lying, manipulation, lack of guilt, shallow affect, callousness, impulsivity, failure to accept responsibility.

Kendall fit them all to some degree. But I was focused only on his mystery and need. The diagnoses Dr. Stone absently mumbled—borderline disorder, narcissistic personality, schizoidal type—didn't tell me anything about Kendall's heart, about where the human ended and the monster began. They didn't explain a fifth grader who wouldn't speak. I thought of Kendall's letters, so desperate to communicate something he had only the haziest grasp of himself. I thought of his googly-eyed smile, his way of swallowing words half out of his mouth. This was no smooth-talking murder machine, no Ted Bundy cliché. Kendall flailed, even in murder.

While Dr. Stone typed, I asked perfunctory questions, unsure that he recalled having consented to an interview. After a few minutes of this, he hoisted two rumpled shopping bags from behind his desk and thrust them at me. They were ripped at the corners with the weight of all the paper inside, piles of reports from women who had survived sex with Kendall. For the next hour I read in silence. Dr. Stone barely seemed to remember I was there.

I read about Kendall picking up prostitutes in the early mornings, after he had dropped off his mother at work. Poughkeepsie was busy with dozens of women loitering outside Dunkin' Donuts at that hour, waiting to attract drunks who had not yet made it home and IBMers on their way to work. Compared to those johns, Kendall was a miserable chore. He smelled awful, and with him everything took forever. He'd drive up, introduce himself as Kenny, and offer to buy a woman breakfast as if they'd been out together on an all-night date. Inside Paulette's car, the invitation would shift into a promise to make them something to eat at home. The women shrugged. They were there to do what they had to, wherever he wanted. The pleasantries were just a tiresome dance. So they rode to 99 Fulton Avenue, followed Kendall inside, and noticed but tried to ignore the foul stench, the tower of old dinner plates sprouting mold so thick it resembled a melted candle, the bedsheets caked with such filth that they crinkled under a person's weight. I read about sex that took hours because Kendall could not climax. "I hate them all!" he'd shriek.

He told one woman that he'd killed Wendy Meyers for giving him HIV. "Call me master!" he commanded another. A third, he warned: "You may never leave." A fourth, beaten into silence, heard him say, "You'll be the victim of a crime if you tell." A fifth, thrashing on a mattress with Kendall's hands around her neck, heard him whisper, "Oh, my God, I almost did it again."

Kendall talked and talked, and almost all of his victims told the police.

Kimberly Beal had been standing near Trinity Church when Kendall drove up one day in the spring of 1996 and asked if she was all right, could he could buy her a drink? A few minutes later they were standing in his filthy kitchen, Kendall staring as Kimberly dutifully drank the wine he'd poured. (He took not a drop himself.) His gaze was odd, Kimberly said later, and she'd wanted to leave even before he reached for her. She told him that she'd changed her mind, had to go. That tripped the trigger.

Kendall dragged her upstairs to his childhood bedroom, threw her down, and bellowed that she was a "bad girl," a whore who needed to be punished, and he was going to call her mother. He tied Kimberly's hands behind her back and pawed through her purse. "I want to know who you are," he snarled, pocketing a birth certificate. Kendall worked himself over Kimberly for an hour, punching her, raping her, screaming at her. But every few minutes he'd stop and peer out the bedroom window, watching for Paulette. They had to finish quickly, he explained, because his mother would be coming home soon.

Afterward, as Kimberly buttoned her jeans in silence, Kendall lectured. She needed help. She didn't belong on the streets. She could be his girlfriend, and he would take care of her, protect her. He insisted on driving her back to the church where he'd picked her up and apologized the whole way. He couldn't stop saying it: he was sorry; he hadn't meant to hurt her; he hoped she would give him another chance. For months to come, Kendall stalked Kimberly, begging forgiveness. He pushed money at her, brought food, told her to be careful and to stay safe. A year later, Kendall had five women stacked in his attic.

By then he'd become brazen, following prostitutes down the street, shouting that he had thirty dollars—couldn't they just blow him? He punched Debbie DiMetro in the Bank of New York parking lot and brought her home, unconscious, to lie on his bed, where he stripped her naked. When she came to, he beamed like a grateful child: "You woke up!" But once Debbie tried to leave, he shoved candy wrappers into her purse, pretending they were ten-dollar bills, and raped her, mumbling all the while about Wendy Meyers. Debbie did not fight. She flattered and cajoled, told him he had nothing to worry about and that she didn't need his money. When Kendall stepped out to get a condom and some Vaseline, Debbie tore out of the house. Reports like hers came into Poughkeepsie's detective squad every few months. Half-clothed women ran screaming from 99 Fulton Avenue. They banged on neighbors' doors. They led police to Kendall's home and repeated what he'd said. Officers typed their words into the department's new computer system and finished off the reports: "No action taken at this time."

━

AFTER AN HOUR of reading, I looked up at Dr. Stone. He was still staring at his spreadsheet of killers, which was fine by me. I did not want him to see how my heart was racing, how sick I felt. My articulate, oversensitive pen pal was nowhere in these pages. Kendall hated women. He pursued only those who needed something so badly they could not turn him down. In the last report, which detailed his confession to Margie Smith, Kendall reeled off a list of discards: His seventh murder victim was "the Yonkers girl." His fourth, "a lesbian." This one was "a lunatic." That one, "the greatest lay of my life." His favorite he'd nicknamed "Snow White."

I asked Dr. Stone if I could make copies, and he nodded distractedly, grateful to have the office to himself again. I spent the next two hours monopolizing a self-service machine at Staples, impatient New Yorkers milling all around.

I read the whole way home and throughout the next day. I did not stop when Derrick came back from work, or while he made dinner, or when night fell. There were hundreds of pages from women who'd been with Kendall. By the last report, I was sweating. This was the bully behind a face as soft as mud. The screeching behemoth who punched matchstick women and apologized compulsively, fantasizing that they might still become his girlfriends.

"A real Jekyll and Hyde," one woman told police. This was not the person I wanted to see at all.

I despised him, finally. But I couldn't tell anyone, couldn't bear the thought of people asking what had taken so long. They would expect me to stop the letters and phone calls. They would tell me to get on with my life. Yet now that I'd seen how brutal Kendall could be, I was locked in even tighter. I was charming the cobra, dancing over fire. I felt like I had him then, a big, floppy fish that had nibbled on my line, and I would reel him in until I'd learned what I needed to know. Of course, he had me, too. But of this, I was hardly aware.

I never told Kendall about reading those reports. Instead I wrote to him about the approaching autumn. For its color and light, its air of expectancy amid shadows, fall had always been my favorite time of year.

"I love fall too," Kendall wrote back. "Or I just hate the other seasons, depending on how you look at it." Then he apologized for earlier notes that had been rude and thanked me for my letter. "I needed it, and it almost sounded as if we were friends."

CHAPTER 8

Close to Home

D r. Stone's shopping bag of case reports included a hand-
lettered chart made by Kendall's legal team—four
graph paper squares that formed a timeline tracing
Kendall's crimes from 1994 through 1998. Along the y-axis, a list
of fifty women he had hired, then assaulted, with a key depict-
ing the cruelties he had inflicted on each and over what period of
time. Some he'd picked up repeatedly over the years. I tacked the
poster to a Styrofoam board and propped it on my desk, staring
at the numbers inked next to each woman's name, an index system of some kind. I followed Kendall's progression from stalking
streetwalkers to testing positive for HIV to a rapid ramp-up of
rape and murder, interrupted with a mysterious murder-free gap
lasting fifteen months, from March 1997 through May 1998, after
which he resumed killing. I stared at the chart for weeks, as Derrick told me the whole case was too miserable to think about, and
my parents wondered what was happening to me, and the rest of

Dutchess County returned to driving between shopping malls on Route 9.

Aside from a few grieving-relative interviews done for the *Times,* I'd avoided the women's families. I told myself that I did not want to force them to trudge once more through memories of a daughter or sister or mother, lost years before Kendall found her. This excuse was more than a little self-serving. The reality was that when I looked at the dead women's pictures I saw challenge, as if they knew we were not so very different. It would have been difficult to explain. Most lived in trailers and highway motels. Not one had a college degree. Yet Kendall frequently marveled at their backgrounds—horse groomer, high school jock, suburbanite. "You never know, I could have been with your best friend," he'd laugh, which showed how little he understood where I'd come from and how far I'd strayed.

In Kendall's mind, there were only three types of women: good, bad, and fallen. Being a journalist muddied my position in his moral hierarchy, but Kendall tried to ignore that inconvenience and slot me into the first group. It was cold comfort. I'd read that in a man like this, afflicted with the conditions Dr. Stone had mentioned, admiration was intertwined with hatred. So labeling a person "good" meant he would almost automatically see her as withholding approval. Any resulting feelings of stress or shame then morphed immediately into overwhelming rage. That sounded right. I'd tried to keep on his sunny side, larding my letters with pleasantries, taking ridiculous comfort whenever he deemed me "a good person." But I kept denying him what he asked for—a photograph, handwritten letters—even while I continued to smile and joke. Now I wondered about the wisdom of this course.

For these reasons, I never told him about my long-ago habit

of stepping into strangers' cars and allowing them to wonder if I was for sale. I'd slip from my New York City bedroom, down the back stairwell of our building, and into the night. My destination was always the same: a town house across the park where a brother and sister held court while their mother holed up in her bedroom, writing. Getting there presented no challenge. Cabs pulled up, the drivers leaning out their windows to ask if I needed a ride. Many told me I reminded him of their daughters. I had no money, I'd explain, climbing into the backseat. Traffic lights smeared red, yellow, green across the black city sky as I thought of my parents bundled into their brass bed and watched the meter tally fares I never paid.

The last time was in Miami. A scorching afternoon during college when I walked a narrow sidewalk, sweat trickling down the backs of my legs. "Girl, it's too hot out there to be walking. You want a ride?" trilled the voice from inside a Cadillac that pulled up alongside. I had not been looking for favors that day, nor thrills, and I kept walking. But the Caddy man kept pace, hugging the curb, driving slow. Cars collected in a long snaking line behind him, horns blaring. Air-conditioning billowed from the front seat. "C'mon now, let me just give you a ride." I turned my head for a moment—looking for an omen, measuring the wind—and stepped inside. I knew what could happen. I'd been throwing myself to fate this way for years, again and again seeking validation from strangers. I was practiced at pushing past fear. Inside the cars, my value would be measured and weighed, and each time I emerged untouched felt like an affirmation. The man in the Cadillac handed me a business card. His front seats were white leather, his face shiny and black, the back crammed with cleaning supplies. His name was Nelson, and he boasted that he could wax cars so bright they caused traffic accidents. I was underemployed myself, trudging through a three-month television news internship. No one at WSVN cared if I showed up or not. Upon learning that I was a literature major, their newest reporter had crowed, "The printed word is dead!" I left for lunch, wandering into the pitiless Florida sun, and kept walking.

"You like to smoke?" Nelson asked after we'd been driving a few minutes.

"Yeah."

"You shoulda found me two weeks ago. I had a brick of hash and I'd break off pieces for every woman who'd let me eat her." He rested one hand on the steering wheel, eyes sliding my way. "I love me that heaven pie."

He rolled past sun-bleached Miami Beach hotels; through Hialeah, where I'd crouched at the edge of a backyard swimming pool filled with sacrificed animals, watching television teams await the outcome of a family-hostage crisis; then back toward Liberty City, known since the race riots of 1980 primarily as an urban ruin. A kid lolling on a corner with a bottle of Olde English 800 peered at us, noting the black man in a Cadillac, white girl in office clothes, then swung himself in beside me. He was lanky and dark-skinned, with an old boating cap pulled down over his eyes. I ran my silent calculations, pictured my legs upside down, sticking out of a garbage can, as the kid handed a tiny manila-paper nickel bag across my lap.

"Do you have a job, other than this?" I asked.

"Denny's. But I'm quittin'."

"Why?"

"Talkin' about sending me for some training in Europe."

"You should go."

The boy looked at me with such disgust it seemed to knock him backward. We stopped at a light, and he was gone. Nelson drove all the way out to Key Biscayne and pulled into a weed-choked park by the bay. We walked between splintered hurdles and worn chin-up bars, smoking, talking. I pointed across the water at a clump of pretty houses.

"Where's that?"

"Coconut Grove. We can't go there."

"Why not?"

"Only time I've been is when they paid me to shine the leaves."

He had to be joking.

"That's ridiculous," I said. I was headed to Coconut Grove for an art opening that evening, but I didn't mention this. I listened to the dirty water lapping in the shallows, a light breeze doing nothing to cool the sticky afternoon.

"I wish we were out on that boat." I pointed at a small yacht anchored like an island of cleanliness a few yards out. "We'd be able to breathe."

"I've never been on a boat," Nelson said, turning toward me.

"You've never been on a boat?" I jabbered, failing to see that my surprise translated as scorn. We stared at one another, the understanding of separate worlds and crossed agendas beginning to darken the sockets around Nelson's eyes.

"You're one of them," he said suddenly. "Get in the car."

I was frightened now, pattering on about a job interview he'd mentioned, offering good wishes. But Nelson did not speak again. He stared straight ahead, driving fast and pulling over at the same square of sidewalk where he'd picked me up three hours before. "Get out," he said, his face rigid in profile, and sped away without a backward glance.

CATHERINE MARSH WAS my age when she died, and her parents, like mine, enjoyed regular trips to Europe. The Marshes were upright folks, educated and solidly middle class. On a gray winter afternoon I drove to their tidy split-level in a development in Schenectady, an hour north of Poughkeepsie, picturing Cathy on the same journey. She'd shuttled up and down the New York State Thruway dozens of times in the year before Kendall strangled her, trying to find her way home.

Marguerite Marsh opened the front door the moment I knocked, as if she'd been standing on the other side with her hand on the knob. She showed me to an immaculate living room lined with rose carpeting. I saw my silhouette in the gleaming coffee table. A framed picture of Cathy stared down from a corner shelf.

At the start of every interview there is a half-second beat, a barely perceptible pause as the parties size each other up and decide how far the conversation will go. Marguerite sat down on the sofa, took one look at me, and immediately stood up to make coffee. I followed her to the kitchen, standing in profile as I gazed at Marguerite's collection of novelty spoons, giving her time to take me in. There were dozens of them displayed around the room—spoons she'd received as wedding gifts, spoons from foreign countries, spoons carved with religious icons and forged of pewter—each set housed in its own case. The rest of Cathy's childhood home was equally well ordered. No sweaters or jackets hung over the stairway banister. No magazines cluttered the tables. I'd grown up in the urban version, every surface buffed to a hazy sheen. No evidence anywhere of lives being lived.

Marguerite was proud of her ability to keep things neat. The worst part of the twelve-year ordeal to reclaim Cathy from the streets had been visiting the county jail when she needed fresh underwear. Twice a week Marguerite drove down with a tidy bundle, standing in line as the guards picked through it. They treated her like trash. None of them cared about Marguerite's impeccable home. None of them understood that she spoke French and had friends in Europe; that her husband had been principal of the neighborhood elementary school and her son was an air force officer. Bringing clean panties to a drug addict was the last thing Marguerite had envisioned for her old age. But this trajectory meant nothing to the guards, only the hard landing.

Though pained by the ritual, Marguerite did not protest. She set her mouth in a prim line and kept her feelings to herself. That was part of the problem, she said as we sat down with dainty china cups full of coffee. She'd rarely shared her emotions, and Cathy had suffered for it. Marguerite's mouth was framed like a marionette's, with deep grooves on either side, parentheses that worked back and forth—pulling tight, then slack—as she composed herself. Alone in the afternoons now, with no more jail runs to make or prayer sessions to attend, she sat at her dining room table pushing through a pile of photos. Here was Cathy on a family trip at thirteen, light brown hair parted in the middle and feathered back like Farrah Fawcett's. There, feeding peanuts to a donkey at Badlands National Park, wearing the same Adidas shorts I'd worn on my own family's western vacation. Here she was at Cape Cod, running through the ocean, and on a towel at Myrtle Beach, a little pudgy, a little sad. *Summer Fun,* her mother wrote at the top of the page.

Pictures in my parents' photo album elicited the same stubborn chorus. Me, at twelve, awkward in a denim hat I refused to remove; at fifteen, my leg wrapped suggestively around the porch column of a New England inn—shorts too short, hair too long, face tanned to hide the ugly truth of my skin. "Children are not tabula rasa," said my mother, who subscribed to the belief that personalities are inborn—our temperaments, strengths and weaknesses, all there in the first moments of life. I flipped to the middle of Marguerite's scrapbook, searching for early evidence of waywardness in her daughter, some hint at what was to come. Marguerite gently pushed me back to the beginning.

"We have a baby girl!" sang the birth announcement when Cathy was born in March 1967. It had taken Marguerite more than a decade to get pregnant after her first child, a son—thinking it would never happen, she'd already adopted a daughter, Marie—and Cathy's delivery was difficult. She'd been premature, just four and a half pounds, and the doctors believed her too fragile to survive. But Catherine Ann Marsh clung to life with her wet baby lungs, and Marguerite, despite her usual tendency toward reticence, told everyone her daughter was a miracle.

In the early snapshots Cathy looks classically wholesome, swinging a baseball bat in a dusty lot, dimpled and blue eyed in her high school basketball jersey. There are pictures of Cathy at holiday dinners, mugging with her older brother, and as a preteen, mimicking jail time inside a fake cell at a colonial tourism site. "I couldn't help putting that one in," Marguerite whispered with a bitter smile. All of Cathy's sparkle and fire had drained away by the time she met Kendall. It perplexed him, the way she lay so still as he strangled her, refusing to fight. Dozens of other pictures told a story Marguerite preferred not to discuss: Cathy drunk at her high school graduation party, shrieking at her mother to buy more beer.

Cathy in her college dorm, eyes narrowed, looking coldly into Marguerite's camera. Cathy in her twenties on a softball field where everyone knew her by another name.

"Hey, Annie," a man called when she showed up for a game in the neighborhood where Marie lived. She smiled and waved back.

"Who was that?" her sister said. "Why'd he call you by a different name?"

"Marie, you don't want to know," said Cathy, jogging across the diamond.

The years slid by. Here was Cathy pregnant in a hospital bed. Now with two daughters—at a park, in a boat. There she was, holding a birthday cake for the eldest. I asked about their fathers, but Marguerite shook her head and turned the page: *29th and last birthday,* she'd labeled a picture of her daughter picking out a Beatles tune at the piano in their rose-carpeted living room. Cathy was pregnant when she died, and I wondered if she'd lain so quiet on Kendall's mattress in an effort to save her unborn baby. Marguerite was sure of it, though she was less willing to ascribe such noble motives to the rest of Cathy's life. After the police found her daughter's journal, Marguerite skimmed just a few pages before burning it. This was the Cathy she did not wish to discuss, the twelve-year-old who guzzled beer in her bedroom, the daughter who got paid for sex acts her mother had never heard of. Only the happy girl in the photos remains. But Cathy wrote constantly, and Marguerite, determined to show me a bright college student who shared my drive to make sense of life through words, thrust a typed essay into my hands. "Frightened Child" told of the first fork in Cathy's road, the moment, at age five, that she realized she was alone in her family.

I looked up toward the house and saw my mother staring out the dining room window.... Then she moved away and out of sight. What took place that afternoon marked the beginning of the end....

When I'd first phoned Marguerite, the day of Kendall's arrest, she sighed the same explanation over and over. Addiction had taken her daughter "places she never wanted to go," Marguerite kept saying. But Cathy traced the genesis of her life on the street to something much earlier, a seed planted long before she ever tasted cocaine. The way Cathy told her story, the day Marguerite stood watching through the window—apart and unreachable—marked a silence between mother and daughter that would widen each year until Cathy was looking back at her family across a canyon of loneliness.

Outside with her father, she'd tromped across the lawn, proud to help rake leaves. Her brother was away at college, her sister out with friends. It was just little Cathy and her dad. Jim Marsh had aged, his daughter noticed. Sweat dripped from his forehead despite the chilly breeze. "Back in a minute," he coughed, dropping his rake and walking stiffly toward the house.

Cathy kept working, ambition speeding her along. She would surprise her father with an entirely cleared yard. She would be different from her siblings, better. She would stand out. But leaf collecting was boring. No matter how many armfuls she gathered, there were always more, and all she really wanted to do was dump the garbage bag, take a running leap into the pile, and lie on her back as pieces of gold and fire fluttered down all around her.

A siren wailed in the distance. Such an exciting sound, Cathy thought. It never made her think of danger, just men flying past in a riot of color and noise. She was captivated by them. Firemen meant action, heroics. Cathy let the rake fall and ran to her front yard to watch the truck rush past, but the sound had come from an ambulance, not a fire truck, and it was idling in her driveway, back doors open wide. Inside the house, Jim Marsh lay on the living room couch, his work shirt ripped open, white suction cups stuck all over his chest. Cathy watched from behind the medics' legs as they strapped an oxygen mask over her father's face. His skin was waxy.

> I felt so scared and helpless. I just stood there. I thought that maybe my father was dead and they just weren't telling me, but I couldn't bring myself to ask.

JIM MARSH SURVIVED the heart attack. But there were more, each year, and Cathy grew up on tiptoe, afraid to disrupt the fragile détente between her dad and death. Everyone acted like something was wrong, but no one said anything. She was sitting in sixth-grade English class when the principal stepped in. "Get your coat," he said. "I'm taking you home." In the car he didn't speak a word, but Cathy knew what was happening. She'd spent her childhood preparing for this moment. At the house, a neighbor quickly ushered her away, into another car, and drove her to Friendly's, where Cathy spent the afternoon of her father's death staring into a bowl of melted ice cream.

The earlier silence, once looming, now settled over the Marshes' home. It stuffed bedroom hallways with cotton rolls of quiet, muffling every question. But in that carpeted mausoleum, Cathy made a discovery. Liquor tore open the hush. Alcohol brightened leaden skies. A six-pack allowed Cathy to forget her trembling mother, so crumpled by grief; made her want to shout and laugh and run. When she drank, she was free. She saw adult faces tight with accusation—Marguerite standing at her liquor cabinet, examining the diminished contents of one bottle after another; a school counselor asking feeble, leading questions and sighing at Cathy's deft deflection. Her grades were good enough—if she refused to talk about the drinking, what could you do? She wasn't failing any classes, and this happened sometimes with kids, the counselor assured Marguerite. Lots of girls just needed to get away from home. When Cathy moved on to college, everything would straighten itself out. The levels in Marguerite's liquor cabinet continued to drop, but she stopped asking about it.

Marguerite paused abruptly in this chronology and cocked her head at me. "Why does this story mean something to you?" she asked.

I mouthed a few words about the opacity of the phrases *street prostitute* and *drug addict,* and Marguerite did not press. She was an accepting woman—she'd swallowed a decade of lies from Cathy—but I could see in her watery eyes that she'd realized how the relationship between mother and daughter haunted me. I wondered if she read Cathy's essay the way I did, as a manifesto of blame. I'd written my own version in college, like Cathy, jabbing at shadows I only half understood. I wrote about sound, as Cathy had written about silence. In my house, rage exploded like mortar shells and anything might trigger it: colors that clashed, the smell of pizza I'd eaten for lunch, the creak of my step on our wooden floors. *"Selfish, thoughtless, careless!"* my mother shrieked, lashed by forces invisible to me, as my father stood by, watching silently. He would not stay her hand across my face, nor utter a word against this sensitive, cultivated woman he loved. "You'll have to be the adult," he said later, as I wept, begging him to explain why she was like this.

In my essay, I framed my father's passivity as near-saintly tolerance, avoiding mention of his cutting sarcasm, the way he routinely reduced waitresses to tears, his willingness to leave a troubled woman alone with two children. I was twenty when I wrote it, unable to name the engine of dominance and submission that fueled my parents' marriage. Their bedroom door swung open once as I stood outside, listening to them fight, and I'd seen them—my mother with her fist raised, my father reaching out to block it— and the three of us froze for an instant, staring at one another. She would come after me now, I thought, racing toward my room. Or she would kill my father. Or they would kill each other. I lay stiff in the dark, waiting. But no one ever came. No one said anything the next day. No friend or relative ever acted as if anything was amiss. So maybe it was me, born with my settings misaligned, misinterpreting everything.

WE SOLDIERED ON, through vacations at the Cape and ski weekends in Vermont, working our New England family myth. To the world, my parents were a dear-looking couple with refined tastes who loved books and theater, voted Democratic, and sent me to elite schools. They bought a second home in Connecticut to live a town-and-country life, though they were not town-and-country people, and gamely, my mother created flower beds and art projects. She potted chrysanthemums and helped us build a gingerbread house that dwarfed the kitchen table. When she wanted stone walls, there was my dad, wheezing as he muscled the rocks into place. We carried our groceries inside through the basement, where a garter snake lived. It was a tiny thing, roughly the proportions of a shoelace, but as an eight-year-old I gave it a wide berth. Other animal intruders had already regretted their trespass, birds that flew down our chimney and broke themselves against the living room windows; bats bludgeoned to death under my parents' badminton rackets. Perhaps the snake sensed this fate, because it darted so suddenly across the floor as we opened the garage door that my sister and I screamed. My mother returned with a poker, and she beat that creature to a bloody smear. I crept back later to find its crooked carcass, split open like an old bicycle tire.

We drove up to the country house on Friday nights, after traffic had cleared and *Donny & Marie* ended, back to the city on Sundays, our route passing the same Gothic asylum where Paulette Francois, mother to toddler Kendall, was then studying abnormal psychology. The mental hospital was a fortress of narrow turrets and stone archways, and it appears in my nightmares, still, obscured by blinding rain.

"Where's Henry?" my mother asked as we sped past one Sunday. She was alone at the wheel maneuvering through the threat of a summer storm, my father having taken to spending weekends in the city. Henry was my hamster, and at that moment he was crouched in his bed of cedar chips on the table in our empty country kitchen. I stared out my window. Even in daylight, the asylum breathed foreboding.

"He's back there, right?" said my mother, still focused on the road and the rain.

What mechanism is it that makes a child freeze? I knew I hadn't carried Henry to the car, and I hadn't seen anyone else do it, either. Yet I never totaled the meaning of those separate facts. I was a dreamy kid who still half believed in magic. Somehow, I was sure, my hamster would be saved.

"I—I think he's back—"

"Goddamnit! What is wrong with you!"

She swerved onto the hospital's wet lawn to turn around, churning soft earth in her wake, and drove the hour back to Connecticut in silence, the only sound our squeaking wipers on the windshield. When I found Henry gnawing seeds in his yellow plastic prison, rain was sloshing across the windows in a blurry river. "Why does anyone have children?" my mother whispered to herself as we tore south again through the velvet night.

MY HAMSTER WAS the only healthy creature in the car by the time we arrived home. A slab of raw steak was set out on the counter, and my father had his spices lined up in sequential order. "Not hungry," my mother said, brushing past. He stood next to the meat, wearing one of the ladies'-cut shirts my mother bought him because, she said, his shoulders were so narrow. He had been called "Fou-Fou" in high school, a nickname I discovered with horror when leafing through the pages of a yearbook from 1946. There was the Most Likely to Succeed, and the Funniest, and the Most Musical, and my own growing confusion. I'd expected his picture above those titles. The night I was born, he'd sauntered home from the hospital as if in a 1930s musical, leaping over low stone walls at Central Park's north end, skipping along curved walkways in his slacks and loosened tie. He might have broken into song. He loved the gentility of a black-and-white time, top hats and grace, ball gowns and rhyming couplets. As a kid he'd taken the train down from Yonkers to sneak into Manhattan's jazz clubs on weekends, underage but uninterested in drinking. It was the music he chased.

By the time I heard those stories, my father had long since put away any dreams of playing music professionally, and considered exercise a practice that stirred up systems better left undisturbed. But he kept my college essay visible on top of his desk for years.

My mother was aghast when she saw it. How dare I write such things?

"*You* wanted to be a writer," I sputtered. "That's what I'm doing—like Philip Roth. He wrote about his family."

"You're no Philip Roth," she snapped.

<hr>

READING WAS THE only activity that went unquestioned in my house, and books were shelter. My mother scoffed at a teacher's disapproval when I read *Catcher in the Rye* in fifth grade. The best thing about *Gone with the Wind*, which she'd given me the previous year, was its length. I churned through the thousand-page paperback three times in succession. As soon as I read the last word, I turned back to the first.

Our truth was complex. My father, a stalwart for the liberal cause, offered our living room for antiwar meetings and provided my first model of a moral conscience. Outside, he was willing to fight any injustice. But at home, where my mother's eyes would grow icy-pale with rage, he was silent. It was bewildering. Teachers phoned to inquire, so very tactfully, about my compulsive hair pulling in second grade. In third grade, I misspelled *the* on a quiz and was hastily taken aside. Was there anything on my mind? Mr. Eyester asked. What child articulates dread? What eight-year-old talks about crouching behind her parents' bedroom door, braced against the verbal knife fight inside?

The older I grew, the more my parents' effort to present a life framed by culture and grace disgusted me. Every gentility was a lie, undermined by their bitter marriage, their petrified kids. Etan

Patz, Lisa Steinberg—when I wasn't buried in books, these were the characters convulsing my mind even into college, lost children whose names appeared in tabloid headlines, kids no one had saved. If *I* were ever in danger, my mother once instructed, there was only one thing to do: "You open a window and scream 'Help!'" she said, her voice trilling upward with a tremor that sealed my resolve. I would never admit desperation like that. I would never cry out.

FOR CATHY, QUIET signaled doom. Everything she did was designed to create enough clatter to keep it at bay. But in my house, noise triggered a crackle of terror. The sound of a step on our wooden floors set my blood vibrating, my ears keen to the direction those footfalls would take. With reading as refuge, I burrowed into all manner of literary darkness—mysteries, fairy tales. Spell-casting stepmothers who wished their stepdaughters harm were particularly compelling. I was training for bravery, and I brought this approach into every corner of my life. People said "reckless" when I got older and ran New York's streets at night, begging cross-town cab rides. They said "high-risk behavior" when I wandered Central Park, consorting with drug dealers and delinquents. But I knew what I was doing. I was trying to vanquish the dark.

The mystery of my mother's fury had preoccupied my childhood and framed my adolescence. Now it dominated my endlessly emerging adulthood. I interviewed teenage hoodlums, wet-eyed pedophiles, and wary gang members—every one of them guided by a logic rooted in wounds. The logic of pain wound itself around every perception, strangling interpretation, coloring vision. Pain could grow until it was as outsized as a sun. It could throb inside you like a second heart.

But in the newsroom all of this remained my secret. Journalists were not driven by their pasts. What of our objectivity, our vaunted dispassion? We all played along with this lie—the reporter who'd lost a son to illness and built her career covering child fatalities; the crime writer who'd been abducted as a youth and went after pedophiles with particular zeal. I embraced the charade. Reporting provided a perfect cover, a shield behind which I might safely study my fears. There were reasons for dysfunction, and you could arrange them on a page. I wrote about explosive violence and felt, finally, in control.

COLLEGE, WHERE NO one knew anything of my frailties, was a chance to start over, and it should have been for Cathy, too. That was Marguerite's hope. But her daughter saw it only as evidence of being pushed aside. A month into freshman year came the first knock on Marguerite's door—just a weekend visit, Cathy said. She missed her old basketball team and didn't know anyone at the state university. Couldn't she come home for a few days to see friends and sleep in her own bed? Marguerite, packing for a week's vacation in Myrtle Beach, wanted nothing so much as time to relax in the sun with Marie and let her worries melt away. Go right ahead, said Cathy, plopping down on the couch. She would be fine on her own. No one would even know she was there. Marguerite had itchy feelings, an uncomfortable sense that her daughter's refusal to tolerate loneliness might be part of a bigger problem. There was something about the sharp cruelty that came out when Cathy drank, the way her voice turned cutting and hard. Marguerite knew drugs might be involved—her intuition hummed like an overloaded electrical wire—but she'd been exhausted by raising a family alone in the years since Jim's death. Cathy's departure for school was something she'd anticipated more than she liked to admit. Marguerite kept packing.

A week later she returned to find Cathy sitting in the same spot on the couch, like she'd never budged. School? Forget it. The community college close to home would be much better, Cathy said. She could live in her bedroom, get a part-time job, and drive to campus.

"So she's back," Marguerite sighed, as the winter afternoon around us tumbled toward dusk. She bought a used car, wrote a check for the new school, and told herself that Cathy would find her way. Kendall's third murder victim rose each morning, ate breakfast with her mother, and swung out the door with a pile of books under her arm. But she never set foot in a classroom. All day long, Cathy loitered on the basketball court, playing pickup games for cash. If she found someone with drugs, she got high. When the thick tar of depression made her sluggish, cocaine wiped it clear like Windex. She had no trouble ignoring those who assumed she was stupid. She cared little about disappointing her mother. What Cathy could not stand was the keening drone of loneliness.

No one in Cathy's family knew about her days on the blacktop. But they could not miss the change in Marguerite. The woman looked exhausted, and no wonder, relatives clucked, the way that Cathy used her. Plenty of kids got homesick—why hadn't she just insisted the girl stay at school? The aunts and uncles could hardly blame Marguerite. Her husband was dead. She'd raised those kids alone. It was a lot. To lend a hand, Jim Marsh's brother offered to check on his wayward niece. He was a teacher at the college, and it wouldn't be much trouble to pop over, maybe take the girl to lunch. When he did, Cathy's uncle learned that she had never been to class. As far as he could tell, Cathy hadn't even registered.

That was the end of Marguerite paying for school. She needed a real vacation now, something much farther away than Myrtle Beach. She flew to Spain to visit friends, and Cathy, no longer bothering with the college-girl façade, found work in a gas station. All of her pay went to buy cocaine. When she needed more, Cathy cashed checks on an empty account, flashing her dimples as she slid meaningless slips of paper across a 7-Eleven counter. By the time Marguerite got home from Europe, her daughter needed a lawyer. But she couldn't find Cathy to discuss it. The girl was living in a section of Schenectady that Marguerite had never seen, parceling crack cocaine into plastic bags from the floor of an empty living room. It was autumn, with short dark days that frightened the aging nurse as she drove back alleys, searching. By Thanksgiving week, she thought she'd found the right house and planted herself outside, a stout housewife in her spectacles and appliquéd sweaters, hollering from the street that they'd better let her daughter come home for the holiday. "Her brother's coming to visit—all the way from South Dakota!" Marguerite shouted at the empty windows. Cathy didn't even call.

Two weeks after Thanksgiving the police raided the crack house and Catherine Ann Marsh, sitting cross-legged on the floor, looked up from a pile of guns and money to go to jail for first time. A few weeks after she'd been released, Marguerite noticed a tiny item in the morning paper: Catherine A. Marsh, arrested and charged with solicitation.

This is how it happens, how you fall from a suburban development onto the rancid mattress in an insane man's bedroom. With loneliness that starts as a bruise and becomes infected. Misunderstandings that go unaddressed, rifts that fray and tear with the years. It starts with a decision, minor as a shrug, to step away. A wrong turn that leads to a detour that brings you so far from the original mistake that you forget there once was a way back.

⁘

CATHY LOGGED SO many trips in and out of rehab that Marguerite lost count. Each time her daughter promised this one would be the last. "If I don't make it now, I'll die on the street," she whispered to Marguerite as they held hands in the chapel of St. Joseph's clinic at Saranac Lake. Marguerite believed her. A few weeks later Cathy signed herself into a Poughkeepsie halfway house. It was only an hour from home, just eight exits down the Thruway, and on weekends she could drive north to visit her little girls, long ago taken into foster care. Marguerite worried about her daughter moving to a place where she knew no one. She told the drug counselors about Cathy's tendency toward lonesomeness and what it always triggered. Not to worry, they said. In Poughkeepsie, Cathy would be surrounded by other addicts starting fresh. There would be a roommate and counselors down the hall. Nobody from before. That was key, they insisted. If Cathy knew no one, there would be nothing to distract her from going to school and finding an apartment, nothing to keep her from building her days forward on a bright, narrow path.

I thought of all the people who'd run from their pasts into Dutchess County. Addicts trying to build new lives. Families from the Bronx who felt they'd made it because they'd found homes with swimming pools. Manhattan refugees like me, thinking the country life must be a better life. I'd shuddered at the missing women—the way Wendy looked so sly in her picture, the blunt fury on Gina's bruised face, the combination of insolence and desperation in Sandy's eyes. I thought about what they did to survive, and

I reviled them. But the longer I sifted my own shames, the harder it became to maintain a convincing distance. I'd never know what it meant to wander Main Street with nowhere to go, what it was to let some greasy guy shove himself inside me for twenty bucks. But I surely knew how it felt to realize that the man fucking you hated you. I'd stumbled through the better part of a decade lying in strangers' beds staring up at cracked ceilings.

THE LAST TIME Marguerite Marsh spoke to her daughter, Cathy was frantic to escape Poughkeepsie. It was impossible to stay clean in that town, she sobbed. She wanted to. She'd tried. But the ache never let her rest. Couldn't she come home to sleep for a few days? The halfway-house apartment had long since been turned over to someone else, and Cathy, pregnant with a third child, was on her own again. Trying to finish school. Trying to find work. Trying to reunite with her daughters. By the time she called her mother, Cathy was living in a car. Worn dull as a callus from conversations like this, Marguerite knew what she was supposed to say. No, she whispered, I'm sorry. It was just too much, too many lies and broken promises. But Cathy begged, her cries ripping through the phone, and once more, Marguerite relented. She listened all night for the familiar knock at her door.

Four months passed before she reported Cathy as missing. There was only weary anger at first, then a stiff, wooden hurt. Confusion when Thanksgiving passed without a call, and Christmas. Only later came the blame—first, for cocaine, then all the drug counselors who'd failed; later, for Kendall Francois, and, finally, for herself. Marguerite smoothed the pages in her scrapbook. "Cathy's going to be thirty-five in March," she said, pressing down on a new script heading. Her mouth was working at the corners again.

CHAPTER 9

Evidence of Things Not Seen

To those left in the wake of Kendall's destruction, the most galling thing was his refusal to attempt explanation or even pretend regret. In court he appeared impassive. The shrieks of his victims' families glanced off him, arrows nicking the hide of a beast. He heard them, he told me later, but didn't know how to explain himself and swallowed every attempt. No sentiment was sufficient, and every word would ring false. Because to Kendall, the story was more tangled, more layered than he could describe, so humiliating he did not want to try. It wouldn't be what they wanted to hear, anyway. The truth about apology, I had to agree, is the terrible inadequacy of the words *I'm sorry*.

I'd made this discovery shortly after Kendall's sentencing. Exhausted by decades of warfare with me on multiple fronts, my parents maintained an awkward silence about their daughter living in a cabin, isolated in the woods. But I circled them like carrion, picking over the past. None of us spoke much about the years before my sister and I left home. It was understood that our memories would be sanitized, packed away, and when discussed, kept within a careful range, bleached of emotion. Yet they festered. In unguarded moments my mother's barbed comments would float back to me on the surface of memory—*You look like a whore. I'm embarrassed in front of the doormen*—and when she felt challenged, even now, the shrill pitch returned to her voice. But beneath it, I had begun to sense something else, something she refused to discuss.

The first clue showed up unexpectedly, when I arrived late to dinner at a crowded Manhattan restaurant. My parents were already seated, and I paused for a moment at the host's station, watching them across the room. My father perused the oversized menu. Waiters bustled between linen-laid tables as New Yorkers chattered over their duck confit. But my mother was not there. She was staring at a world I could not see, a memory that made her eyes widen, jaw go slack, expression vaguely sick—the face of a person confronting horror. I will go all my life wondering what scene was replaying in her mind, but I am certain it took place in the cavernous Park Avenue apartment she knew as a child, where the dining room was lit by flickering sconces and the help ate their meals at a card table in the kitchen. We saw my grandparents infrequently, though they lived a ten-minute cab ride away, and I retain only two memories from those visits. In the first, my grandfather was yanking my three-year-old sister out of his leather lounger and hurling her across the room. She crumpled in another chair like a rag doll, too stunned to cry. No one moved. I remember only silence, then a hasty dinner at the long table in the shadowy dining room. On the other visit, my grandfather was dying. He lay on a divan in his study, the shades drawn against afternoon traffic as we watched him sleep. My mother never touched him. I don't think she spoke a word.

I heard he was an angry man, forced to accept a job in his brother-in-law's firm and seething with bruised pride. I heard he was brutal, an amateur boxer who issued threats my mother recalled through gritted teeth, sixty years later, though she closed off the faucet of memory as soon as I asked for more. Even as an elderly woman she would cross to the opposite side of the street when walking through her old neighborhood, uncomfortable tracing the same stretch of sidewalk she had as a girl. But she refused to talk about her early life in any detail, so I spent years collecting clues, alert to the moments when a story might be unearthed like pennies dug from the crevice of an old pocketbook. She told me about staring into the deep end of a drained swimming pool during a weekend in the country. Summer was over, the air turning cold. Breaking an arm or leg might delay her return to the apartment with the big dark rooms, so my mother—not yet out of elementary school—took a deep breath and jumped. A silly idea, she laughed dryly now, waving off the recollection like a bad smell. She'd landed scratched and bruised, mostly by shame, and nine years later left home for good, her father watching from his lounger as she muscled her bags out the door.

These scenes she narrated with airy detachment. But on paper they smoldered. I found a fifty-pound trove of her writing pushed into the back of an old desk and lugged the folders around with me for a decade as I moved from one apartment to the next. She'd tried to publish short fiction throughout her twenties, the stories typed on yellow paper, rejection notes neatly attached. She'd found work as a secretary in an advertising agency and there had met my father, her writing soon filed away behind the needs of two little girls who knew nothing but the white-fire fury in her eyes. "You are a narcissist!" she'd shriek at my childish transgressions—a game left on the coffee table, the laundry unfolded. I had no idea what that word meant, but among her array of curses, *narcissist* was the worst.

Nothing builds a liar like fear, and I became a prolific one, protecting every corner of my small life from attack. I wore the clothes she told me to but hid my real outfits in the back stairwell of our apartment building, changing before school in the chilly draft. I wanted to dress like my friends, girls worthy of approval. My secretiveness increased as I grew, wandering Manhattan for hours during high school, entertaining advances from drug dealers, pornographers, Scientologists. The shadiest street person frightened me less than my mother in her proper suits.

Only once did I defend myself from her attacks. I was sixteen, leaving for my usual Saturday ramble around Central Park, seven hours untraceable and free.

"Where are you going? I'll need something to tell the police tomorrow morning," she snapped as I passed her in the kitchen, my father wordlessly chopping onions for their eggs. I sneered, and she swung at me. But this time, I grabbed her arm midair and held it. My strength shocked us both. Her hand kept pushing down toward my face. I kept holding it away. There we hovered, her arm suspended and trembling between us, until I slammed her into the refrigerator. "Don't you touch me," I whispered. "Don't you ever hit me again." I was shaking when I left, but elated.

⸻

THESE WERE THE moments I had in mind when I invited my mother to a summit on my country road strewn with dead leaves. The particular battle that prompted this meeting in Pleasant Valley is lost to me now, but all of our latter-day fights were rooted in the same bottomless swamp, my sense that she'd gotten away with something she never had to answer for—a crime, of sorts, within our family.

The wood-burning stove crackled as we pulled our chairs close, sloshing through waves of memory. The insults and incessant criticisms, the burning hand. "You never apologized for any of it, not even once," I said. "You never explained *why*." This had been my goal all along, not a meeting of partners-in-fault building the future, but an autopsy of the past. I wanted an inventory of her wounds, a tale of childhood misery to equal my own. I wanted stories I'd never heard, incidents that would provide the connective tissue. I wanted her to remember, and I wanted her to atone. She made a sound like an animal being gutted. "I'm sorry," she wailed, sinking to the floor. "What more can I tell you? I'm sorry."

—

DESPITE MY STATUS as a stringer working for hourly pay, I was still a writer for the *New York Times* and a tantalizing threat in Kendall's eyes. He leaped at the chance to schedule phone conversations, during which he took great satisfaction in reminding me of the shallowness of my profession. Reporters were not writers, he lectured, just parasites and liars. Derrick, settled into his new public relations job, agreed. It was tacky, the way I'd attended the wake for Heidi Cramer's mother, pathetic, he said. Why hadn't I just left their family in peace? The growing divide with Derrick was only mildly troubling to me, but his observation about the morally slippery nature of my job gnawed. I called Heidi to apologize for my intrusions, and let her harangue me like I was child again, standing in the kitchen on Central Park West.

Navigating these hierarchies often distracted me from the fact that we were all the same generation—Derrick, Kendall, most of his victims, and I—children of the 1970s, raised to believe opportunity was assured for anyone willing to seize it, even as IBM atrophied before our eyes and the Mid-Hudson Railroad Bridge crumbled. Across the country in Silicon Valley, technologies were gestating that would remake everything in the next five years—decimating standards for news coverage, democratizing communication—but we didn't know that, tucked in our historic valley where the clouds hung low, capping views of what was possible.

Derrick had tried to move away. Much like Kendall, he despised the hypocrisies of his hometown and appeared ashamed to be living there, darting behind pyramids of canned food in the grocery store if he spied an old classmate while we were shopping. He disdained the white boys from Spackenkill High who drove into Poughkeepsie to score cheap weed on Main Street, their cars bulging with heavy bass and shoulder punches. Kendall shared this point of view. It was important to him that I understand he had never crossed into Poughkeepsie's squalor before turning eighteen. As a child he remained on the suburban side, chasing suburban success, and by high school that appeared to be working. The mysteriously quiet boy from Ralph Forsythe's homeroom had been pushed deep down inside. Now, Kendall impressed with his eloquence and wit. Other students slouched in their chairs, waiting for the bell to ring, but Kendall leaped to add his observations to class discussions, particularly in history.

Ninth-grade World Cultures allotted just two weeks to the study of Africa and religions other than Christianity, a small opening into which teacher Anthony Grabowski felt it important to squeeze in a few words about the history of human bondage. He lectured on slavery in America and watched students go glassy eyed. He described auction blocks where children were torn from sobbing mothers and saw his star pupils doodling. Kendall, however, was rapt. The subject electrified him. So vocal was the class's only black student on the matter of slavery that Grabowski worried his new favorite might be ostracized. But he appreciated the way Kendall wrestled with the story of his people without ever sounding resentful. What this kid wanted to talk about was morality, not blame. Over and over, Kendall asked Grabowski how it was possible for one person to ignore the humanity of another.

"That was how he looked at everything, in terms of right and wrong and the ability of people to do things that were so obviously wrong," Grabowski said as we walked the Arlington High School football field. "I don't think his target was women, in general. I think it was prostitutes, like Kendall thought he was ridding Poughkeepsie of the stench of prostitution, a moral crusade." If true, this theory accounts for only half of the story. Kendall pined for the women on Main Street even as he deemed them trash, writing them letters, fantasizing about building families and white-picket-fence lives.

By the time the history teacher and I were discussing his most infamous student, Grabowski had long since retired. He was taut and tan, a gamy old buzzard. But during the years Grabowski knew Kendall, he passed gray winters in a fluorescent-lit classroom and was nearly as blubbery as his star pupil. They'd shared something, Grabowski thought, as overweight men and observers of history. Remembering those years, he had no trouble using the word *love* for an inquisitive, thoughtful kid who humanized textbook discussions. He spoke of *waste,* for a boy so clearly intelligent, so obviously different.

Kendall pushed everyone hard up against themselves. His fascination with slavery reminded me of my own Nazi fixation in the tenth grade, a common teenage deviance, though impossible for a Jewish girl to admit. I knew nothing about that heritage. My family celebrated Christmas and sent me to an Episcopal high school. At my grandmother's funeral I'd been stunned to hear my father murmuring the Kaddish. But sitting in Modern European History class I got the message: Jews had been labeled ugly and weak and worthy of extermination. To be associated was unbearable. I was lost in a prep school full of lacrosse players and would-be debutantes. At home, I twisted in secrecy and loneliness. But when I adopted the Nazi gaze, I was armored. In class, while blue-blazered boys sprawled their legs in the aisles, I sat primly in the front row, waiting for Dr. Majors to turn off the lights so I could go dizzy with the power of propaganda beamed onto a pull-down screen. The midnight rallies dazzled. The flickering torches quickened my heart, and I'd slip on my coat of hatred—disgust surging at the frightened people lining up to board death trains, the way they looked at the ground, avoiding eye contact, so intimidated and meek—until the lights came on and I'd startle to consciousness, aware that I'd been talking to myself in the voice of someone else.

I knew enough to be concerned. I asked to speak with the school chaplain, wondering where to begin. He was a man of milky skin and gentle disposition, so I trod lightly, first mentioning my interest in the medieval tapestries that hung in the Metropolitan Museum and showed witches being burned at the stake. It was their agony that drew me, I said, and I assumed everyone shared this view, riveted by the women in the fire. The chaplain shifted uncomfortably. We sat on a patchy plot of grass in a community garden as I blurted my confessions one by one, stumbling to an awkward silence. I wanted to tell him about the afternoon I sat alone in a dark theater watching *A Clockwork Orange,* too ashamed about the narcotic allure of violence to confide in anyone afterward. I was a timid kid, a bookworm at heart. But tales of sadism created in me a dreamy sensation like floating. As I saw others brutalized, my own humiliation eased. I couldn't tell that to the chaplain, either.

Grabowski, too, had missed the significance of what he was hearing from the teenager seated before him. Kendall's fixation with slavery, I strongly suspected, had been sparked not by horror but by recognition. He had adopted the gaze of the enemy, the white master, and made it his own.

I CHASED THE riddle of the Francoises like an addict, frenzied to understand the ingredients of abuse that could add up to a man like Kendall. I envisioned the worst—beatings and incest, starvation and ridicule. But no official source suggested anything of the kind. This void in an answer for cruelty left me with a curiously empty feeling. And it was in this emptiness that I began to form a new picture.

Aside from his teammates and teachers at Arlington, everyone Kendall knew growing up was part of the congregation at Central Baptist Church. Paulette had been a member since childhood. But McKinley rarely joined his wife for the three-times-a-week prayer sessions she insisted their children attend. And in 99 Fulton Avenue, McKinley slept in a separate bedroom, on a separate floor. I stared at crime scene photos showing the gold-leaf wallpaper in their stairwell, the pathway to Kendall's attic tomb, and wondered if his parents had ever been united enough to paper it themselves. Surely, the place had been habitable when they moved in, but now there were tiny footpaths winding through piles of garbage that

Kierstyn would walk from her bedroom in the back, through the kitchen, and out the door to school. Kendall did the same from his room on the second floor, skipping a shower because the upstairs plumbing rarely worked. By that hour, McKinley was long gone, out the door at dawn for his commute to the DuPont plant in Connecticut. And at day's end, the Francoises rarely gathered for dinner. There was no clearing large enough for a table where they might sit and share stories. No sense of the family as a unit, one detective would tell me later, describing bonds as wispy as an abandoned cobweb.

I thought of their home as a cave, a warren of dim rooms where everyone kept their heads down, looking neither left nor right, to avoid seeing what surrounded them. "It's the way they kept the family together," a forensic psychologist hypothesized, many years later. "They know how they're living is crazy. But they all had their secrets. There was something really bad going on in that family, and everyone was in on it. There's more bodies buried, so to speak, than just the bodies."

Within these claustrophobic spaces, Kendall's mind twisted like a scrub tree on a barren hillside, whipped by winds of yearning for success that would forever elude him. No wonder he loved fantasy. No wonder he found comfort in games built upon hierarchy, where power flowed to those who followed the rules.

His older sister, Raquelle, had moved out as a girl, raised by relatives, and she grew up to work in conflict mediation. Years later Kierstyn, the youngest, would pursue a degree in family studies.

Family was important to Kendall, at least as an ideal, though he was curiously preoccupied by the notion of illegitimacy. Those born out of wedlock were irreversibly stained, he told me, referring to the self-described cousin who'd incurred Kendall's wrath less for talking to reporters than for being "a bastard" who'd never known his own father.

No child is born with such judgment. It is implanted. Paulette's own parents, lifelong churchgoers, had married with Mittie already pregnant, and Paulette followed suit when joining her life to McKinley's. Appearances, obligations—these things formed the scaffold of their lives. Kendall's father set him to work keeping the sidewalk clear of snow, and Paulette dispatched him to help a family friend with yard work, while inside their own home order and upkeep had fallen away decades ago, if they had ever existed. Detectives guessed that the place hadn't been vacuumed in twenty years. For public occasions—class-picture days or holiday gatherings—mother, father, and children fixed themselves up acceptably. But they never invited anyone in, they forbade their children from having guests, and, day to day, Paulette appeared so disheveled at work that colleagues assumed she was wearing the same clothes she'd slept in.

In her impoverished marriage, solace for Paulette came through ties to church. She'd skipped teaching Sunday school only once, the weekend after Kendall's arrest. After that, she was at Central Baptist every day, driving forty minutes into the country to pray.

On the Sunday morning I visited Central Baptist, two years later, Pastor Richard Butler was preaching about the hopelessness streaming through American culture and the cynicism of media. "Never let it get inside you!" he bellowed as row upon row of elderly black women raised their hands in silent assent. Every few minutes, parishioners yelped affirmations, the shrieks and cries coming faster and louder, like popping corn, until the whole room rocked with tears and song. I sank low in my pew, wishing I could dissolve into belief that strong.

KENDALL TOLD ME that he had stopped "talking with God." But earlier, when his classmates at Arlington were combing Led Zeppelin lyrics for yearbook quotes, Kendall looked to the Hebrews: *Faith is the substance of things hoped for, the evidence of things not seen,* he wrote. In the class of 1989 volume, most students beam from the glossy pages. A few look stoned. Kendall, in a V-neck sweater and tie, rests his chin on a fist, expression intent.

The junior-executive attire echoed his judgment against neobohemian style so popular with the Vassar students who congregated in torn jeans and baggy sweaters down the block from Kendall's home. He listened to their blithe chatter, their easy sense of importance, and his stomach torqued. I imagined him on the night he'd described attending a folk music concert on campus, putting such care into his outfit. In rooms filled with rot he'd trimmed his hair, cleaned his glasses, and pressed each item of clothing. Seated amid the students later, he couldn't understand. Those kids were rich. They could have anything they wanted. But they dressed like the bums on Main Street. He'd missed all the signals, the language of casual irony, because, for Kendall, nothing was casual.

Since I was consumed with tracing what had happened to his heart, Kendall's yearbook quote reverberated like a gong. *Evidence of things not seen.* I pored over Bibles to read the full passage exactly as he had. The Good News edition was no match, nor the gold-leaf volume in Vassar's library. Not until I was assigned to cover Rudy Giuliani speaking at a Syracuse University graduation in May 2002, did I find the correct version: the Gideon Bible inside my hotel nightstand. Kendall had selected the most hopeful portion of the passage. The rest directs believers to understand punishment as proof of love.

No one from Arlington knew about Kendall's afternoons at Central Baptist Church, nor how he sifted the Bible for meaning. All they knew was that he was huge and black, and for this reason assumed he would be a natural on the football field. But Kendall trudged onto that hard flat turf knowing he would be beaten. That was the drill. Someone drove a shoulder into his gut, and he bent to block, push back, resist. Stronger players girded their thighs and remained upright. But Kendall fell, and fell again. He took a shove and tumbled to the ground. Stood up, got slammed, and stumbled. It was always this way—after freshman year no one expected anything more. The biggest guy on the team could barely run. He looked like a monster, but could be pushed aside like a child. Soft, the jocks smirked, a mama's boy. Rolls of flesh bulged from his uniform as he lumbered across the field, stretch pants peeling away to expose his ass crack. His helmet, too small, left a shiny patch of chin open to every hit. Most players just tried to ignore him.

One afternoon in the middle of a drill and for no apparent reason, the monster lifted his head and screamed. It shocked Arlington's happy, athletic boys. It froze them motionless. A sound like whales crying, animals dying. Floundering in the dirt, Kendall wailed and wailed, his cries so loud they seemed almost visible, so raw they became embarrassing. The players stood by, kicking at the ground. No one looked away. Nor did anyone offer help. They waited until Kendall grew quiet, smiled meekly, and staggered to his feet to begin the drill again.

Other than this brief outburst, the popular belief about Kendall was that he never got angry, never appeared flustered or upset. This placidity became an identity, his rung on the ladder of Arlington's social order. He was the gentle giant, a teddy bear, people said. Kendall cringed at the label. It was a yoke around his neck, turning him into a photo stand cutout. And behind it, a metamorphosis was under way. The paranoia that would soon order all of his thoughts had wormed inside Kendall's mind, making every joke sound like a cutting dig and casual friendships an elaborate ruse. But this happened silently, stealthily, and other than Anthony Grabowski, few noticed. There were odd moments—the time Kendall tore a gold chain off a boy's neck, the day he waggled his head from side to side, moaning, when he thought something had been stolen from his locker—but they passed, and afterward Kendall shifted back into the same agreeable guy he'd always been.

Grabowski had tried to keep up with his favorite ninth grader through the years. But Arlington is vast—at graduation, students hear the names of some classmates for the first time—so by twelfth grade Kendall knew nothing of his former mentor's summertime transformation. In three months, Grabowski had shed eighty pounds and chiseled himself into a trim, toned bantamweight. The sight hit like a gut punch. Other kids were high-fiving in the hallways, embracing one another after time apart. But Kendall saw only Grabowski. What of their bond, their solidarity in size? No, here was the truth, kicking him in the face, again. His onetime friend just another smiling lie. Another person proving that kindness was a sham and his flesh, repulsive. Kendall sucked in his breath. The voice that came out was so sharp and cold Grabowski couldn't be sure he was speaking to the same kid.

"So you think you're something now, because you've lost all that weight?" Kendall hissed.

The teacher reached out, tried to make a joke, but Kendall

was already walking away. "It was sort of like I'd betrayed him," Grabowski said. They never spoke again.

Within a few months Arlington's class of 1989 would begin pondering the future, sizing up one another to predict who would be stuck forever in Poughkeepsie and who might build a life beyond. Dwayne Gordon from the football team was headed to college on an athletic scholarship, and probably the NFL—everyone knew that—but few others stood out. No one gave Kendall a thought. Still, when the graduates-to-be were invited to submit their senior wills for the yearbook, Kendall dutifully compiled a list of dopey jokes and saccharine memories, all of them written for his teammates. To the lineman who lived on a farm, he bequeathed "a cow"; to his coaches, "a winning season"; and to the quarterback so genial and popular everyone assumed he could go anywhere, Kendall wished "a world of success." A decade later, most were still living in Dutchess County. The quarterback took over his father's trash-hauling company. A few jocks found coaching jobs at neighboring schools. The best-looking boy in the senior class grew up to become a bartender. Each was stunned to learn from me that he'd held any significance for Kendall. "You know, I never even looked at his senior will. I mean, it wasn't like Kendall was going to become a CEO or anything," the bartender said.

These chosen children of Dutchess County would soon find themselves dismissed as townies by Manhattan commuters migrating north. But in the late 1980s, they were still golden. Arlington's football players were state champs, and IBM was handing out paychecks to all their dads. From that happy perch they could afford to be generous, joking with Kendall in the hallways, slapping his broad back as they galloped past. He went about his business quietly, not like the other losers groveling to be popular, and the jocks appreciated that. It was weird the way he trudged down the hallways dragging his book bag—hair a mess, pants hanging off—but they'd see him later at practice, and in uniform everyone looked pretty much the same. "I never saw him get in a fight, never saw him act violently, he was just a really good guy," said the wrestling team captain, now married with a family. "We called him Kamala—for King Kong Kamala, the pro wrestler."

Kendall remembered that, too. He'd laughed at the nickname along with everyone. But he knew what they were saying: He was a gorilla. He stank. They were saying no girl would ever get near him.

CHAPTER 10

Man and Monster

S everal people had urged me to get a professional's advice about corresponding with a killer, though they were clearly more concerned about my own mental health than about aiding my quest to understand Kendall. Two years into our correspondence, my personal life was falling apart. Derrick, disgusted by the letters that came like clockwork twice a month, now slept on the floor in his office, and by the time Kendall's calls from jail began interrupting dinner, our relationship was over.

"You're more interested in a fucking serial killer than me!" he screamed one night after I hung up the phone. It was true. A fixation as obvious as infatuation, uncontrollable as a reflex.

Among family members, my choices incited less outrage but more bewilderment. "I just don't understand—you had all the advantages," said Aunt Ruth, sitting across my parents' dining room table at Thanksgiving. She lived just outside the city and came in for Broadway shows, preening in the reflected light of her brother's ascension from working-class Yonkers to a home on the Upper West Side. She could not comprehend taking this pedigree and choosing to live on a rundown road in the middle of nowhere, pondering the interior life of a multiple murderer.

I waved off such questions but, in truth, I often ached for a way out. I was driving straight toward everything my parents had raised me to be free of—ugliness and deprivation—everything they'd hoped I would never see. I couldn't even tell them why. I couldn't say that what they had shown me was gracious but narrow, elevated yet hollow; that talking to a killer on the phone felt realer, somehow, than a life lived in university libraries and well-reviewed restaurants. I couldn't tell them that Kendall's rage matched something in me; that it held a significance I could almost smell, drawing me closer.

While tinged with particular bitterness, Derrick's scorn for my pursuit was only a close-up version of the general response: certain acts were so depraved they defied meaning. And it wasn't hard to miss the implication that there was something wrong with me for searching. But if Kendall meant nothing, then the women in his attic also meant nothing. They were reduced to abstractions, colorless silhouettes of misfortune. He'd hoarded the bodies because it was convenient, police told me, suggesting that Kendall was simply too lazy to dispose of them. A rather shallow interpretation, it seemed to me. Subverted desire, Kendall's sense of being "ripped off"—none of those feelings added up to the wreckage in his attic, the tomb in his basement, the hints I saw in autopsy reports about what he'd done to some of the bodies. How could anyone walk away from the chance to understand more? But this question itself was received as immoral by everyone around me because it suggested that Kendall Francois once had been reachable, a human being. That he was, in fact, one of us.

I lay in my bed watching years blow by. Years when the rest of my generation grew flush with stock-market success and dot-com delirium; when my sister met the man she would marry and invited me to drinks with writers for *The New Yorker*, academics at Columbia, editors from the *New York Times*.

"You could be one of them," my mother said.

"I thought I was," I shot back from my hideaway life in the woods.

Many mornings I awoke exhausted, as if I'd spent the previous eight hours running up a mountain. I knew I hadn't lived up to what anybody expected. A cold ocean of self-loathing sloshed inside me, and I began to luxuriate in ugliness, letting my hair grow matted and dirty, wearing pajamas until late afternoon when I'd finally rouse myself to begin preparing dinner. In New York State's gray and moody autumn, I trudged to the farmers' market, eavesdropping on mothers planning holiday meals with their grown daughters, gazing at young couples as they laughed over shared secrets. Then I'd turn toward the greeting cards, searching for a picture—crashing seas, lonely lighthouses—that matched whatever I was trying to convey to Kendall that week.

"Stop trying to identify with me," he wrote.

But I couldn't stop. Awkward and inscrutable, unseen and unloved, Kendall personified everything I felt myself.

DR. STUART KLEINMAN, A forensic psychiatrist, agreed to meet me for lunch in Manhattan because he was interested in violence and, he said, in journalists. He also seemed intent on ensuring that our meal met the standards of a man accustomed to being well paid for his time. He advised me to make a reservation at an

Italian restaurant in Midtown, popular with media types. Younger than I'd anticipated, Dr. Kleinman sauntered in a few minutes after me. He wore gold-framed glasses, a gold-buttoned blazer, and the air of an Ivy League hotshot, not someone devoted to the study of misery. Our interview fell on one of the worst single-day point drops in stock market history, leaving the linen-spread tables around us mostly empty, which was a relief. The psychiatrist ordered all four available courses, and as our appetizers arrived, he ticked through the serial killer canon. Ted Bundy, John Wayne Gacy, Jeffrey Dahmer—men unable to feel true emotion for anyone other than themselves, the doctor said. They wore the veneer of a personality, looked and acted like people who could relate to others, but they were robots faking a human heart, unreachable and profoundly unmoved.

Kendall turned those qualities inside out. He looked monstrous, yet was so fragile and easily upset, so protective of his family and starved for the kind of fairy-tale romance he imagined to be love. Everything about him was outsized and confused, hardly robotic. When I'd mentioned working on a story about abused circus animals, Kendall said the subject angered him too much to discuss. Locked within the stone walls of Attica, he was determined never to become angry again. "It is never quiet in prison, but I try to stay peaceful," he said.

For Dr. Kleinman, I sketched the basics of Kendall's case and received the psychiatrist's back-of-the-envelope diagnosis: A borderline personality, he said. A man with only the shakiest grasp of reality, unable to credit the legitimacy of any experience outside his own. I told the doctor that my killer was a sci-fi fan who devoured tales of right and wrong, obsessed with the relationship between Luke Skywalker, *Star Wars*'s paragon of good, and his father, the dark lord Darth Vader. Dr. Kleinman chewed his egg-plant and wondered aloud which character Kendall identified with most. This was not something I could ask directly. The notion of identification sent Kendall into paroxysms of fury. When I pointed out that he was someone whose feelings had serious implications, a person the rest of us needed to understand, Kendall threatened to sever our connection completely. Surely, he saw Vader as a doppelgänger—the honorable warrior who gives himself over to evil until it corrodes so deeply that he becomes less man than machine. I'd been captivated by Vader myself since the fifth grade.

After the roll call of famed psychopaths, Dr. Kleinman carved into his veal cutlet and offered a tutorial on borderline-personality criminals. These were highly manipulative people who would design a plan for murder in exacting detail. They thrilled at playing cat and mouse with the law. This sounded right. Kendall had delighted in his ability to elude Poughkeepsie's police, and still giggled to recall their fumbling investigation. But he hardly seemed the careful plotter. Everything in the police reports I'd received from Dr. Stone suggested that Kendall was a man overtaken by gales of fury that rose up and drowned him. His chief survival tactic was an ability to quiet these storms and resurrect the gentle-giant silhouette.

"I think he's triggered by betrayal, or the sense that he's being set up for betrayal," I told the doctor. "And his mood can turn instantly."

Everything about me incited Kendall's rage—irregularities in the pace of my letters, a postponed phone call—all of it seen as evidence of a universal design to undermine and ignore him. Everyone was part of the pattern, the women he'd killed and those he let go, former classmates, teachers, teammates, and me. Only his family remained absent from the list. I would apologize for angering him, only to hear Kendall insist, with mounting irritation, that he never got angry with me. He used other words—*frustrated* or *annoyed*—but never, ever *angry*. This he said he'd learned from his mother, who also never got angry. "A saint," Kendall called her, noting that jailhouse guards had commented on what a lovely woman Paulette seemed to be. "Probably the nicest person on the planet."

Dr. Kleinman was intrigued. "Look for contradictions between what he's saying to you now and what he's said before."

I ticked off a half-dozen while the psychiatrist buttered his roll: Kendall was mesmerized by women, but disgusted with them. He described himself as sexually insatiable, yet had been unable to climax. He sneered at frailty and failure in others while stumbling through the most rudimentary shop-class assignments himself. At Arlington he'd scrunched his face in concentration, glasses slipping down his nose, while he carved wooden figurines for a chess set as other students laughed and watched the clock. "Nothing ever comes out as good as I want," he told me. "I'm like a perfectionist that way." This pattern repeated in the army. While the rest of his battalion cleaned their weapons with a cursory sweep and left for dinner, Kendall spent hours ministering to his machine gun. In the Attica welding shop other inmates snickered as Kendall labored over file cabinets destined for a bureaucrat's basement.

"This is a person who feels like a nothing, a laughingstock," said the doctor, brushing bread crumbs from his sleeve. "I expect you'll find that he lived in highly self-defeating ways, constantly setting up problems for himself. A very ineffectual kind of guy."

All my adult life I'd wondered about mental health professionals like Dr. Kleinman, drawn to dissect darkness. Those I'd encountered had sad eyes and wise hearts, none of the crisp businesslike

air evinced by the man sitting across the white linen tablecloth, pe-
rusing the dessert menu. But nothing in my search for the meaning
of Kendall Francois had unfolded as anticipated. The most soulful
interpretation I'd heard so far came from an FBI profiler.

"You see someone who's that big, and you say, 'He should be a
macho football player.' But that's not who Kendall was at all," Special Agent Charles Dorsey told me. "For the most part, when we
deal with prostitutes as victims, they're thrown out a passenger
car door—but that's when the offender feels comfortable in his
surroundings. This is the rage that comes from not being able to
be who you are."

Dorsey's analysis matched much of what I'd found, and it was
the only theory that suggested Kendall's handling of the bodies
pointed not toward slothfulness but deep discomfort in his hometown, a profound lack of ease with his surroundings. As far as I
could tell, the only place Kendall had truly felt at home was the
wrestling gym at Arlington High. No other team had a heavyweight
like Kendall. He anchored the squad, and long after graduation he
continued to haunt the mats, wandering back into the bowels of
Arlington during furloughs from the army. Even as he sat in jail
awaiting Grady's decision on the plea bargain that would save his
life, Kendall clung to his memories of high school wrestling, asking
if I would attend an Arlington meet and report back because the
Poughkeepsie Journal's coverage of sports was as lousy as its coverage of everything else. I demurred.

Kendall had not swept every contest. As in football, boys half
his size could often outmaneuver him. But losing never dimmed
his enthusiasm. He'd been Arlington's ace, the big man who strode
onto the mats at the end to clinch victory. Into his twenties, Kendall would return for Francois vs. Francois reunion matches at

Christmastime, pinning Aubrey to the floor while the rest of the squad gathered round, screaming for one brother to thrash the other. Their teammates had liked both boys well enough, though their stench was unbearable. It got so bad in the locker room that other athletes had to breathe through their mouths. Coach Fred Perry told his crew to ignore it. The smell was "natural for the boys' African heritage," he explained.

A stocky man with small dark eyes, Perry toured me through the dim warren of pipes and hallways that led to his gym, and seemed to be working hard to keep his temper in check—at what, I was unclear. In front of his team Perry did not hold back. When Kendall performed poorly, the coach ripped into his three-hundred-pounder before crowds of howling spectators, his neck turning rash red, the cords going taut. Kendall hung his head. "Yes, Coach. Okay, Coach, I'm sorry. I'll try harder." Often, Paulette and McKinley were watching in the stands, Perry recalled, silent and impeccably dressed.

People grew accustomed to seeing Kendall, at twenty-one or twenty-five or twenty-seven, still hanging around, keeping score, straightening the locker room. His old teammates were long gone by now, but there was a new generation, and the younger kids loved him. They hung off his broad shoulders, trying to pull him to the floor while Kendall gently picked them off, a mother dog enduring the play of pups.

A regular at hometown contests, Kendall had been absent for weeks in the winter of 1998. But no one mentioned it. No one inquired. No one knew that he'd been sitting in jail, charged with assaulting a prostitute, nor that he had five dead women secreted in his home. Anyway, now he was back and up to his usual pranks, whisking a chair from beneath the bottom of a skinny boy about to sit down, roaring with laughter as the kid fell flat on his back. It was typical Kendall—he loved slapstick—and afterward he was up again, striding across the mats to prepare for the next event. A guy with responsibilities. A man who commanded respect. Hell, he thought, practically an assistant coach. When Kendall returned to his seat, the skinny boy was ready. He kicked Kendall's chair aside to share the joke, and a multiple murderer toppled to the floor as the whole gym pointed, screaming with laughter: *buffoon*. Kendall was stunned—taken by a kid, just a little punk. Fury came as a shrieking wind. There was no progression from confusion to insult to anger. No feelings connected to ideas. Only blind rage. He reared up, grabbed the boy, and hit him so hard the kid's baseball cap spun across the room. Arlington's gym was packed, but Kendall didn't see anyone. He barely saw the boy. He was a force beyond thought. "He went down on the floor, and we saw this side of him that nobody had ever seen—just intense rage and embarrassment," said a teacher who'd been sitting in the bleachers, watching the whole thing.

DR. KLEINMAN SEEMED EAGER to get on with dessert, so I hurried to lay out more details for his interpretation. I talked about Kendall's interest in slavery. I mentioned his preference for white women and noted that in their basic size, shape, and color, many of his victims bore a passing resemblance to me. Dr. Kleinman nodded slowly as he chewed. "It's a role reversal," he said. "He is creating a scenario where the white women are property, bought and paid for, and he is the master. You need to find out what white people have meant in his life. It's possible that killing might have been stressful for him."

"Does that mean he might feel guilt?"

The doctor swallowed.

"Ambivalence," he said. "If he feels ambivalent about his crimes, there may be some capacity for remorse."

During our phone conversations, I sometimes thought I heard a kernel of this pinging around inside Kendall. It might surface for an instant—"I deserve to be dead," he'd mutter. "Those women didn't deserve to die like that"—only to sink again. Kendall hated to talk about remorse, either having it or not. The entire topic made him shrink away.

"Your subject hates himself," the doctor said. "Particularly as a man."

This seething mountain of force felt like a quaking failure, someone with no more effect on the world than a bug, and his self-loathing was volcanic. He would set himself up to fail again and again. I thought of Kendall in the army, kicked out for being obese. Kendall, who went to one of the best high schools in the county and graduated to clean middle school floors; who aspired to live in white suburbia and chased that dream by pantomiming relationships with women he had to pay.

"Pathological narcissism is ultimately deep insecurity," said Dr. Kleinman.

Yet Kendall reveled in what he considered his superior intelligence, bemoaning his isolation in a world of mediocrity. He had been steely calm while answering questions from police, but a giggly, guffawing mess the first time I visited him in jail. Relaxed while hooked to a polygraph, denying murder, but streaming with sweat around women he desired. So often, he'd been haphazard and disorganized about his crimes, leaving corpses exposed in the attic and garage, telling some women what he'd done to others, then letting them go free. As a psychopath he appeared to me suspended, with one foot in our daylight world, where he struggled to negotiate shame, aspiration, confusion, and love; the other in Dr. Kleinman's nether-realm of ghouls who felt nothing at all. Neither a functioning man nor an outright beast, but something malformed and caught between. Such paradoxes delighted him. Kendall boasted that criminologists found him interesting precisely because he did not match a traditional serial-murderer profile. "That actually makes me happy, not fitting into their nice little categories," he'd told me. "I don't even believe in violence."

Whatever his mood, bombastic or depressed, I could never shake the sound of torment on the other end of the line, the sense of a mind struggling with the impulse to reach out, connect, communicate. Most of Kendall's heart was indeed gnarled and dead, but some crippled sliver, I felt sure, remained alive. It was not always evident in our phone conversations, but Kendall's letters displayed a poignancy that made me wince, and the delicacy of his drawings tore at my heart. Dr. Kleinman glanced up from his tart as I spoke. His round glasses glinted with every bite.

As far as connecting with Kendall, the doctor's advice was clear. "Your subject is a paranoid, and paranoids need facts, consistency. Make sure you are always the same, utterly reliable. Keep every phone appointment. Follow through on every promise."

I stared at my plate, thinking of our endless games, the way I sometimes let months elapse between letters or ignored Kendall's phone calls—mostly to remind myself that I had the power to do so. I stood near the phone, watching it ring, picturing Kendall on the other end in a prison hallway, waiting. I saw his face, hopeful, then hardening.

"Kendall will idolize you at first and then turn," Dr. Kleinman said. "Psychologically, this is a very fragile guy. And his rage against women is enormous."

I nodded and took notes, trying to look like a grad student.

"There will be no end to his sexual fantasies," the doctor continued, wiping his mouth with care. "They'll be explicit and disturbing, and a good deal worse than that if he feels betrayed. I don't envy you. It's going to get intense."

THE ESSENTIAL TRUTH about borderlines is their inability to understand or care about the feelings of another. This defect precludes connection and, by extension, true communication—both of which Kendall grasped at with ravenous need. That was my trouble with diagnoses. They turned a person into a specimen, a checklist of traits, rather than a human being with a destroyed soul. Still, Kendall fit the profile. Borderlines split everyone other than themselves into categories—good or bad—and they can change a designation instantly, dragging you from saint to pariah with the speed of an electric shock. They are, simultaneously, mystified as to why their relationships never work out. They have no idea that they come across as cruel. Psychopaths, sitting just next door on the spectrum of mental illness, catalog insults and incubate them for years, brooding over offhand remarks and magnifying the smallest slight to obscene decibels.

The question in my mind was whether these tendencies had been part of Kendall all along, or was there a point when he turned? If so, did any strand of his old self remain, a rope bridge that he might inch across? I'd never believed Kendall's cruelty was inborn. He'd told me about holding his little sister's hand as they strolled the lawns at Vassar, Kierstyn brushing the velvety flower tops with her fingertips, then bending to pick a few. Kendall nearly choked on the memory. He told me that college students, seeing his little sister pull a few daffodils, had run at her, shouting, "Open your hand! Open your hand!" terrifying the girl. "She was just a baby," he said. I mulled this unprovable story for years. Even if an invention, it suggested Kendall had a deep attachment to his little sister and seething resentment for the privilege that surrounded them. He told me about fashioning dresses for Kierstyn's paper dolls when he wasn't losing himself in video games, and I didn't see a born monster. I saw an introvert. A shy kid, an ugly kid. I knew that kid.

Research into the neurobiology of personality disorder was then in relative infancy. But it would make great strides in the years following Kendall's imprisonment. Simon Baron-Cohen, a British psychology professor who built his career on the study of autism and wrote *The Science of Evil,* describes borderlines as people who lack an essential sense of self. Tellingly, the portion of their brain that forms the seat of empathy is physiologically different—thinner and smaller than average—just as it is among the autistic. Baron-Cohen and others theorize that while physical predilections may be inborn, negligent parenting is the catalyst, igniting a reaction that can become full-blown personality disorder. In Poughkeepsie, however, all authorities said there had never been any suggestion of abuse in the Francois home. At first I assumed all of these people were lying—squadrons of teachers and social workers covering for their failure to act on something that must have been obvious. But Dr. Kleinman shook his head, no. Neither physical nor sexual abuse were prerequisites for depravity like Kendall's, he said. What did the most damage was a home life of such disconnection and neglect that if abuse had occurred, no one would have done a thing to stop it.

I thought again of Paulette, who'd forbidden her children to invite friends over; insisted that Kendall and his siblings attend church three times a week, yet allowed them to sleep in garbage. Kendall kept telling me that his was an average family and he no monster. But psychopaths lie to hide their true nature. It is their hallmark, a defining trait. Was this all that lay behind Kendall's self-portrait—deceit proffered for his own amusement? Or might he be trying to explain, with Delphic riddle-speak, that no single entity was to blame, that manipulation was as much a part of him as nearsightedness or brown eyes?

CHAPTER 11

Solitaire

Elf,

I don't know how this is for you, but talking about all of this is hard. It is not as simple as being a killer. Is that how you still see me? You want to lay things on the line, Well here it is I like you. You seem to be a nice person, but you could never understand what I'm going through. I don't like what I do, and I don't like who I am in the big picture, but you don't seem to be able to appreciate anything except this fucking book.

This was the first letter Kendall wrote me from Attica state prison, where he resumed his campaign to get my photograph and demanded to know why I continued to withhold this sign of good faith. There was the inappropriateness of crossing that line, I explained; the deaths of others whose pictures he'd kept; my terrible fear. All of these excuses he rejected as baseless. I was incorrectly comparing myself to the women on Main Street, which revealed more about me than any snapshot.

A few weeks later, he added: "You are a cruel, lying, manipulative person. The perfect reporter."

I had imagined that when done with the court system and officially imprisoned for life, Kendall might become more pliable. I'd hoped he would serve up a buffet of anecdotes intertwined with history that added up to answers. Instead, he maintained a surprising hauteur, schooling me on his rights, though the right to hold on to his story was almost all he had left. I kept on, trying to reason with a man who acted largely on instinct.

> *Ken,*
>
> *I do not just see you only as a killer. I never have. I see you as a person who has been in pain for a long time, and whose pain is a big part of what ultimately happened. It is difficult to understand how someone who writes and thinks the way you do, someone as interested in spirituality and Shakespeare, someone who cares about right and wrong and obviously feels for certain people, could grow up to commit the crimes you've committed. This is why I want to write about you. I have a hunch that your story is important to understand. Don't you?*

He was surely the only person on the planet who would characterize me as a perfect reporter. This remark had been prompted by a chance meeting at the post office, where I'd noticed an elderly black man collecting his mail and wondered if he was a Francois relative. The number of African Americans then living in Pleasant Valley hovered below two hundred, and I knew the surnames of many in Kendall's extended family. The type on the man's envelope confirmed it. He was tall, in a plaid work shirt and jeans, smudgy old cap jammed on his head, and I watched him walk stiffly across the road to sit on a bench. His appearance suggested a life of hard work with no time for idle imaginings.

"I don't mean to bother you, sir," I said, following him out the door. "I'm a reporter, and I've been writing about the Kendall Francois case."

"No," he said quietly. "I don't want to get involved in that."

"Do you know the family?"

The barest trace of a nod. "My wife—she's a cousin."

"Did you know him—Kendall?"

He nodded again.

"Did you have any idea how things were for them?"

"Well, we were pretty surprised when the news came out."

There are people who believe any expectation of privacy is eliminated for someone even remotely associated with crimes on the magnitude of Kendall's. Journalism depends on this belief, gluing together scraps of detail from widening circles of acquaintance. Everything is relevant. Anything might provide insight. But all I saw on the bench in Pleasant Valley was an old man, encircled in shame.

"I'm sorry to bother you," I said, quickly walking away.

I was on my way to Nine Partners Cemetery anyway, in search of the Francois family burial plot. I'd wanted to see McKinley's grave, but Paulette's friends at the mental hospital told me I'd never get the chance. McKinley's body had been shipped back to the family compound in St. Martinville, Louisiana, for fear of vandals desecrating the site in Dutchess County. So I resolved to look one generation earlier, hoping the headstones of Kendall's grandparents might tell me something. The cemetery sat on a generous hilltop that caught the sunlight even when the valley below remained in shadow. I found the Blackwells' section easily. They had short humble stones that bespoke Mittie and Roy's belief in service to God, country, and forces more important than selfish human struggle. I sighed and turned to leave. But there on my right rose a shiny brown marker with the name MCKINLEY L. FRANCOIS freshly engraved. There were no aphorisms or epitaphs, nothing beyond the dates of McKinley's fifty-three years on earth, with space for two more names, though he had four children and a wife. Of course, Kendall's name likely was not one McKinley would have wanted to include, Raquelle remained separated from the family, and Paulette hadn't even shared a bedroom with her husband. So perhaps the spaces were reserved only for Kierstyn and Aubrey. In any case, I had been lied to again, or misdirected by someone who'd spoken in ignorance, which paralleled everything about this case—a furious impulse toward shutting doors and maintaining darkness. Someone, however, had been here very recently. On newly turned earth sat two potted plants, a miniature pumpkin, and a few stones arrayed in the shape of a cross. I sat down and leaned on McKinley's headstone, as close to a member of Kendall's family as I had come.

No newspaper editor would consider sitting by a grave to be significant, nor a ten-second conversation with a distant relative. Yet word of my latest effort to speak with his kin brought a thundering response from within the stone walls of Attica.

> *Things are going to have to change, especially your tactics and attitude . . . my family has been through enough without you going around stirring the pot. Don't take me for a fool. It hasn't worked so far. . . . The worst part is that when your not being 'a reporter,' I actually like you.*

Battling over insignificant trespasses was only my most obvious problem. Far worse was the truth that any reporter hates to admit: I wanted to be liked by my source, even if that source was a serial killer. Perhaps especially because he was. Kendall followed up with a phone call soon after his letter.

"That thing you're writing about me—your book, what's the name of it?" he demanded. This interest was new. For years, Kendall had refused to look at anything I'd written about his case.

"I'm thinking maybe 'Evidence of Things Not Seen'—from your yearbook quote."

"Hmmph. Okay, I guess. But I think it implies a double meaning. When are you going to hurry up and finish so we can get to know each other?"

"I am trying to get to know you this way, through writing. I know you won't talk about your mom and dad, but what about your older sister—is she still studying to be a minister?"

"How did you know about that?" Kendall barked. "She doesn't even speak to me."

"From you—you told me."

Kendall hated my writing about him, yet he carefully tended the coals of our relationship, imagining friendship from a reporter who could pantomime it only while writing about his case, which was precisely the self-sabotage Dr. Kleinman had described.

"Maybe I should write a story about you," Kendall said, trotting out one of his favorite weapons.

"What would you say in a story about me?"

"None of your business. When are you coming out here?"

Interesting. He'd been putting me off for nearly a year since our conversation at the Dutchess County Jail. Every time we talked about a visit, I reminded him that the conversation would be an interview, which shattered the illusion of friendship he so desperately wished to maintain. But touching his family, even tangentially, seemed to inspire a change.

"I could come next Sunday. But you know what I'm going to ask about."

"I'll think about it."

A few days later he called again.

"I'm kinda nervous about our visit," Kendall began. Apparently, it was on, though he'd never explicitly accepted my terms that this was an interview, an effort at fact-finding and investigation—not a social call.

"Why are you nervous?"

"I don't know if I'll be seeing Elf, which would be nice, or if it's going to be that megabitch reporter, which would ruin my whole day."

"I'll try not to ruin your day. What worries you, in particular?"

"I'm worried that we'll argue, because you're a very aggressive person and I'm a very passive person—normally, anyway. It's probably hard for you to believe that a guy who killed eight people could call himself passive, but it's true. I have a big problem with being too respectful and not saying what's on my mind, even to you."

"I think you make yourself pretty clear."

"But I never want to be disrespectful."

"Well, thank you for that," I said.

"You're welcome. See you Sunday."

"HOW ARE YOU doing with your project?" my mother asked before I left for Attica. Since our fireside reckoning about the past—

hers, mine, and our family's—the tone of our conversations had begun to shift. She phoned often, treading carefully, trying to re-connect.

"I don't know, Mom. The guy's impossible. He says I pick fights, ask too much, push too hard."

"Well, you *can* be very antagonistic," said my mother, siding with a serial killer in their mutual assessment of my deficiencies. Clearly, we still had a ways to go.

⁂

I STARTED OFF for prison on a steamy Saturday in August 2002, the skin on my face tight with dried tears. Derrick and I had al-ready agreed that I should move out, but he'd made a mix tape for my drive, track after track of Grateful Dead and the Band, music I listened to only when I had a stomachache. He meant it to be calm-ing, I suppose. We'd never been well matched, but Derrick had a physical grace I admired more than I'd ever let on. Even as I drove toward Attica in the muggy heat, I thought of him the winter be-fore, on a Sunday morning when he'd laced up his hockey skates to see what he could do on the frozen pond behind our shack. It was hypnotic, the way he swung one booted foot behind the other and propelled himself backward with a dancer's fluidity. "That is beau-tiful," I called from the water's frozen edge, Moses barking crazily by my side. Derrick shrugged off my praise, and I knew then that we were over. He wouldn't accept anything that came from me, not even awe. So much of early love is rooted in what the other person makes us feel about ourselves. For me, Derrick had been validation that I was acceptable, finally, to the kind of men who'd previously offered only scorn. I wondered what I could have possibly meant to him.

Now he only wanted me gone. But I'd stalled on my way out the door. I was terrified. After all the letters and phone calls, this would be my first interview with Kendall free of barriers or restraints. Apparently, he was worried, too. He fretted that anything he said could be "used against" him, as if anyone, other than me, maintained a vision of Kendall as something more than irredeemable. I'd asked several people for advice about our meeting. Assistant District Attorney Smith and the Court TV criminologist who'd mailed her head shots to Kendall waved away my concerns. Sitting thigh to thigh with a man who'd strangled eight women should pose no problem, they said. And they were right, of course. Kendall was unlikely to throttle me in public. But neither of them knew the tone of our fraught phone conversations, the cat-and-mouse quality of our relationship.

"Kendall Francois has asked me to visit him, and I'd like to know the procedures for speaking with inmates who have a history like his," I'd asked his case manager a few days before.

"Francois? He's in here for eight life terms," the man laughed. "It won't make any difference to him if you're number nine."

"Where will we be talking?"

"You'll be in the visitors room."

"But with barriers, or some sort of glass between us?"

"No, it's just a big open room."

"Will he be shackled?"

"Not unless he does something during your visit. Then, the next time, you'll be in a booth."

Charles Dorsey, the FBI profiler, was more generous. "Let him do all the talking. He's the teacher and you're the student." I was to convey submission, gratitude, appreciation for Kendall's taking time out of his busy schedule. Psychopaths were chameleons,

Dorsey said, adapting to the circumstances before them. Kendall would take on the role of teacher if I treated him as an expert, the master. "Build him up. Flatter him. Don't go in with a list of questions. They enjoy talking about themselves. Just sit back and let him run. And don't challenge him. Only ask about something if he broaches the subject."

The most important thing, he added, was never to show fear.

OUTSIDE ROCHESTER, I pulled into a Days Inn. The motel chain had symbolized relief during my cross-country pilgrimage with Derrick five years before. It had hot showers and free coffee and that was all we wanted. But now my room felt stuffy and dank. I turned on the television but snapped it off three minutes later and went to eat at the Olive Garden across the parking lot, listening to other diners as I poked at my plate of creamy pasta.

Motels had always been a comfort to me in their Cloroxed uniformity, a pleasant suspension from regular life, where no one knew me and I could almost disappear. But anonymity meant enduring in silence if reality barged in. Many years earlier, I'd been booked into San Antonio's fanciest hotel for a reporting tryout. The place was grand, with multiple lobbies and glittering ballrooms. Filigree-frame mirrors tracked me as I walked carpeted hallways, a success en route to applause. I snuggled into a bed of crisp sheets, imagining my glorious future, and awoke at two A.M., to shuddering moans. It was a man, weeping on the other side of my wall. Then a woman, cackling. A couple's fight, I thought. It would crescendo, then resolve. But the cries and cruel laughter continued until dawn, so chilling I didn't dare call downstairs. The following night it happened again, with a two A.M. crash that shook my headboard, then sobs and the sound of a man peeing. Several years later, in a Montreal motel, I heard a similar brawl—furniture breaking, racking sobs, piteous jabbering—but this time I rang the front desk. When the night clerk knocked, he found only a solitary man inside, throwing himself against the walls.

"Things aren't always what they seem," Kendall lectured me time and again.

Dorsey had advised that I let Kendall lead our conversation, and I'd underlined his directive in my notebook: *Do not challenge.* But he'd offered no strategy for handling Kendall-as-inquisitor. I tried to prepare myself for possible scenarios, imagining how our conversation might unfold, but my mind kept veering to the question of contact. This was the real reason I'd asked about a barrier and shackles. I didn't know how I would negotiate a handshake. A criminal psychiatrist I knew had famously kissed Ted Bundy on the cheek just before his execution, which suggested a level of confidence and composure I could not conceive of mustering toward Kendall.

AT SEVEN A.M., I startled awake, chaotic dreams shattering into fragments, and stumbled to the window with a Styrofoam cup of coffee to sit in the morning light and scan my notes. First, I'd follow up on what Kendall had told me about his father and the family farm in Louisiana. Then the army, which seemed to be a turning point. Then I'd let him lead. I opened one of Dr. Stone's police reports—I'd brought the entire stack along—and a rumpled piece of paper slid onto the floor. It was a letter I'd never seen before, slipped mistakenly into the file, but I recognized the handwriting.

... You're ALL I can think about. I want to hold you and protect
you from the world. I can't even put down everything I'm feeling
for you right now. I want to be the person you laugh with and
cry with. I want to be the person that you share your hopes and
dreams as well as your fears and problems. Someone that will
stick by you no matter what happens. Just tell me what I have to
do to prove myself to you. I want you, I need you, and someday I
hope to love you. I also hope to be someone that you can truly love.

Kendall had written it to Christine Sala the summer they were
pretending friendship. He'd strangled six women by then.

⸺

UNLIKE A MODERN cement-block penitentiary dropped by
the side of some lonely highway, Attica sits in the midst of a small
town, around the corner from the Little League field. I drove up
Main Street, made a right turn onto Exchange, and there it stood,
a towering fortress, pointed gun turrets piercing the sky. The town
of Attica had been founded in 1811 and looked it, with small buildings arrayed along a two-block shopping area. Kendall complained
bitterly during his first snowy winter up there, refusing to set foot
in the courtyard of his stone fortress until he saw green grass for
a week. But this morning was sweltering. In the parking lot hundreds of cars lined up under a glaring sun. I leaned against mine
for a moment, enjoying the warmth against my back, lingering as
it started to burn.

Just as the notion of someday coming face-to-face with a killer
had haunted me since childhood nightmares about David Berkowitz, the name *Attica* lingered, too. I'd been mesmerized by its stac-

cato sound since the sixth grade, when I heard John Travolta aping Al Pacino—"At-ti-ca! At-ti-ca!"—as he dressed for the disco in *Saturday Night Fever*. At twelve, I knew nothing of the facts, the thousand prisoners who'd rioted there, black inmates marching white officers to the roof for execution. The police firestorm that ended their four-day siege had been the bloodiest single encounter between Americans since the Civil War, so tangled in chaos and rage that it took another three decades to resolve the question of blame.

Not until I saw the village name printed in a road atlas near a little black dot did I realize that the word Attica held no power itself. It was just a place, not a force. The main entrance to the prison was merely a small door hung with a wooden sign: ATTICA VISITORS AREA. When I arrived at 8:50 A.M. (already five minutes late by Kendall's count), a large fan was blowing gusts of warm air around the reception room. Guards smiled and chatted. Inmates wearing utility-green jumpsuits pointed me toward the sign-in sheet. It asked for my name and the person I'd come to see. I grabbed one of the stubby golf pencils provided, wrote *Kendall Francois,* and felt a jolt of electricity shimmy up my arm. The box marked *relation to* posed a greater problem. Kendall had never authorized me to visit as a journalist, and a white woman coming to see a black inmate was an unlikely blood relative. I worried that writing *acquaintance* might raise questions, and I didn't know how to answer them. So I scribbled *friend* and for the hundredth time silently begged the families of his victims to forgive me. Then I sat on a bench to wait with the others who'd shown up that morning: a mother and father with two young children, a tattooed woman with frizzy hair, a busty blonde wearing a tennis visor, and a well-dressed black man who kept his gaze down, hands clasped in his lap.

WHEN THE GUARD called Kendall's name, I was to empty my pockets, remove my shoes, and walk through a metal detector. He had already told me not to wear hair clips, buckles, or an underwire bra (an attention to detail both accurate and unnerving), so I got through without trouble, though the cough drops and a letter I'd brought had to be stored in a locker. The stocky blond officer looked at me like I was an idiot for not knowing this rule, but she buzzed me through one set of iron bars, then another, and I stepped into a sunny courtyard within the prison walls. A few inmates were digging in the dirt, close enough to nod to, but their voices sounded far away. The silence surprised me. I'd imagined Attica as an echo chamber of shrieks and manic laughter. But the prison felt serene. I crossed the yard on a narrow walkway, guided toward a steel gate by a scrawny man who motioned without speaking and pointed me toward a hallway lined with prisoners' artwork. I walked alone, nothing in my hands but a slip of paper bearing the name of a killer. In the visitors room an officer reached down from his elevated command post, took the paper from me, and carefully spelled *FRANCOIS* in neat letters on a ledger. He passed this over a pot of coffee to another guard, who peered down. Which was the first name, he asked, Kendall or Francois? A serial killer who'd made the front page of the *New York Times* was nobody here. I assisted with the formalities. The first guard nodded toward a small card table with two orange chairs and told me to wait there. Was there anything else to know, some procedure or warning I should be aware of?

"No heavy making out," he said.

I sat at the table for twenty minutes as other inmates walked in to meet their guests. The room looked like a high school cafeteria with its inspirational murals and linoleum floors. A bank of vending machines hummed against the far wall, and prisoners were neither escorted nor announced. They simply materialized, drifting in from every direction, silent as ghosts. I considered my position at the table. Two chairs had been placed next to each other on adjacent sides, but the prospect of sitting thigh to thigh with Kendall horrified me, so I moved one chair opposite the other and sat there. This way, we would be facing, with less chance of contact. Within seconds, the guard who'd assigned my seat was marching my way, telling me to put the chair back where it was. I would be seated at Kendall's right hand. No one seemed to understand why this might concern me. Minutes slid by. Kendall did not appear. I bought a can of cranberry juice and sat down to fidget with the deck of cards he'd told me to bring, every few seconds jerking my head up to scan the room, always expecting that he'd be there, watching from a distance and laughing. A half hour later, he finally walked in.

Even fifty feet away, Kendall cut an enormous silhouette. His hair was combed straight up like Don King's, or the Bride of Frankenstein, and he lumbered toward me—six feet, four inches and almost four hundred pounds—uncertain and squinting because his eyesight was poor and because he'd never really believed I would come.

"So how you doing?" he said, settling himself on the dinky plastic chair.

He was wearing a fresh beige polo, Converse high-tops, and the same cheap aviator glasses I'd seen at the county jail. Rivulets of sweat poured down his face, though the room was air-conditioned.

"I like your Cons," I began.

"They're Pataki's," he shrugged, referring to New York's then-governor. He peered at me as I chattered about the drive north, how pleasant it had been, dotted with farms and livestock.

"The farms make me sick," he said. "I hate the smell of manure. The worst is at night, when I'm trying to sleep."

Kendall had breathed gas from rotting corpses for two years while slumbering on Fulton Avenue, but manure made him squeamish.

"Really? I kind of like that farm smell," I said.

Manure reminded me of sleepy barns I'd known during the days in Connecticut, the comfort of an animal's flesh rippling beneath my hands. It suggested warmth and earthiness that felt like solace. But Kendall knew nothing of that. He whined about creature comforts—bad weather, the bugs in his cell—though he'd lived in squalor at home.

He glanced down at my hands, fiddling with the cards.

"I've been trying to remember how to play solitaire," I said.

The idea of playing cards with a serial killer was so cliché it almost made me laugh. But this had been Kendall's idea, and he seemed grateful for the opening. Gently, he took my deck and began to teach me "clock," a stupid and tedious game, nearly impossible to win, though Kendall whipped through it undeterred by his inevitable loss. He laid the cards down smartly, flipping them over with a quick slapping sound.

"So how's work?" I asked.

Kendall was a welder in the metal shop, building the same file cabinets Poughkeepsie bureaucrats used to store property records.

"I make thirty-eight cents an hour," he said.

"I figured the pay would be low—"

"That's a raise!"

"Well, a raise is good."

He grinned, fat lips pulling away from his teeth.

"Actually, you can go up to sixty-eight cents an hour, but you have to be on a high-protein diet for that and I have bad knees."

I laughed, weakly.

"Do you know any of these guys?" I gestured at the other inmates sitting near.

"A few."

"Are most of them here for life, like you?"

Kendall smiled.

"They'll have the chance to get out, though that's up to the parole board. Most of them aren't in here for good, like me."

"Do they know what you did, why you're here?" He was already nodding. "Are they afraid of you?"

"Some are. Others are like, it's cool. Most people don't believe I did it."

I scrunched my face into a question mark.

"Because I'm such a nice guy!" Kendall guffawed. "Just because someone's a murderer doesn't mean they're a mean person."

This was his favorite refrain.

I wanted to know how a nice guy could strangle eight women.

"Sometimes things happen that are out of character. Stronger forces were at work."

"What forces?" I said, leaning forward, my face inches from his. Kendall cast his eyes down and pulled away, tracing the cards on the table. Despite his size, I never felt crowded by Kendall's physical presence. He was, if anything, retiring, keeping his girth to himself, making sure his arms never took up too much space. Though whenever he looked up and held my gaze, I went witless again.

We switched to politics. Kendall had voted, usually Democratic, in every election since turning eighteen, and he spoke easily about current affairs. "Your president is an idiot," he said, referring to George W. Bush. I asked about his feelings on capital punishment, now that he had been spared the death penalty.

"I don't care about dying, really. If it could have been done in a few months I would have gone right ahead. I told my lawyers that if they could promise no app— What do you call those?"

"Appeals?"

"Yeah, if they wouldn't do any appeals I would have gone ahead. But of course they couldn't do that."

I'd often wondered about Kendall's thoughts on his own death. Our phone conversations withered whenever I mentioned his HIV or asked how he was feeling. "My health is none of your concern," he'd sniff. But at his sentencing, when Heidi Cramer shrieked that she couldn't wait until he fell to AIDS, Kendall told me he'd wanted to yell, "I plan to live a long, long time!" He disapproved of capital punishment, abortion, and euthanasia, but thought if one or two were legal, all three should be. He relished his ability to point out such hypocrisies, and he saw them everywhere, unacceptable contradictions in everyone he had ever known, inconsistencies that proved he was being lied to at every turn.

"In my ethics class I told the teacher that society survives on lies," he said.

This was it—right here. The remark I could use as a crowbar to peek beneath Kendall's bombast and study the rot below, the casual clue that might open up his past and confirm all my suspicions. He'd grown up in a home of darkness and deprivation, his youth structured around rigid adherence to church teachings about love and forgiveness, though there was little evidence of that in his parents' marriage. Outside their home, his family pantomimed middle-class success—Arlington schools, steady jobs, and college degrees—but inside 99 Fulton Avenue life bore not a shred of resemblance to the world Kendall had been taught to reach for. Was that disconnect meaningless? Was the riddle of Kendall merely a happenstance of genetics, a little seed of paranoia that had found fertile ground and flowered into pathology? Maybe, but the notion of hypocrisy enraged him in a way I found relatable. And he'd always maintained that his biggest mistake was coming home after the army. Not killing women, coming home.

"How do you mean 'survives on lies'?" I probed.

"Men lying to get women into bed has kept the human race going for centuries!" he crowed, delighted that I hadn't seen the punch line coming. "People are corrupt by nature—narrow, limited, racist, nationalist, arrogant. They always need to pigeonhole others, divide themselves into categories and groups. Everybody's got to be something, they can't just be human."

Fuck this, I thought. He's whining in clichés.

"You want something to drink?" I asked. "A soda?" I needed to breathe without him near me.

"Get me a grapefruit juice. Ruby Red."

I walked toward the bank of vending machines and glanced back at Kendall as I plunked my coins in. He looked so much smaller now, playing clock again, a gigantic kid lost in make-believe games. Much of what he said made a kind of sense, but it felt so flimsy, a worldview of slogans and sound bites.

"So how do you feel about your life now?" I asked, sitting down with the juice. Kendall took a long drink.

"It's a waste of energy to feel. Didn't you get me a napkin?"

During our conversation, Kendall consumed five cans of grapefruit juice, six peanut butter cups, one bag of microwave popcorn, and a sausage and pepperoni microwave pizza. I paid for all of it, serving each item at the table because inmates were not permitted to use the vending machines. In his letters, Kendall had always made a point of showing good manners—thanking me for writing, apologizing for off-color language, and spewing indignation about visitors who showed up without asking for permission first. "So arrogant!" he'd say. "So rude!" But he offered not a kernel of popcorn, nor any appreciation for my bringing it. He was the king holding court, and I should be grateful that he tolerated my presence.

I found a paper towel, and after he wiped his mouth Kendall went back to the cards, surrounded by rapists and murderers, yet muttering a sanitized "Oh, sugar!" when the game didn't go his way. The cards became a running commentary on our interview. I'd ask my questions, and Kendall offered answers based on the suits he turned up. Hearts and diamonds meant he had to respond truthfully. With spades or clubs, he'd smile and shake his head. Soon he began asking the cards about me. Was I lying? he wanted to know. (No, they said, I was not.) Being deceptive? (Somewhat, they found. This I did not dispute.)

As he ate, the behemoth who'd slept on sheets stiff with dirt made dainty place mats for his food, sweeping the table between courses and carefully cleaning his hands before peeling each wrapper. He nibbled at the tiny bits of cheese stuck to his cardboard pizza carton—his movements meticulous, precise, unhurried. "I'm going to get all I can out of you during this visit because I don't have much food left in my cell and I don't get to buy more until tomorrow," he said.

Kendall hated the cafeteria, preferring to cook on a hot plate in his cell and avoid other inmates. He was fearful of people and had rebuffed repeated invitations to play on the Attica prison football team.

"I hate football," he said.

"Were you ever injured during a game? Some psychiatrists think head injuries in people with a genetic predisposition can lead to violence like yours."

I was referring to Dorothy Otnow Lewis, the psychiatrist who'd kissed Ted Bundy. She was convinced that nobody—not Hitler, nor Stalin, nor even Bundy—was born a killer. I'd read her book so many times the spine broke. I told Kendall that Otnow Lewis hoped to meet him.

"Well, she's old enough that her wants won't get her into trouble."

"What does that mean?"

"Something my father used to say."

A number of other researchers have since taken Otnow Lewis's basic premise—that killers' brains, shaped by trauma, are physiologically different—and run in the opposite direction, suggesting that the seeds of psychopathy may be detectable in kids as young as five. Like Kendall as a fifth grader, these fledgling psychopaths show little emotion and appear untroubled by the prospect of punishment. One child I'd read about gradually cut down the tail of his family cat over a period of weeks. Another, age nine, pushed a toddler into the deep end of a swimming pool and pulled up a chair to watch him drown.

"I don't think it's genetic. Otherwise, my parents would have had other bad children. I have a good family," Kendall told me for perhaps the tenth time. "A close family."

I did not challenge him. I stared at Kendall and waited for elaboration. It's the first trick a reporter learns. You let your source stew in the quiet until they become uncomfortable enough to fill it. The loser in this contest is the one least able to tolerate silence.

"I always look for the best in people and rarely find it—that's one of the things that got me in here," Kendall said.

We stared at each other for another long moment, and again he broke first, the words tumbling out.

"I asked for an anger management class. But the waiting list is months long and my counselor said I'd have to go through a sex-offender program first. I told him he was crazy—I'm not a sex offender! My problem is anger."

He looked like he was trying to stifle a laugh.

"Do you think you would have killed other women who angered you, women who weren't prostitutes?"

Kendall threw down the cards.

"Never," he said, locking my eyes. "I can guarantee that."

"What do you mean guarantee?"

"I just wouldn't, is all I can tell you. It's just the way my mind works. I wouldn't hurt any woman who was married, especially if she was the mother of my children. But I can tell you that if I hadn't confessed there would have been more. If I'd wanted to keep going, it would have gone on and on, and they never would have found a thing."

Detective Siegrist had admitted as much already. So why had Kendall confessed on that summer night three years earlier? There were other opportunities. Had he woken up that morning and decided this would be the day?

Kendall shook his head. He'd had no idea. He'd picked up Christine Sala (*I think I love her soul*), and had his hands around her neck when he decided to let her go. This had been the moment that broke open the whole case. But while the circumstances were clear—Christine talking to police, a subsequent interview with Kendall on assault charges, and the preparation of a warrant to search his home for the shirt he'd been wearing—no one ever brought up the missing women. It was Kendall. They'd left him alone in the small gray interview room, and he made his decision.

"It just came to me when I was sitting there by myself," he said.

"What did? Were you tired? Was it getting to be too much?"

Kendall smiled his sad, secret smile.

"Something like that. But you're making me think about things I don't want to think about."

"What things?"

He laid out four cards in a diamond pattern between us, three hearts and a spade. Kendall looked up.

"I was thinking I want to throw you down on this table and fuck your brains out."

My hands began to tremble, so I sat on them. Kendall leaned back in his plastic chair, beaming.

"You were pretty good," he said. "I feel like I need a cigarette."

Kendall's sexual fantasies were a black hole in my ruminations, something I'd avoided pondering throughout our correspondence. I rolled my eyes when he wrote "how pretty" I'd look pregnant with his child. I responded with silence when he penned nauseating passages about giving me oral sex. I could almost hear him chuckling. In one letter he asked if I masturbated. "Assuming that you do, do you ever think about me? I think that would be 'check!'" In fact, I had pictured sex with Kendall, though hardly out of desire. I imagined him with the women he'd killed and transposed his heaving flesh onto me. I saw his jiggly arms gripping my throat. I smelled the chemicals coming off his skin. It was an exercise I practiced to see how much I could stand.

"You're like a child, afraid of me," he sneered. "You do think I'm a monster."

I couldn't let it end like this. Kendall frequently told me that he never set out to kill anyone—his victims weren't saints, he'd say, but none deserved to die. Speaking of such things, his soft voice would dwindle even lower until it trailed off altogether. This didn't feel like sorrow, but something closer to bewilderment at what he'd done with his life. It sounded, faintly, like shame.

"You say you wouldn't have killed anyone except prostitutes. But the police keep telling me that I should be worried about you."

Kendall got very quiet.

"You have nothing to fear from me," he said.

I'd been running circles in my mind for three hours by now, and I was spent. So wrung out that I forgot about the power of words.

"I've got to go soon," I said.

"Why now?" Kendall growled, the gentle voice suddenly as hard and cold as a rock in November. "Why do you have to go right now?"

He heard the remark as rejection, a woman's judgment that he had failed to perform adequately. And he was not wrong.

A long drive home, I said. I needed to be back before nightfall. Kendall appeared to accept this. Wordlessly, he pushed my playing cards into a neat stack, preparing to put them away. This was the moment I'd envisioned while driving the New York State Thruway and watching television inside my stuffy motel room, and during our insipid games: the end of the interview. Would we shake hands, recognize our common humanity? Would I be able to extend that gesture toward a man who had crushed the vocal cords of eight women and left them slumped in the corners of his home? Kendall slid the cards into their packet. I breathed long and slow.

He handed the deck to me. Our fingertips were within millimeters. But they did not touch.

"I have a question for you," he said as I pushed away from the table. "But I know what the answer's going to be."

"Try me."

Kendall ducked his head and grinned.

"Can I have a hug?"

CHAPTER 12

U-Turns

I tore down the interstate at eighty miles an hour, not stopping for so much as a bathroom break. At home, I ripped off every shred of clothing and threw it in the laundry. I didn't want anything that had touched the prison touching me. I drummed my fingers across my computer keyboard, spilling out every eye flick and nuance of the conversation with Kendall. I'd walked into a dungeon, sat next to the man who terrorized my dreams, and managed to play cards. My revulsion at the idea of touching him nagged quietly—I knew he'd seen my fear. But mostly, I felt triumphant.

Derrick was unimpressed. He came home, glanced at me writing, and began to pack kitchen equipment into boxes.

"I found a place," he told me. "I'll be moving in two weeks."

"You found a place since I left yesterday?"

"No, I'm buying a house—from someone who works at the college."

"You're buying a house?" I was beginning to feel queasy.

For years Derrick had perused the real estate flyers that piled up beneath community bulletin boards, inky circulars listing page after page of one-inch ranch homes. I'd never given them a glance. I never expected to build a life in Dutchess County, and I'd assumed that Derrick felt the same. He refused to attend the weddings of old friends or even catch up with them over a beer. Now he was talking about buying a whitewashed Victorian with gingerbread trim. He was telling me that he'd saved thousands of dollars toward the down payment, and that his parents would lend him the rest. He was telling me that Moses would live there, with him.

"He needs a yard," Derrick said. "You don't even know where you're going."

It was true. I had no idea. I'd made attempts to find another rental but slunk away from each, heartsick. I stepped into the flashbulb-bright kitchen of a mother-in-law apartment and sat in my car afterward, numb with loneliness. I peeked into a hippie house where purple sheets separated one living space from another, and walked out despondent enough to consider couples therapy. But Derrick was moving on, so I answered an ad for a studio in a barn across the river, in a town where I knew no one. The rent was bearable. The floorboards had a warm dark sheen, and the kitchen boasted a butcher block island where I imagined myself sipping tea.

During our last week together Derrick and I stood in the living room of our tree-house home, surveying the detritus we'd collected over five years—sofas claimed from street corners, tables belonging to dead relatives, ceramic kitchenware my mother neither wanted nor could bear to throw away. We tallied who owned what and to which home it would go. I insisted on keeping a framed picture of Moses as a puppy, despite its cracked glass. But Derrick fought for items that left me speechless: cookie sheets his sister had given me as a birthday gift; two dozen ancient issues of *Gourmet* discarded by his mother; every Christmas ornament his parents had sent us as a couple. It seemed that he wanted to obliterate every connection I had to his family, wipe from my life any evidence that we'd ever been together.

"And the rolling pin," he said, pulling the marble cylinder from its spot on our kitchen shelf.

"You're kidding, right?"

He'd presented it to me as a surprise, a gift, I'd thought, since I was the only one who ever used it. I didn't know whether to laugh at the idea of a thirty-year-old bachelor coveting Williams-Sonoma bakeware or crumple to the floor. Clearly, Derrick had been preparing his inventory for weeks.

"Fuck it," he said with a sigh. "I'll take the TV. You can have the bed."

⁂

THOUGH MY BARN apartment was fifty miles north and west, I kept my old postal box in Pleasant Valley, driving two hours each week to check for mail from Attica. I'd become exhausted, not to mention impoverished, by answering Kendall's monthly collect calls, during which he'd natter on about the weather or what he was cooking in his cell. So I said nothing to him about my new phone number and ignored his scrawled complaints about being unable to reach me. Often I went days without speaking to another person. Sometimes I closed my eyes and envisioned myself in a better, future time. I was on a hilltop in front of an old house overlooking the ocean, a ring of children dancing around me. I was fat in that image, and old, and happy.

"Do you ever write outside of your job?" Kendall often asked me in his letters. "Stories, poems or anything creative?"

For years I'd imagined showing my writing about him to others. Then I'd freeze, anticipating Derrick's derision. Every time I drove to the city to visit my family or friends, Derrick complained. The place was a cesspool, he said; it had destroyed me. I'd written an essay about the upended power dynamic when older women dated younger men—our relationship was Exhibit A—and he forbade me from publishing it. But alone in the quiet, I began to think again about putting my life on the page.

In a bookstore I'd noticed a writer's workshop advertised on a bulletin board and scribbled the number. I had never participated in anything like that. I could hardly maintain a journal, so loath was I to confront myself. But in this tiny mountain town no one knew me. No one need learn that a serial murderer was my most reliable human connection. Nor that our twisted relationship was now the most sustained Kendall had known with any woman outside of his family. The writing group met in a doctor's office, after hours, our pens scratching on paper the only sound. I wrote about cutting high school French class to get an abortion and drinking a milk shake afterward at Schrafft's. I wrote about mounding my bedsheets into awkward bundles at the Laundromat because there was no longer anyone to help me pull the corners tight. I wrote about a life of false starts and dead ends, typing through Christmas while my family gathered at the glossy table in New York and wondered what was happening to me.

How illusory was the power I'd felt as a journalist, hiding behind my reporter's notebook. That skinny pad of lined paper had always conferred such mysterious authority, though I knew it was unearned. Most subjects willingly acquiesced, as if being caught in a news story were part of the natural order. Kendall, naturally, had a different view of my profession—its shameless seductions, rapid intimacies, and shifting balance of who was being exploited by whom—but I had been unable until now to see how deftly he deployed my own tactics against me. Looking back over his letters, I could almost hear him chortling as he designed his test, demanding to tromp through every corner of my life—my first kiss, first computer, the dress I wore under my high school graduation robe—every fact and thought and feeling. Of course he recognized the way journalists manipulate and devour, savage people and toss them aside; the way we become expert at rationalizing our acts, telling ourselves all is acceptable in service to the story.

As I sipped tea in the silence, it became easier for me to see why Kendall felt control would remain his if we corresponded, not as writer and subject, but as "friends." This, we had never been. But by insisting that I give up my notepad, Kendall forced me to know him through experience, rather than question-and-response. He goaded me to trust my perceptions, something I'd never done with confidence before. When Derrick slammed Moses down, smashing his skull on the floorboards, I told myself that I'd misinterpreted those actions, hadn't seen what I thought. Derrick just got angry. He was unhappy with me and hated his job. He felt stuck in his life and took it out on the dog, but he loved Moses. I knew that. So I swallowed my protests, assuming I was wrong, always wrong, my reactions off base, my questions out of line. I was the crazy one, chasing after murderers. Derrick said so all the time.

Kendall knew nothing of these mental gyrations, nor would he have cared. He was focused only on my next trip to Attica. Our previous interview had been both the best and worst visit he'd had since being imprisoned, he said. He'd stayed up all night thinking about it and was exhausted for days after. He'd told me too much, let too many things slip. *You didn't learn what you wanted to know, but you learned a lot*. To my mind, it had been as elliptical and ex-asperating as all our other conversations—I still hadn't found any equation to explain his cruelty—though it did count as one of our least fractious exchanges. Even this glimmer of a connection sent Kendall reeling. Belittling criticism was where he felt at home. When he asked for my opinion of the visit, I wrote:

> *It seems like a part of you wishes to connect with people, at least with me. But it's a pull in opposite directions—yes?—the wish to stay isolated, pulling against the wish to connect. I know you'll tell me if I've got this wrong.*

On Mother's Day, Kendall sent a card. I had by now received a half-dozen drawings from him, but none like this profusion of but-terflies and curlicues floating through space. It looked like an explo-sion of joy. *All I thought of was you as I made each butterfly. I don't know if the card was any good, but I know it was meant for you*. On my birthday, Kendall sent another: three flowers sketched with such concentration and delicacy that I wondered again what I meant to him—a white woman who wanted to know his mind and his heart, who did not seek money but something more difficult to give.

"Emotions are a tricky thing," Kendall said. This comment was his response to word that Marguerite Marsh wanted to visit Attica and hear what he had to say. Kendall was apprehensive. Margue-rite might ask questions he could not answer. He was "fearful of her making a scene."

DURING THAT LONELY winter in the mountains my mother mailed news of a start-up writer's colony, and I made my leap, sending a dozen pages to a panel of anonymous readers. Seven months later I was driving north on I-95, invited to live in an island cabin off the coast of Maine and do nothing for the month of July but pour myself onto a page. It was the first time anyone, other than Kendall, had expressed interest in my writing outside of journalism.

Once, I had been fearless about such journeys. At twenty-three, I'd driven from New York to the tip of North Carolina's Outer Banks, clacking away on my mother's manual typewriter in moldy motel rooms along the way. I'd taken a boat trip in Haiti, crammed into a creaking hold with hundreds of frightened, vomiting people as we hit a storm at sea, and when we docked in a tiny fishing village under a calm moonlit sky, I felt reaffirmed about my place in the world. But now I emerged from my barn apartment like a mole in daylight, a snail without its shell, sensitive and exposed. Where had I lost myself? How far had I drifted? I drove north, so keen to reverberation that billboards shouting "Assert your independence, eat dessert first!" felt heavy with meaning. At the dock in Maine where I was to phone for a boat ride to Norton Island, I dawdled, wandered, stalled, afraid someone on the other end would tell me there had been a mistake.

In Maine, fog shrouded every morning. I picked through loamy forests, listening to birdcalls and the sound of my feet snapping dead twigs. I followed shady trails that led to hidden coves and hiked back, breathless and muddy, to sit in my pine-box room and write about the ways a monster was forcing me to reinterpret my life. I was shy around the others—the literary magazine lothario, the bawdy lesbian, the luminous, poetic blonde, and the bright young light now teaching in Boston. All of them had published books to acclaim. They lived in Brooklyn or respectably intellectual college towns. They did not subsist on Campbell's soup from the Grand Union. Who had let me in, with my lowly news clips and miserable obsession? At dinner, a Russian journalist also staying on the island regaled us with stories about covering wars and "investigate KGB." Each day she trundled across our stony island astride the seat of a golf cart, and when it toppled, its burned-out motor whirring in the mud, Irina-of-the-formidable-bosom pushed it a quarter mile uphill to the main lodge. I'd hear her in the mornings stomping past my door and hang my head as I tried to make sense of my fun-house-mirror conversations with a killer.

On the fifth day, I went for a walk. It was possible, said our host, to hike the perimeter of this rock in the Atlantic, so I set out with a notebook, quite pleased with myself. Words alone had propelled me here, to a place where people wanted me to tell my story. I sat on a slab of stone, breathing in sun and wind from an ocean at the edge of the world. A few swigs from my water bottle, a few notes jotted, and I'd be on my way. But now, turning into the brush, I could no longer find the path. I searched, tearing at brambles, bogs sucking my feet into swamp. I hacked through dark woods, doubling back, then plunging in deeper, my mind confused, making addled decisions. I was not dressed for this. I was not prepared. I considered calling out. But this was an island—it didn't matter that the way forward was unmarked. If I just kept moving ahead, water to my right, I would eventually come round, and surely at some point the trail would reappear. After two hours of thrashing I arrived at an inlet, impassable from where I stood on the shore. This was the breaking point. The end of the line. I could admit failure here and backtrack, or give up the comfort of dry clothes and slog through the shallows. I eyed the crabs skittering across nearby rocks and thought of Kendall, who said he'd wanted to be a marine biologist but hated the ocean. What was he? Every advance turned into a retreat, canceling itself, adding up to nothing. He fell through my hands like water. I jumped off the bank and gasped at the cold, sloshing twenty yards before I could stagger to shore. The writers would be gathering now for wine on the lodge's sunny porch. They would ask each other how the day's work had gone and offer encouragement. I'd arrive looking like a yeti, covered in mud and blood and brambles. But I'd arrive. And I'd have a story. I'd be able to look back and see the path I'd traveled, understand how one part connected to the next and finally brought me home.

Fed up with the silence, Irina left a few days later in a thunder of baggage, and slowly the other writers emerged. We met at night to eat lobster pulled from the ocean, cooked over open fires in a wok filled with seawater. We read to each other in a chilly barn where beams creaked against the wind. Back and forth we marched from the lodge to our writing rooms, joining at dinnertime like a family. Sometimes I imagined Catherine Marsh sitting on the bed behind me as I typed. Despite her essay's therapy-couch language, "Frightened Child" was still, undeniably, the artifact of a mind trying to connect. It could kill you, that wish for connection, that need to be seen. It left Cathy aching, and Kendall destroyed, and it had led me down a hundred wrong roads. But I saw now that it could also be salvation. At night I dreamed I was Cathy, traipsing from car to car. I was Kendall, my hands around the neck of a well-coiffed older woman. I was in grade school, pummeling the first friend to betray me—until someone hugged me from behind with a love so powerful I awoke with a gasp.

⸺

WHEN I GOT home, there was a message from Derrick.

"I have something to tell you," he said when I returned the call.

"What?"

"I need to talk to you in person."

I half hoped to hear that he missed me, half expected to learn that he had a new girlfriend and was already proposing marriage. He'd want to torture me with the news, see my face bewildered and hurt, fighting off tears. I stared at myself in the mirror, practicing an expression of composure, while I awaited his arrival.

In an hour Derrick was knocking at my door, stepping from his Victorian house on the hill into my musty studio to sit on the threadbare couch we'd once owned together.

"It's about Moses," he said.

In the ten months since our breakup, Derrick had called me several times about the difficulty he was having with our dog. Moses had become the neighborhood menace, tearing after flocks of sheep, barking and snarling as he chased them to the main road. He'd snapped his leash trying to kill the cat next door. Every weekend I'd visit like a noncustodial parent, Moses greeting me at Derrick's front door, his thick body wriggling with joy. He'd always been like that, lunging toward me across parking lots, heaving forward with the force of a freight train.

Derrick had indeed begun a new relationship—he and his girlfriend had watched me shopping one night at the Grand Union, spying from the baby-goods aisle while I gathered my cans of soup. She had two young children who often stayed at Derrick's house. That was the problem. Moses was the problem.

"There's nothing you can do when a dog's out of control like he is—everyone knows that," said Derrick, looking at his hands. The tight knot in my chest began to slide downward, creating a flutter around my heart, a nauseous, empty feeling in my stomach.

"Where is Moses now?" I asked. But I knew.

Derrick's voice caught. "I brought him to the vet's after you left for Maine. I made an appointment— They said there's nothing you can do—"

"Are you telling me you had him put— You killed—"

"You don't understand! You've never understood! He didn't even act scared. They barely had to hold him. It was like he was proud!"

I no longer cared about maintaining impassivity. I could barely breathe. The tiny picture of Moses that I'd rescued glared from its cracked frame.

"You couldn't wait until I got back from Maine? You couldn't give me a chance to come up with another answer? You couldn't let me say good-bye?"

"I didn't want you to make a scene."

How little I'd understood this man. I was tempted to mention how much he sounded like Kendall. Our pup, not four years old, had been cremated after the execution, his ashes wrapped in a fur cap and buried in Derrick's yard. "So he won't be cold in the ground," my ex-boyfriend sobbed.

ONCE, I WOULD have imagined pouring out the whole miserable tale to my correspondent in Attica, thinking he might be able to meet me here, or at least validate my sense of betrayal. Nothing about that idea attracted me now. Though alone as never before, I'd grown better at keeping Kendall tucked into a secret corner of my life. For weeks, I staggered around my apartment, telephoning Derrick to shriek at him. He picked up every time. Meanwhile, my letters to prison, once so cloying, now became almost breezy. I sent light updates about my travels, described the vagaries of weather, news of little consequence that created a certain constancy between us. I no longer cared about currying favor. I told Kendall about visiting a Mexican art museum in Chicago and being struck by a single piece of tin, a small rectangle on which the artist had painted pictures of his parents and friends who had died, churches and graveyards, gang life and prison guards. A life story set down in pictures. I wondered what Kendall would come up with if he tried something like that. He answered by acknowledging that while he liked art, he had never been to a museum. "I would have loved," he said, "to go with you."

CHAPTER 13

Ghost Story

Every few weeks, I'd check in with Detective Siegrist, who believed you could trace the outlines of a person's past by examining how they lived in the present. Homes spoke to values, to the things people held dear, and other than those inhabited by the desperately poor or clearly insane, Siegrist had never seen any place like the Francoises'. It suggested a lifetime of hidden chaos. They were hoarders. Kendall collected corpses in a manner not so different from the way his parents collected garbage. He kept telling me to look beneath the surface of life in Dutchess County, while insisting I skip over his family. But bodies in the attic were surely not the only secrets buried at 99 Fulton Avenue.

Most hoarders, when interviewed about their early lives, describe critical, intrusive parents and childhoods marked, as a result, by a preference for objects over people. I'd seen a picture of Kendall's mother in high school, before she was Paulette Francois.

And despite her pearl necklace and graceful hairdo in the 1965 Arlington yearbook, Paulette Blackwell did not look like a happy girl. She looked frightened, like someone who did not wish to be seen. The term *hoarder* was little used in upstate New York circa 2001, though the condition had been noted on police blotters for more than fifty years. At least since 1947, when the stiffened bodies of Langley and Homer Collyer were pulled from their Harlem apartment, barricaded inside tunnels of newspaper, car parts, old pianos, and baby carriages.

Lots of people attribute sentimental meaning to objects—Marguerite Marsh had her spoons, my mother her 1970s pottery—but hoarders freeze, locked in a kind of emotional paralysis that leaves them clutching the useless until a home is consumed. The condition—recently recognized as a mental illness affecting 5 percent of the population—has no correlation with deprivation, at least not of a material nature. The Collyers, for instance, began life with great promise—Langley as a concert pianist, Homer as a lawyer—sons of a successful doctor and a renowned opera singer descended from the Constitution-signing Livingstons. Mr. and Mrs. Collyer were, however, first cousins, ostracized by their families after marrying. Among hoarders, shame is a hallmark and secrecy its result. The primary requirement is not poverty but profound disconnection, the ability to keep readjusting one's blinders until brokenness is woven into the fabric of a life. "Like when a guy comes home from work and drinks until he passes out in front of the television every night. Okay, he's an alcoholic. But to the people in the house it's normal, just something you kind of grow to accept," Siegrist said. "It was like that for the Francoises." Shuffling through the stench and darkness, they had never allowed themselves to realize what was happening, though Siegrist believed this was a choice.

Denial powerful enough to ignore corpses in your home might be impossible for the upright citizenry of Dutchess County to comprehend, but I cringed with recognition. Living with Derrick, I'd slid from being a college valedictorian full of fire and promise to a semi-hermit living frightened and ashamed in the woods with a man who despised me, and refused to admit what was happening. I absorbed Derrick's attacks on my past, education, family, and work until I hated who I'd been and did not know who I was. I curtailed my social life, rarely left home, and smiled through Derrick's insults about my taste in clothes, haircuts, and interior design. I could not bear to call this what it was. Standards downshift. Aspiration falls away until it becomes possible, in the midst of decay, to fool yourself into believing everything is fine.

Of course, the police in Poughkeepsie didn't know anything about my disheveled personal life. Siegrist, in particular, welcomed my presence as an opportunity to unspool his theories about Kendall, which he explained to me one Halloween night as we cruised the city, the aging investigator never changing speed as he maneuvered through crisp new cul-de-sacs and decrepit older streets. He knew every traffic light and whether it would be blinking red, yellow, or green. He drove through them with an easy rhythm, like breathing in sleep. After thirty years with the department he had been inside most of Poughkeepsie's homes. Here, a man had frozen to death wearing twenty T-shirts and six pairs of pants, all the clothes he owned. There, a mother had died leaving a husband and two grown sons. Siegrist had visited to offer condolences. Fifteen years later, he was back with condolences again after one son put a pistol to his head. The family was typical Poughkeepsie, white and working class, regular as rain, but Siegrist wasn't surprised by the suicide. Soon after the mother's funeral he'd popped in to say hello and found the father sitting with his hand clamped around a beer, staring at a television set that never went dark, the household disintegrating into a sigh of cigarette smoke and dust.

At ten P.M., Siegrist steered his cruiser into the parking lot across from Kendall's old home and slumped in his seat. "You don't know how many times I've sat here, staring at this house," he said. I didn't mention how often I'd done the same. Ninety-nine Fulton Avenue, rebuilt from the ground up, was unrecognizable now, polished and cheerful, with orange decorations for the holiday tacked to its front door. Waist-high goblins tromped up the porch steps swinging plastic jack-o'-lanterns. The new owners doled out candy bars from a bright front hall, the only place on the block to open its doors to trick-or-treaters. "Odd that this should be the one," Siegrist said.

Tracking a serial killer was nothing the detective had envisioned when he joined the force in 1969. In those days, the only time his town made national news was when its swashbuckling prosecutor G. Gordon Liddy set out after Timothy Leary, dragging the disheveled acidhead from his Millbrook mansion into the courthouse downtown. Siegrist's days were spent walking a beat in his stiff blue uniform, chatting with shopkeepers and investigating traffic accidents. Public drunkenness was as wild as things got. Sex crimes accounted for less than 1 percent of reports. Homicide didn't even make the chart.

Siegrist had done his time at Dutchess Community College, same as Margie Smith, same as Donte Turner, Catherine Marsh, and Kendall Francois. But he never considered himself university material. "I didn't have that kind of talent. Not book smart," he said. It didn't seem to bother him. Law enforcement had never been a big burning desire, but he liked being outside and his father had briefly been a cop when they lived in the Bronx. After the family moved upstate his older brother joined the Town of Poughkeepsie force. Bill, to his mother's great disappointment, signed up with the city. He rose unremarkably through the ranks, ruffling few feathers, and made chief of detectives just a year before he tapped on Kendall's car window, stopped at a traffic light in January 1998.

"I'm Lieutenant Bill Siegrist," he said. "I'd like you to come down to the station to talk."

Kendall agreed readily. He never asked why.

Siegrist acted as if the conversation was a spur-of-the-moment idea, but he had prepared weeks for this moment. Kendall drove to the station house and Siegrist followed, ushering him into a conference room arranged like a theater set. There were file cabinets with the name of a missing woman labeling each drawer— Wendy Meyers, Gina Barone, Catherine Marsh, Kathleen Hurley, Michelle Eason, Mary Healey Giaccone. Boxes of paper had been positioned to look like stacks of evidence. Photos of 99 Fulton Avenue and others from the 1989 Arlington High School yearbook were tacked to the walls. "It was all bullshit," Siegrist said as we sat in the car staring at Kendall's house. "We didn't have a thing."

If Kendall had ever wondered about the police, his questions were answered then, alone in a room surrounded by yearbook pictures of his clean-cut teenage self. He allowed Siegrist to hook him to a polygraph machine in another office and sat politely as an investigator questioned him about each of the missing women. *Did you know Michelle Eason? Did you have anything to do with her death?* Kendall passed easily, offering one-word denials, and walked out of the interview smiling. "Yeah, I heard from some prostitutes that you thought I killed those girls," he said with a sympathetic sigh as the detective drove his chief suspect back to downtown Poughkeepsie, then bought him lunch. Siegrist and his swaggering protégé, Skip Mannain, watched Kendall down burger after burger as he chatted about women and rough sex.

The conversation was instigated by Mannain, who believed he'd found a way into Kendall's psyche. "He started talking about 'these fucking bitches,' so I played right into it—'Yeah, fuck them. I like fucking slapping them around, too. Yeah, that's what they want,'" Mannain told me, recreating the scene. "I'm pretty good at talking to people and getting them to tell the truth and confess. And I'm thinking, if the professional cop image isn't going to work, let me be a fucking sexual predator. I mean, I was getting really rude with him about the women. I thought we could maybe build a friendship there, or something. And I guess we did, because by the end of that afternoon he allowed me to go to his house."

Pliant and well mannered, Kendall showed Mannain into 99 Fulton Avenue, guiding the detective up the stairs to his filthy bedroom, but cautioning that he must walk only in prescribed areas. His parents did not allow visitors, Kendall explained, insisting that Mannain's more experienced partner wait outside. The junior investigator smelled urine and rot—five decomposing bodies lay in the attic right above his head—but he failed to recognize this as the reek of death, and a few minutes later walked out, shrugging his shoulders. Four years later, in the Attica visitor's room, Kendall howled at the memory. I had never heard him sound so pleased.

SIEGRIST LOOKED EXHAUSTED recounting these humiliations, but he'd brought me to 99 Fulton Avenue quite purposefully, and had more to say. It was a confession, of sorts. By the summer of 1998,

Kendall had murdered six women, and fresh reports about him were streaming into the detective squad monthly. Siegrist wanted a dog team, but he had no crime scene, no hard evidence, and a disturbingly long list of other suspects: family guys who lived in the country and came into town to hire prostitutes three times a week, whispering things they could never say to their wives; an ex-air force officer who'd raped an eleven-year-old and now camped in the woods along the river. Mannain was convinced this was their man. But Siegrist put his faith in the dogs. It took him weeks to convince the handlers, all volunteers from Ramapo, to drive an hour north to Poughkeepsie. Where, exactly, would the dogs be working? For Siegrist, the lack of a crime scene was the biggest problem of the case.

On a sweltering Saturday in July the team arrived. The dogs nosed through garbage-strewn fields and scraggly shrubs. They tracked down to the river and along the weedy shoreline. They dug up animal bones, and the day dragged on. Siegrist mopped his brow and thought about his family. He was never home, spending all his time on a case that went nowhere. No one seemed to care if he solved it. The newspaper ran no stories. The mayor asked no questions. "It's your case, Bill," they kept saying. He wondered whether to walk the dogs past Kendall's house, but the handlers were losing heart and the sun was going down. "I just said fuck it. I told them to go home," the detective sighed. He would second-guess that decision for the remaining days of his life, dreaming even in retirement of women's bodies buried in a basement that he was unable to find.

Kendall slid Audrey Pugliese into his basement a few weeks later. Catina Newmaster joined her two weeks after that. "There are no heroes in this one," Siegrist said.

COMPLAINTS ABOUT THE investigation began quietly, with a few parents grumbling about inattention to their long-estranged daughters. The noise increased to muffled outrage over the summer, when FBI investigator Dorsey finally visited from Quantico. After Kendall confessed in September, it exploded. Women walking Poughkeepsie's cracked sidewalks besieged any reporter who would listen with claims that they'd been reporting Kendall to police for more than year. Siegrist attended a law enforcement banquet and tried to hold his head up as laughter rolled around the room. "Hey, Siegrist!" yelled a major from across the hall. "You get a lead on that serial killer yet?"

The problem was the women themselves, police said. They reported Kendall's assaults too long after the fact. They were difficult to track down for follow-ups. If they were missing, it was safe to assume they did not want to be found. "Yeah, we had complaints about Kendall from some of the prostitutes," Mannain said with a shrug. "We found a girl that Kendall beat up and brought her in to sign a complaint for assault or something. But she winds up sitting in the office, getting her period. She's sitting there and her pants are just turning to blood. All she wanted to do was leave. We wrote this up, what she was telling us about Kendall. But she wouldn't stay to sign it, and it took us like three weeks to find her again. Kendall was beating up these girls, but they were all living to tell about it—so?" His blue eyes drilled me. "So Kendall was into some rough shit." He sighed and fiddled with a paper clip, bending it into strange shapes.

Mannain ducked me for four years before agreeing to talk

about the case. We sat in a Mexican restaurant—his choice—as he recounted this story and then invited me to his home. No police officer I'd ever met had made such an offer, and I was puzzled by it. But I went.

"So is Kendall infatuated with you?" Mannain asked as we stood in his spotless living room, dominated by a couch so overstuffed I felt as if the room might tip.

"Maybe." I was careful to keep ample space between Mannain and me, me and the couch. "Sometimes he says things that suggest that."

"I'll bet."

Forty-one and single, Mannain claimed to love his life. Being a cop in Poughkeepsie might not sound exciting, but he considered it the world of a frat boy. No shortage of women or bars, and on weekends he could ride his Harley into the mountains, obligated to no one. He'd invested his salary well, purchasing a small ranch-style home just outside the city limits where he kept his bike in a roomy garage and played with his dogs out back. Mannain would never describe Poughkeepsie as idyllic or quaint, but he found ways to have fun. As a boy growing up there he hadn't thought much about what he might do with his future, just imagined living it somewhere else. High school graduation did not inspire much action. Mannain slid into a job selling athletic equipment at the mall, worked weekends at a car wash, and drank most of his pay. When three friends suggested they all pack up and move to Los Angeles, Mannain could think of no reason not to. They would rent an apartment by the beach and screw all the beautiful women they could. That was the plan.

Los Angeles turned out to be exactly as advertised. A real city where real things happened. Those shivering bastards suffering through winters back in New York State were fast becoming a distant memory, and Mannain vowed he'd never go home again. This was the life he'd been made for. He applied for a job with the LAPD, fantasized about busting high rollers in classy bars and pictured himself riding into the sunset. When he passed the police exam, Mannain went out to celebrate with a frenzied joy. He was the East Coast boy who'd made it, decked out in gold chains and cowboy boots, discoing across the floor of a beachfront bar. The DJ laughed, called him a faggot. Chairs flew. Fists flew. Police arrived, and within hours the LAPD rescinded its job offer. Mannain slunk home to his father, joined the marines, and returned to Poughkeepsie two years later to don yet another uniform. He was twenty-five years old, walking a beat in the city he'd always wanted to leave.

Siegrist had known the younger cop since Mannain was a teenager chucking rocks off his father's roof, with a coiled energy that set him apart. An angry kid who'd grown into an angry man. You could not call Mannain an easygoing guy. But Siegrist took an avuncular interest. He'd been chief of detectives for only a few months when he promoted Mannain off patrol and assigned him to the missing-women case in 1997. The younger officer hated his new duty. Missing-person cases were thankless. They meant endless phone calls and long paper trails. Mannain dawdled. He whined. He felt he was ready for bigger things and took pride in telling anyone—suspects, hookers, other officers, city officials— exactly what he thought of them. I left his home through the back door, where refrigerator magnets and wall hangings offered cheery reminders about always being brave enough to go your own way.

LIKE MANY WOMEN on Main Street, Catina Newmaster had been attacked repeatedly by Kendall Francois, though he was not her only assailant. By the time Catina taped on a wire to set him up for Mannain, in the spring of 1998, she had come to accept beatings as an occupational hazard.

"Do not get into the car," Mannain told her. "Lean in, chat him up. Under no circumstances do you get into his car."

But Kendall would smile his wistful smile, and Catina jumped inside. The police had to rush after her again and again, inventing excuses to pull Kendall over and extricate their wayward informant. It was ludicrous. How could you protect a woman like that, Mannain kept asking me in tones that suggested this was not a question.

Catina was tiny, barely one hundred pounds. Siegrist had known her since childhood, watching her grow up through regular visits to the Newmasters' for domestic violence calls or child endangerment claims or drug charges; Catina's parents were fixtures on the police blotter, and no one was surprised when their daughter came of age with a crack addiction so vicious other users shook their heads in disbelief. Her utility to investigators, however, was unexpected and exceptional, a shrill, baby-girl voice that came through clear as glass on a hidden mic and pointed them toward dozens of drug arrests. She was, quite simply, the best informant city police had ever seen. So they busted Catina when they had to, found ways to usher her through the system, and developed a grudging fondness for the waiflike junkie. They used her for years.

The news stories I wrote during this period were built around the assumption that women like Catina came from failed families spouting one defective child after another. Grist for the court system, a sinkhole of societal drain, and that was the idea I had in mind, as I turned onto the narrow lane that led to the home of Catina's older sister. Tammy lived in a tidy cottage on a manicured cul-de-sac just north of the city, and when I parked in her drive-way, surveying the pretty white house with its curved walkway and joyful flower beds, I thought I'd made a wrong turn. Not until I noted the address on her front door did I realize how close Tammy lived to the streets where her little sister hustled blow jobs.

I had noticed Tammy at Kendall's court dates, always in a long black dress, gently guiding her mother by the elbow, and I associ-ated the willowy woman primarily with poverty and broken lives. You could not miss it in her mother's face. Barbara Newmaster limped up the courthouse steps clutching a framed portrait of her dead daughter, and her huge eyes, underscored with a fine mesh of bags and wrinkles, were the saddest I had ever seen. But if you'd glimpsed her before, perhaps stepping out of a liquor store, or hur-rying across a parking lot, you might have stopped and stared for a moment at the traces of beauty in this drawn, ravaged woman. She was tall and gaunt, like Tammy, with long auburn hair gone brittle and a pale heart-shaped face. I gazed at mother and daughter, not-ed their resemblance, and assumed that Barbara and Tammy were time-lapse versions of the same person. But I was wrong.

Tammy lived the way people in Dutchess County were expected to, in an immaculate home where her son ate peanut butter sand-wiches at a spotless kitchen table. She was married to a quiet man who strung cable for the phone company, and might have been standing at her kitchen window, washing dishes and gazing out through the frilly white curtains, while Catina sold her services a mile away. A year older than her little sister, Tammy had been raised by a circle of relatives and friends, ferried from home to home de-pending on the mental health of whichever adults were around. The sunny kitchen on a quiet street was still not enough distance. Think-ing back, Tammy acted as if the past might rear up and swallow her whole. Her knobby hands clung to the home that smelled of Pine-Sol, while the newspaper, slavishly covering crime-scene postmortems, now ran Catina's picture almost every day.

Tammy agreed to discuss her family only until her boy came home from school. She pushed at her hair and apologized for that limitation, and for greeting me in sweatpants, and for not having coffee ready. We stood in the kitchen doorway making small talk as she brewed a fresh pot and I surveyed the rest of her home—the living room anchored by a gleaming glass coffee table displaying photo albums stacked with geometric precision; hallways lined with thick carpeting that led to bedroom doors firmly closed. Not one dirty dish lingered near Tammy's kitchen sink, and the floors had been carefully swept, then mopped, then polished.

"We can talk in here," she said, gesturing toward the breakfast nook. Tammy folded her delicate hands. Even doing housework, she had the grace of a dancer. Every time I glanced from her face toward the sunny garden and unlived-in living room, Tammy's determination to build a clean, quiet life made me ashamed of what I'd come to ask.

THE LAST TIME Tammy had seen Catina, a week before her death, the younger sister was preening and posing in a new denim dress. She'd been clean for days, she said proudly, and the dress was special. Once, it had been Tammy's. But Catina admired it so much that the older sister sighed, pulled open the snaps, and handed it over, off her own narrow back. People were always doing things like that for Catina. She was so needy, so girlish in her wishes—a horse to ride, roses on her birthday—though by the time Kendall put his hands around her neck, it had been years since Catina's name appeared on anyone's gift list. How did you shop for a person if you never knew when you'd see her? Tammy asked. She realized the dress might be worn while Catina was jerking off men in cars. She understood that its pockets would soon hold any number of homemade crack-smoking devices. She knew the money police paid Catina for her work went only to drugs. To Tammy, none of that hardened the image of what her little sister had always been: a kid, starved for acceptance.

"A follower," corrected one of the Main Street prostitutes who'd attended high school with her. "A major wannabe. She would do anything to be popular."

Working for the police, Catina found her niche, and it thrilled her. She told friends she had a new project going, something much bigger than the same old drug busts. In the winter of 1998, as she sat in the back of a Poughkeepsie courtroom, waiting for her latest charges to be dispensed with, Catina spied Kendall in the front row, waiting to be processed for his own most recent arrest. He'd assaulted yet another girl. "That's him! That's the killer!" she squeaked in the ear of a friend who'd accompanied her. She hummed with excitement. She could barely sit still.

AFTER IT WAS all over, after police had removed Catina's body from Kendall's home and word leaked out that, at their suggestion, she'd worn a wire to set him up, public outrage was curiously muted. Tammy, in particular, choked down the urge to accuse. She needed to believe the authorities were good, she told me. Unquestionably good, those men who'd used her little sister, then knocked on Tammy's door one night in early September to say they'd found Catina's body with all the others in Kendall's home. A copy of the

Journal lay face up on his bed, its front page displaying a phalanx of officers arrayed behind District Attorney Grady as he introduced the new Missing Women Task Force.

It had been raining for days before she disappeared, the streets humid and empty over Labor Day weekend as families grabbed their last chance at a summer holiday out of town. I thought of Catina watching kids she'd known in high school driving past on their way to end-of-summer celebrations, children in the backseat, as Catina stood in the doorway of Dunkin' Donuts, waiting for a customer.

> . . . . All alone on a Sunday morning outside, I see the rain is falling. Inside I'm slowly dying but the rain won't hide my crying, crying. And don't you know my tears will burn . . .

She'd written those words, from a song by Lisa Lisa, on a scrap of notebook paper that had been folded and smoothed so many times when her pimp passed it to me that it nearly fell apart in my hands. Catina knew people looked at her as trash, a creature no one wanted to touch. For a woman like that, what might it mean to bring down a killer, to be the pipsqueak who put away Kendall Francois?

"What're you lookin' to do?" she asked, walking up to his car.

It was late morning, and she'd eaten nothing yet, according to the autopsy report that I would read later.

She wasn't wearing her wire that day, the police insisted. And no officer ever expressed personal regret to me about what had happened to their favorite informant—such a statement would border on admitting responsibility. But her fate hung heavy around the necks of many, making their eyes sag, their cheeks grow sallow. "I don't think really we could have done anything more than what was being done," said Walt Horton, a detective with thirty years on the force. "But this was the hardest part to swallow."

She had been warned, they said. She knew who she was toying with. "Her drive for dope, I guess," said Horton, struggling for an explanation. "If I knew that you had thirty dollars in your pocket, and I knew that I wanted that money to get high, I might just say, 'Well, I don't care if you beat me up again.'"

Maybe. But Catina had told her sister that she was clean in the days before her death. And she was proud to be doing important work for the police. In that last hour of life maybe she believed she could go with Kendall and slip away from him once more. Maybe she thought the police were watching. Maybe she was so high she didn't think at all. Or maybe she was ready to die.

I COULD SEE Tammy working to push these ideas from her mind, trying to arrange her face in a placid smile as she quashed questions about police officers who had used Catina and failed to protect her. The word that came to mind was *expendable,* but Tammy couldn't stand to think of her little sister like that. "I try not to think along those lines. I need to believe what the authorities have told me," she said. Kendall must have pulled Catina into his car, Tammy decided, because her little sister would never knowingly sit next to a murderer. She would never have been that desperate. Yet everyone who knew Catina said she was exactly that desperate, that she would have gone anywhere, with anyone, for the promise of one more hit.

"I know how my sister died," Tammy said, rinsing her coffee cup. "I don't need to know what happened leading up to it."

CHAPTER 14

A Day in the Life

A week after killing Catina Newmaster, Kendall drove Paulette through the quiet morning streets to the Center for Change. They cruised from Fulton Avenue, on the better side of town, to his mother's office on the ramshackle north end. Paulette had long ago been moved off the psychiatric hospital wards and into a desk job, then away from campus altogether. Now she worked as a vocational counselor for the mentally ill, telling them they could achieve anything they wanted. Kendall dropped her off at 8:30 A.M., as he did every morning, and went looking for Christine.

They had been friends all summer—no sex, just Kendall stopping by her motel to lend Chris money, talk to her, watch her get high. He bought her breakfasts after she'd been out all night and he'd been holed up in his bedroom, scribbling fantasies in a spiral notebook. Sometimes Kendall imagined marrying Christine. He couldn't stop thinking of her long red hair, how the two of them would live in a white house filled with children, Christine serving dinner when he came home from work. That morning, he found her walking toward the Family Dollar store, where shoppers burrowed through bins to buy cheap Pampers or jumbo cartons of cereal. He beeped. She turned.

"What's up?" Kendall said. "Are you working?"

"Getting something to eat. What are you doing?"

"Making tapes. Want to come over and listen? You can get something to eat at my house."

Kendall opened his car door, and Christine stepped inside.

EVIL, AS I'D always conceived it, was precise. It involved planning and required control. Evil was intentional and unabashed. It knew itself. Kendall, however, often seemed bewildered by what he'd done. Speaking to me, he never referred to his crimes as anything other than wicked acts. But he thought of evil people as dispassionate, unencumbered by anger—psychologically powerful in ways he knew he was not. Kendall considered himself part of a separate class, schlumping through his days, making snacks, drawing birthday cards. "I don't feel as if I'm evil," he told me. "But then, I don't feel as if I could even do the things that I've done, so what do I know?"

Investigators had theorized that the person responsible for Poughkeepsie's missing women was a white man, the rogue air force officer down by the river or a charming suburbanite—the serial-killer stereotype—not Kendall, whom they routinely busted for beating up hookers, saw afterward wolfing down hamburgers, and laughingly referred to as "Fat Albert." Kendall had been a shambling oaf to the cops, a nothing, and he confirmed their bias when he passed the polygraph. Later, when they knew better, officers would attribute their mistake to a chilling mental divide in the man. They would speak of him as evil, and of evil as a force that operated like a machine, immune to confusion or shame. He was a freak, they said, an aberration. It allowed them to shake off his story as one might a baffling dream.

In my attempt to decipher the riddle of Kendall I imagined the little boy his cousin Mon-Ray had known, a fat kid burrowed into electronic battles on a handheld screen, the pings and squawks a presence that never talked back or changed the rules, never acted different one day to the next. I pictured him dressing for school, sliding through liquefying newsprint and moldy chicken bones, telling himself it was okay that the sinks were clogged, the toilets broken. "So we had a messy house," he snapped at me. I thought of the humiliating football practices, the failed weigh-ins at Schofield Barracks, and Kendall's return home to spend his afternoons pushing a broom at Arlington. Always, he'd loitered around schools, more comfortable when surrounded by children. At night he circled Main Street, tearing up one block, wheeling around the corner and down the next. Faster and faster he drove, round and round, blowing through stop signs and scanning the sidewalks, chasing someone he could never find.

In the early mornings he crawled back into the white Toyota to drive Paulette to work, two huge people in a compact car littered with condoms. He dropped her off at the Center for Change, hired a girl to beat, and spent his afternoons in ethics class at Dutchess Community College.

Kendall liked ethics. His teacher, Janet Winn, was Vassar schooled and broad-minded, a liberal thinker who led her students through Hobbes, Hegel, and Kant, demonstrating how each might have handled questions of punishment and justice. Kendall's papers were nothing much at first, though Winn appreciated that he could string a sentence together better than most. He paid attention to her comments—she could practically feel him sucking them in—and his work improved. During class he wouldn't shut up, punctuating discussions with a constant patter of jokes and commentary until Winn pulled her ninety-eight-pound frame tall and straight, a wisp of hair coming loose from her bun, and snapped in her well-bred French accent, "Cool it, Francois." After that he was meek as a lamb.

This had not been easy for her to do. The first time she saw Kendall, red flags began snapping like a gale was rolling in. *Do not undermine this man. Do not embarrass or humiliate him. Do not make a joke, even a gentle one, at his expense.* There was something fragile about the guy, stretched to quaking, Winn thought. A lot of kids at the community college had issues. They came from homes where education was not necessarily prized. They had multiple jobs, multiple kids. They were all so insecure. But Kendall triggered a different feeling in her. Was it only her own self-conscious liberalism, his being black in a sea of white faces? Winn wasn't sure. But she listened to the voice inside, and it said, *Do not challenge this student in front of his peers.*

Kendall enjoyed her class. He liked wrestling with real questions, speaking up and showing everyone in there that he was smarter than any black man they'd ever seen. He even liked tiny, white-haired professor Winn. When they debated the death penalty, Kendall announced his opinion with pride: anyone who killed should be put to death, he thundered. Most of the class appeared to agree. Winn could see them nodding along, punishers all. She did not share this view, and shifted the debate to euthanasia and abortion—how could it be legal for the state to sanction one type of killing and not another? she asked the class. A fair question, Kendall thought.

After the lesson, Winn walked out of the room right behind her garrulous student. Unlike the social misfit he'd been in high school, here Kendall was a clown, a flirt. And he was often surrounded by girls. This intrigued Winn, since he was not much to look at. But Kendall charmed his classmates, she could see, and he clearly enjoyed the repartee, playing the joker, the jiving ghetto black, nothing like the earnest wannabe jock he'd been at Arlington. Around older women, he was noticeably quiet, Winn observed. The middle-aged housewives who'd returned to school after watching their husbands question the security of an IBM career leaned away, making no effort to hide their disgust as Kendall caromed past their desks. But the younger girls took pride in showing they had no prejudice, no fear.

"I think any woman who has an abortion should be killed," Kendall bellowed as students jostled out the classroom door. Winn froze. His voice was granite cold. It sent a sick chill through her stomach. Morality was a matter of absolutes with this man. You were on one side of the line or the other, with no space for gray areas, complexities of the heart. This was the antithesis of how Winn tried to live her life. She noticed Kendall's girls hanging back now, looking up at him oddly, questions flickering across their faces. He slouched upstairs to his next class, leveling under-the-breath insults at every person he passed.

There might be a few rounds of Dungeons and Dragons later in the cafeteria or, if it was Monday, a Magic tournament at Donte's house. Then it was back to Fulton Avenue and another night of zigzagging Main Street.

WITH CHRISTINE, KENDALL decided the games were over. It was time to get what he was owed, stop playing puppy dog, find what he'd been looking for all his life. Kendall drove her two blocks to 99 Fulton Avenue, Paulette's crucifix swinging from the rearview mirror. Main Street that morning had been sweltering, but the air on Fulton Avenue was clean and fragrant. He opened the garage, pulled the car inside, and closed the door behind them. Christine sat in the dark, a twitch of worry tightening her throat.

"Aren't we going into the house?"

"In a minute," said Kendall, unbuttoning his pants. "I want to talk to you here first. I've missed you. I want to have sex."

"That's crazy—you know I'm not going to do that. Take me back to Main Street."

"You are not going anywhere."

Kendall grabbed Christine's slim neck and straddled her in the passenger seat. Now the bitch would pay for all the meals, the loans, the flirting and teasing. He punched her in the face, reached backward to open Christine's door with one hand and work himself to erection, while the other pressed down on her throat. Christine felt the nausea of breathlessness. She bucked and writhed. Kendall couldn't get her pants off. *Sleazy crack whore in her tight pants.* He opened her door and got out, right hand still digging into her throat, and tore off her shoes and pants with his left. Christine's eyes were bulging. She knew she was going to die. She couldn't believe he was the one, though she'd heard the talk. She couldn't believe he would do it to her. He pulled out his penis, but it was only half erect.

Thank god, now he'll let me go.

"Give me a blow job," Kendall growled, pulling Christine out of the car by her hair. He towered over her. Once hard, he shoved Christine back into the car to jam himself inside her. But Kendall's penis went flaccid again. His condom kept falling off.

"I'll kill you!" he screamed. "I'll kill you!"

Then, faintly, from somewhere outside the garage, a girl's voice: "Kendall? You know I need that car! Kendall, what are you doing in there?"

TWO BLOCKS AWAY Detective Mannain, in the blue uniform he hardly ever wore anymore, was stopping cars, handing out Xeroxes of Catina Newmaster's elfin face to every driver who passed through the intersection at Main Street and Grand. This had been Dorsey's suggestion, the primary strategy to come out of his visit from FBI headquarters: stand at the exact spot where Catina was last seen, at the exact time on the same day of the week, and hand out flyers. A rather low-tech solution it seemed to the Poughkeepsie police, but Dorsey kept talking about "matching the internal clock" of the offender. "Have you seen this woman?" the fluttering papers asked in bold type. It was grunt work, as far as Mannain was concerned, something Siegrist should have assigned to his beat cops. But Grady had just held his dog and pony show reassuring people that there was a task force dedicated to solving the mystery, and the *Journal* was finally running stories. People were starting to talk.

Around the corner in her filthy bedroom, Kierstyn Francois was dressing. The day would be busy—first school, then a shift at Montgomery Ward—and where was her brother? He knew he was supposed to drive her to class. "Kendall!" she called out again, thinking she heard him in the garage. "Kendall! You know I need that car!"

His head jerked up at the sound, and he stopped moving, straining to listen as Christine choked and wheezed beneath him. Her hair was everywhere, in his hands, on the car seat, the floor. Swiftly, Kendall threw the garage door open, gunned the Toyota backward out the driveway, and, wheels shrieking, tore around the corner. Immediately, he began the stream of apologies. "I'm so sorry, Christine. I never meant to hurt you. I wanted to take care of you. I'm so sorry, Christine. Please let me take care of you." He made his first right, headed toward Main Street, and stopped at the traffic light, stretching to open the passenger-side door. "I'll call you later!" he said as Christine stumbled from the car. He noticed police covering the street, handing out Catina's smudgy picture. Drivers glanced down at it, then up at her face beaming from a billboard, wisps of blond hair curling up at her chin. He waved at the officers from his car. They waved back.

"Hi, Kendall, you fat fuck," Mannain said to himself, as Kendall made another right turn and headed home to take Kierstyn to school.

CIGARETTES, THOUGHT CHRISTINE, staggering into the corner gas station. Just need cigarettes.

"You okay?" the clerk asked, noticing her torn T-shirt, her tangled hair. Christine waved him off. But he persisted.

"You got red marks all over your neck!"

Christine began to cry. She couldn't swallow. Words fell out in random order: Attacked. Need cigarettes. No cops.

"You got to talk to a cop!" the clerk said. "There's one right out-side."

Christine was shaking her head—she was wanted on a heroin charge—and she lunged for the door. But Mannain and his part-ner were walking straight toward her, summoned by a customer yammering about some girl who said she'd been attacked. They strode in, tall and businesslike, annoyed at having to talk to a nineteen-year-old hooker who didn't want to see them anyway. A rape case, thought Mannain, just another rape at the hands of that slob, Kendall. Same shit every day. He sighed. He brought Chris-tine to the station house and took her statement. All she did was complain about wanting to go home and take a shower. He drove her to St. Francis Hospital for an exam and phoned Margie Smith, who handled sex crimes for the district attorney. The thumbprints on Christine's neck, the attack in Kendall's garage, so similar to the reports from Catina, now missing, and a dozen other women—Mannain still hadn't put it together. None of them had.

Kendall's activities between that morning and afternoon when police knocked on his door remain a mystery. He had changed the shirt he was wearing when he raped Christine. Kierstyn, now back from school, was pulling the Toyota out of the driveway on her way to work when a young officer walked up and told her to step out of the car. McKinley opened the side door to another detective ask-ing if his son wouldn't mind coming down to the station to answer a few questions. McKinley shrugged and turned to call upstairs. But Kendall was already there, standing behind him. He nodded hello to the officers. He knew them well.

"Hey, Kendall," said the younger one, normally assigned to traf-fic duty. "We need you to come back to the station to talk."

"Okay."

There were no questions from father or son about what had precipitated this request.

"It was like asking to interview a teddy bear, for chrisssakes," said the officer who drove Kendall to the station, gagging at the smell of rot that began to cloud the car.

MANNAIN AND HIS partner showed Kendall into interview room 112. It was small, carpeted in gray, and windowless save for a little square in the door. They turned on a tape recorder at 4:38 P.M., and for eight minutes fed Kendall questions about the assault on Christine, trudging through his one-word answers until Kendall began to summarize the rape himself. Then he became formal, loquacious, uttering Christine's name with a lilt in his voice. He said she began to "disrobe." He said they stopped "upon her request." He said he'd asked for permission to continue.

"Was she scared at this point, scared of you?" the detective asked.

"Yes."

"Ken, what you did, was it right or wrong?"

"Wrong."

"Did you want to talk about your anger management at all? Do you have a problem controlling your temper?"

"Yes," he said, perking up.

"And you have problems to the point where you hurt people?"

"Yes," Kendall continued with emphasis.

"Do you think this problem is getting worse?"

"It's not getting any better."

AT 4:46 P.M., the officers snapped off their tape recorder, and Kendall affirmed his statement with a slovenly scrawl that looked nothing like the tight cursive he would later use when writing to me. The police explained that they needed to prepare a warrant and go to his house to get the shirt he'd been wearing while raping Christine. Kendall nodded, and the detectives stepped out. He was alone. He was amazed. No one had said a word about the missing women. They'd asked if he wanted to add anything to the story about Christine, and he'd almost told them right then. But no. They saw him as a rapist only, nothing more. He peered out the little window, scanning. Sat down for a moment, then peeked out again. Across the room he could see Mannain marching in and out of some big shot's office, waving his arms around, acting like he was on top of it all. Same as the jocks at Arlington who'd clap you on the back and make jokes later about your smell. What did they think, that he couldn't hear, didn't care? Hadn't he tried to get help? Hadn't he'd told the damn courts nine months ago that he needed to talk to someone about his anger? That stupid judge, what had he done? Forced him into group therapy for sex offenders so he could spend twenty dollars talking about girls he'd just paid thirty to fuck. It was so ridiculous, he had to laugh. He was sure it would end the day he let Mannain into the house, but the guy had seemed like he barely cared, like all he wanted to do was get out of there. Now, this thing about the shirt he'd been wearing with Christine—there might be other cops looking around, and they would be smarter. They'd check his room. They'd see the newspaper on his bed, opened to the story about Tina and that ridiculous Missing Women Task Force, and they'd figure it out with his father standing there, his mother just home from work. They'd find Tina and Sandy and the Yonkers girl, then the others—what was left of them. He thought of Janet Winn's class and the day they'd talked about the death penalty. They'd execute him now, he knew that.

Kendall studied the roomful of men in button-down shirts bent over their desks. The place looked more like an insurance office than a police station. No wonder these cops couldn't keep anyone safe. He tapped on the window. He'd take control, do everything for them. Save his family the embarrassment of standing there while these idiots made their discoveries. He hoped Kierstyn would forgive him. He'd always liked her best.

An officer opened the door, his face pleasant, inquiring.

"I want to talk to the head prosecutor about the missing women," Kendall said.

WAS THERE NO end to this day? thought Margie Smith. Was it not enough that she'd been standing in front of a judge when the call came in reporting that a girl had been raped, and then scrambling to find someone who could take over her caseload, and then arranging to have her personal gynecologist oversee the exam? She was exhausted. And now, at five o'clock, some joker wanted to talk about the missing women? Smith drove the ten minutes from Poughkeepsie's courthouse to the town barracks in Arlington, glad that the building was air-conditioned, at least.

"I'm Marjorie Smith and this is state police investigator Arthur Boyko," she said, making introductions and extending her hand. "I understand you want to talk about the missing women."

He nodded. This was the head prosecutor, a woman? She was kind of dumpy—not his type at all—with curly blond hair and a snub-nosed face. Mannain was standing there too, grinning like he had a joke he couldn't wait to spill. Kendall looked at the three of them. He was going to tell everything now—well, not everything, not about sawing up some girls, or tying Mary or gagging Kathleen, and he wasn't going to talk about the black girl—but most of it, and then it would be over. He'd be done. A movement caught his eye as they prepared to sit down, a quick flash of something shiny, and then a phffft, and Mannain cackling as a mist of Mountain Fresh Glade settled onto Kendall's skin. The ball of hatred in his stomach felt like it was going to blow right out of his throat. "Get out," he hissed.

Mannain chose to view this as an endorsement. Kendall probably felt bad for lying to him all these months, the detective decided. He shrugged and left.

For hours Kendall told his story, his voice bored, weary, as if he could barely be bothered. Nowhere was the teasing tone he would use with me. Here he exhaled in long sighs as he spoke of women gasping for air before he drowned them. He described moving bodies up and down the stairs, from the garage to the bedroom, from the attic to the basement, with a striking lack of detail. He ate two slices of pizza, drank a soda, and talked about folding Catherine Marsh into a suitcase. He was silent for nearly a minute before describing Catina sitting naked in the front seat of his car, and only then did his voice betray the barest tremor, as if he had just realized the full import of all he'd said.

"When we go up to the attic to look," said Smith, "what are we gonna find?"

"Bones."

"Is that all that's left?"

"There's maybe a little bit of flesh."

"On who is there flesh left?"

"Excuse me?"

"Who's got the flesh left on them?"

"I don't know. They're all mixed together."

"How are they mixed together, Kendall?"

"Some of them are in a large bag together and some of 'em are in an old kiddie pool."

Smith was fighting to keep her face composed, but she'd always taken her job to heart. In the end, it usually came down to families.

"Kendall, was your mom or dad or anybody else home when this was going on?"

"No!" he said, startled.

"What about Catina? Was anybody home when you killed Catina?"

"I think my sister may have been at the house."

Kendall chose not to detail his nights in the attic, the eyebolts he'd screwed into beams, the way he'd gagged Mary with duct tape, bound her arms, and tied a rope around her neck. But Boyko suspected. And he was disgusted.

"Did you ever have sex with any of the bodies?" Boyko asked.

"What do you think, I'm sick?"

Kendall had been in the police station more than nine hours by this point, Smith and Boyko nearly as long. It was time to wrap up.

"Is there anything we've forgotten to ask you?" Smith concluded. "About how you feel about all of this?"

"I felt bad," Kendall snorted, as if being forced to recite from a book of rules. "That's why I confessed."

"Why did you do all this?" she asked.

"I think I'm crazy."

Bullshit, Smith thought.

"Anything else you want to add about who Kendall Francois is? What makes you tick?"

"I don't know anymore."

Smith knew there were a dozen things she'd done wrong. It was nerve-racking with Boyko sitting there, noticing every stumble. He was the one with experience in these interviews. She remembered, suddenly, about Christine Sala and how they'd all come to be sitting there.

"Why are some of them dead and some of them aren't dead? Why is the woman from this morning—why isn't she one of the eight? Why isn't she number nine? What made you stop?"

"I care about her," Kendall said quietly.

CHAPTER 15

One of Our Own

Being black did not make Kendall particularly unusual as a serial killer. But choosing victims from another race did. District Attorney Grady maintained that bias had never been the motive behind Kendall's crimes, though that could be true only in the most narrowly legalistic interpretation. Kendall had pined for a girlfriend throughout his years at Arlington, told me all of his rage stemmed from high school and that "you don't want to rock the boat when you're one of the only black kids." Later, he'd penned lovelorn letters to former classmates, all of them white. His brother and uncle, both successful professionals, had married white women. But Kendall could barely get one to speak to him even when he paid for her. He was, simultaneously, horrified to be associated with the blacks lolling drunk and indolent on Main Street.

Kendall's plea deal required that he speak about Michelle Eason, the only African American on investigators' list of the missing. She was a longtime prostitute and had disappeared from Main Street during the same period as Kendall's other victims. Flipping through photographs during his confession to Margie Smith, he had treated Michelle's picture differently than the rest, setting it aside to discuss later but never returning. He had known her, certainly. Kendall told his younger sister, long irritated by his preference for white women, that he was finally dating a black girl and her name, he said, was Michelle. But if Eason's mug shot was any indication, Kendall would have despised her. So wasted and beaten was Michelle, she could barely hold her head up. It would have enraged him, in his obsession with morality and judgment.

All along, the police had maintained bemused interest in my go-rounds with their cipher. They viewed our correspondence through a Hollywood lens, applied the standard story line, and believed Kendall might lay out for me all the mysteries they'd been unable to solve. Detective Walt Horton, assigned to the Michelle Eason case, had perhaps the greatest motivation. Years after the file folders were all packed away, there was still no sign of her.

In the summer of 2001, Horton called and invited me in to talk. It was embarrassing. I knew he would quickly recognize that my conversations with Kendall were driven by something far afield of journalism. But I arrived, as requested, and was shown to the same interview room where Kendall had sat facing pictures of himself, his home, and his victims. A battered old desk and two chairs—one with ripped red upholstery, the other new and blue—were crammed inside. I chose the red one.

Horton never would have reached out on his own, not without prodding from Siegrist or possibly Mannain. He was a by-the-book cop, unimpressed with shortcuts or miracles, though years earlier, in desperation at the growing list of missing women, he had consulted a psychic who said she "saw" one of them lying on a concrete slab near the Taconic Parkway. Somewhat sheepishly, Horton spent hours off-duty trudging through woods along the narrow highway. And now, three years after Kendall's confession, the detective was still so tormented that he was turning to me.

A silver-haired man who favored short-sleeve button-downs like a cop from the fifties, Horton had been on the job for thirty years. He'd heard other departments snickering about the bungled investigation in Poughkeepsie, watched Mannain deified on television as the hero who'd brought Kendall down, stood by as the younger man basked in acclaim from crime-story celebrities (pathologist Michael Baden had autographed his most recent book to "the handsomest super-cop I know"), and kept quiet. But now Horton heaved a fat file onto the table between us and let loose. His voice sounded like shifting gravel.

"Look, the police department doesn't deal with the greatest clientele, but the feeling about them missing was, so what?" He hung his head. "These ladies are out there, and they're creating problems for our city. People are calling us all the time, complaining about them, saying 'move the prostitutes along.' The community didn't really care about these missing women because they were the problem, and the problem was going away."

He stared at his knees. I thought of Sandy, the horsewoman and grandmother with gleaming auburn hair; and Cathy, plinking out pop tunes on Marguerite's upright piano. I thought of Wendy, making long-distance calls to her little boy in Florida every Sunday, and Gina, running from her broken home to drive off with boys in the night. A week before our meeting, I'd passed the gas station where Christine Sala stumbled from Kendall's car. There was another young woman there—a girl, really—standing on matchstick

legs, scanning for customers, so tiny that her extralarge polo shirt
served as a dress, so ugly that she discouraged closer examination.
She bent over to tie her sneakers, exposing her underwear like an
animal offering itself.

"Were you surprised at how long it took the *Journal* to run anything about the women?" I asked Horton.

"Absolutely. Maybe they didn't think it would sell newspapers—
what motivates editors to print any story? I mean, even their families
weren't calling. With these women, there was just no pressure to follow up. But what I'm saying is, these are the people we deal with, and
they deserve as much attention as somebody that's of a higher stature."

All the women Kendall killed had been damaged, and I suspect
they recognized something kindred in him. Kathleen Hurley had
confided about her mother's death as she sat next to Kendall, en
route to her own. He was easy to talk to, sympathetic, as if he knew
what loss felt like. Though he dodged the idea of remorse or apology, Kendall had always acknowledged that some of his victims
never did a thing to anger him. He was upset at someone else, he'd
say, declining to identify whom. But he'd taped Kathleen's mouth,
the autopsy report suggested, and I wondered if it was something
she'd said. Kathleen was not a Main Street regular. She'd had a fight
with her girlfriend and stormed out, wearing nothing warmer than
a Russell Athletics sweatshirt in the January cold. She grabbed
her cigarettes and left a toothbrush behind. She didn't plan to be
gone long. Kathleen held regular jobs—line worker at IBM, bus
driver for disabled children. She lectured her little brother when
he made jokes about retarded kids. He'd watched in awe as she ran
down a mugger who'd swiped an old woman's purse. A brawler. An
avenger. Someone I might have liked to know. Kendall dumped her
in a plastic bin, and over eighteen months her body liquefied. She

dissolved like the Wicked Witch in Oz. Yet unaccountably, Kathleen's rib cage remained partially intact, curving over to shelter a skeletal hand which bore the bone of a single raised finger, and on that finger remained a bit of skin sufficient for a print. This was the factor, this insistent, defiant finger, that told Kathleen Hurley's story. Without it, no one could have said with surety that she had ever been there.

Horton's face was carved with deep grooves. He rubbed his knuckles as he spoke.

"I think Kendall Francois is very clever. I think he's a lot smarter than people gave him credit for. Did he ever talk to you about Michelle?"

I wanted to help. The detective looked so hopeful and sounded so weary. But all I could offer was limp sincerity.

"Whenever I ask about the case he dodges my questions, even now."

"And how does he appear in prison—does he smell?"

"No, not at all."

Kendall's lack of body odor had been the first thing to strike Horton when they met for the plea-deal interview about Michelle. Before, he'd believed that the cloud of odor hanging about was due to something chemical in Kendall, something internal. But now, sitting opposite this fresh-looking killer two years after his confession, Horton realized it was just a function of home.

"I killed those eight women," Kendall began. "If I'd killed another, why wouldn't I tell you?"

"Well, let's say Michelle got into your car and triggered you to do what you did with eight other women. Let's just say that happened, and you still didn't want to tell. What would be your motivation?"

"She's black."

"Why would that matter?"

"I wouldn't want people of my own race to think badly of me for killing a black woman," Kendall said.

Not quite a declaration of guilt, but it was enough to convince Horton.

"I really think those are the reasons," he said to me. "Michelle just fits his profile in every way, everything except her race."

Kendall felt that confessing to the murder of a black prostitute would disgrace his family and everyone in the Central Baptist Church congregation, so to shield their dignity, to spare them this shame, he was keeping Michelle a secret even now, Horton believed.

"Are you saying that Kendall thought only white women were low enough to be prostitutes, that only white women deserved to be killed?" I asked.

"Well, he's black, the victim's black, and he said he wouldn't want people like him to think—"

"That he'd killed 'one of our own'?"

"Exactly."

"Do you think he'll ever cop to it?"

"No, I don't."

NEARLY EVERYONE HAD a theory about Kendall's motivation, but these ideas generally revealed more about the speakers than they did about him. He was a mirror, an opaque pool reflecting us back onto ourselves. Teachers believed he'd once possessed an inner light, a spark of goodness, brutally extinguished. Therapists spoke of inchoate rage triggered by the humiliation of rejection, and the simultaneous thrill of having a woman compliant in your hands, in your bed. Someone who would never leave. Donte Turner, steeped in politics and sociology, interpreted his old friend's crimes as a comment on the powerlessness of black men in America. For Kendall, the meek, to wield a decision like life or death over a white woman would have been the ultimate affirmation, he thought. "I bet he freaked out the first time," Donte said. "You take a minority who cannot project power over the system, then this happens and you don't get caught? I think that was the catalyst." The murders became a game to Kendall, like those he'd played each week at Donte's home. "Kendall loves games," Donte said.

We were talking in the Palace Diner, which Donte had chosen, proclaiming it a white-people's restaurant. Unbeknownst to either of us, Skip Mannain was sitting in a nearby booth, listening. He later offered his evaluation of Donte's theories with undisguised scorn. Investigators favored cleaner story lines devoid of political overtones. To them, Kendall was a big black kid in an all-white school who wanted a girlfriend but could never get one because he had never learned how to take care of himself. "So he turned to prostitutes," Siegrist said. "Taking them out to eat, imagining they were dating, talking about getting married. I think every man's dream is to have a house with a white picket fence and soccer with the kids on Saturday, church on Sundays. But prostitutes aren't people you want to have that kind of relationship with."

What I saw was a man who obliterated women by crushing their throats, their vocal cords, the place from which they might have told their stories. And he looked into their eyes as he did it.

⸻

PSYCHOLOGICAL NUANCE MAY have held little interest for most of Poughkeepsie law enforcement, but it mattered a great deal to the city's lone black detective. Teddy Alston had arrived from the South as a child, around the same time as Kendall's grandparents. He'd been raised in the same Italian American neighborhood where Donte now guzzled iced lattes, living there through the race riots of the 1960s, then the crackling tension of the Brawley period, and he could not miss the unspoken messages transmitted every day—in the supermarket, between cops, ricocheting from one person's eyes to another's. "Racism in Poughkeepsie?" he said with a bitter laugh. "It's damn intense. Look at the suburbs around here. All those white guys moved out there for a reason, and it's not economic. Look, it was never against me. I always had white friends. I was surrounded by white people, actually. But pain? Rage? My god, it never ends." Years later, after Horton, Siegrist, and Mannain had retired, the three white detectives would meet for lunch, talk over the old days. But Alston never joined their table.

He and I sat in the same room where Horton had questioned me several weeks earlier, and Alston's memories came in a torrent, as if no one had asked for his impressions before. He'd been the only Poughkeepsie officer to interview Kendall's family, and they were still the true quarry in my mind, the source of answers. But for Alston, that source was me. He'd never been able to speak to Kendall. And so we had the terms of our trade.

"Kendall always tells me, 'There are a lot more awful people who are white than black,'" I began. "But he also calls the black people who live here 'trash.'"

"He's a racist—it's obvious—and not just against white people," Alston said. "He's racist toward anyone who's other."

The detective and I looked at each other for a long moment, the same sort of staring contest I'd had so often with Kendall. But this time I broke first.

"So you spoke to the Francoises the night Kendall was arrested?"

Alston had knocked shortly after midnight, and McKinley answered the door. Kendall was still at the police station talking with Smith and Boyko, and crime scene investigators were on their way to tear the Francoises' home apart. Alston said nothing about that. He'd been sent to extract the family without raising alarms. "Hey, use the black guy," he explained to me. "That's how we did it all the time."

McKinley did not appear overly concerned when invited down to the station to talk in the middle of the night.

"Is this going to take long?" he asked. "I have to be at work early in the morning."

There were no questions about where his son had been all afternoon, or why Paulette and Kierstyn were also wanted for questioning, or why squadrons of police cruisers were lining Fulton Avenue. None of the family spoke during the ten-minute ride, though in the front seat Alston was struggling not to retch.

"Everybody in that house reeked of death," he said.

I imagined the dread unfolding in their hearts. Paulette and Kierstyn had emerged behind McKinley, holding hands and weeping as if on their way to a funeral. At the station house they were separated, Kierstyn sent to sit by herself while Alston spoke to her parents. He seated himself at the head of a conference table, with Paulette directly opposite and McKinley to her left.

Alston had been assigned only to babysit and keep the family distracted. But he began asking questions anyway, addressing them to McKinley, who kept his eyes locked on Paulette. And she never stopped staring back at him.

"Other than this staring thing between Kendall's parents, did they appear bizarre in any way?" I asked.

"There was something wrong with Dad, without a doubt. It may have been his health—I don't know. But she ran the show."

"Mom?"

"That's correct. I'd ask him, 'What's been going on around your household for the last few months? Didn't you smell all those people? I mean, didn't you smell the bodies?' And he's looking right at her, saying, 'Nothing abnormal, nothing abnormal.' He hears me, but he answers to her. Like he won't make a move without her say-so. He won't take his eyes off her."

"What was Paulette doing?"

"Staring directly at him with this look like 'Don't say anything else.' I'm sitting across from her, and she's got his attention the whole time. You know how Kendall told us he went upstairs and poured bleach on those bodies? She gave him the money to go to the store and get it."

This story had become legendary, a tale about Paulette demanding an explanation for the stench in the attic, the maggots raining onto her bed, and Kendall brushing her off with an excuse about a family of dead raccoons huddled together in a foul nest. An interesting image, I thought.

Kierstyn had been present for this discussion between her mother and brother, the detective told me, and she wanted to see the dead raccoons for herself. Kendall forbade her.

Now Alston turned to me.

"If your brother was that adamant about not going someplace and his behavior was so bizarre, would you or would you not go up there and find out what the heck he was hiding?"

"I would."

"I would, too. The minute he left the house I'd have been up there to see what the hell."

He let that hang in the air between us.

"So what does that say to you?" I asked. "That she was afraid of Kendall, or afraid of what she might find?"

"That's a possibility," said Alston, sounding unconvinced. "But if a normal person suspects something—enough to say 'I'm going with you'—then why on earth would she not at some point go?"

"Do you think she's a normal person?"

"I don't think anybody in that house was normal."

"You mentioned that there was something wrong with McKinley, and this staring thing with Paulette. But did their relationship seem close—the parents'?"

"Not at all. They didn't get along. They didn't sleep in the same room. They didn't even sleep in the same part of the house. They lived under the same roof, but they didn't live together. It seemed to me that he couldn't stand to be anywhere near her."

"Did McKinley strike you as a scary person?" I asked, thinking of Kendall's gritted comments about McKinley's considerable size.

"No."

"A meek person?"

"Yes."

"So Paulette struck you as the stronger personality?"

"Yes. Although she was quiet, I felt as though she's the one that ruled the house. You talk to Kendall, right? Ask if his parents ever fought in front of him, physically fought. See what he says."

I'd done so, years before, and been thrown down a well of memory.

"All parents fight—didn't yours?" Kendall had retorted, sending me back to the tall bedroom door where I'd stood in my nightgown listening to shrieks on the other side. My sister never understood this need to get right up close to the fear. But it always seemed safer to me than blindly waiting for the ax to fall. Among the four Francois children there were similar alliances, though as a unit the family displayed all the solidity of an abandoned cobweb.

"There was no wholeness to them," Alston continued. "No closeness between the mother and the father when it came to the kids. It was my feeling that the mother was not just the matriarch, but"—he slammed the table so hard that I jumped—"the aggressor."

"Why do you think Kendall's so determined to shield his parents?"

It was the question that had become more intriguing to me than any other. Kendall's determination to curtain the facts of their lives as provocative as the facts themselves. The avoidance of truth within Kendall's family was the biggest unanswered question of the case. How was it possible to build denial so strong that you could live in a home where maggots dropped from the ceiling and do nothing about it? To ignore the stench of death enveloping you in sleep?

Alston thought Kendall had controlled life at 99 Fulton Avenue to the point where all the Francoises were afraid of him—even now, while he was in prison. This was what kept them from talking to me, the detective surmised.

"He's the different one," Alston concluded. "A predator, and it is my opinion that he has quite a few more secrets than he's told."

The detective peered at me.

"A white female, dark hair. You don't wear a lot of makeup. How many times have you met with him?"

"Twice—once at the jail, once at Attica."

Alston looked me up and down, then held his palm in front of my face to demonstrate what so many others had: Kendall's huge hands, almost mythic by now, with fingers thick as steel cables, palms hard and broad as the head of an ax.

"Do me a favor, will you?" the detective said. "Don't go visit him again. Don't get yourself in a position where he can put his hands on you. I think he has plans."

CHAPTER 16

The Face in the Mirror

I doubted that. I'd grown used to the idea of visiting my beast in a cage. Still, the late-summer visits were an annual ordeal, weighing on my mind for months before.

"What if I went with you?" my mother asked.

Her offer stunned me. She'd never been anywhere near a prison. She'd built her entire life as a bulwark against looking at poverty and pain. I couldn't imagine her in the forsaken emptiness of western New York or inside the soaring walls of Attica. I wanted, suddenly, to spare her.

"Thanks, Mom. But these are long conversations. I'd worry about you getting bored. I don't even know where you'd sit—it's not like they have a waiting room."

"Couldn't I just wait in your car? I'll bring a book."

My chest was aching. For years I'd longed for caring like this. But I'd made my path, and I'd walk it alone. It seemed safer that way. The story of Kendall Francois was the sort that made my mom stiffen and go distant. The kind she skipped over in the newspaper because it forced confrontation with the differences between a family's public face and closeted reality. It begged questions about who is valued and who is not, and whether certain lives are more worth saving than others. All of it likely to lead to tense conversation, then miles of silence.

"There's really no need, Mom. I'll be okay."

⸻

THIS TIME, THERE was no breaking down in terrified tears before starting out. I was all grim resolve, and there was no one to cry to, anyway. I rolled through upstate farm country listening to the tapes Derrick had made for my first drive, snapping off the music when memories took up all the air in the car. I no longer believed the tale I'd originally told myself about good intentions enabling an innocent to discover the truth within a monster. I was no innocent, and Kendall knew it, much as we both wanted to believe otherwise. I looked down at my fingers, clenched and ringless on the steering wheel.

Other than the incessant demand for a photograph, Kendall's most frequent request, reiterated in letter after letter after my first visit to Attica, was that I allow him to hug me. I'd laughed this off as an absurdity. Yet, like everything else he seized on, the subject of contact anchored in affection, dependent on trust, pressed bruises I had skirted all my life. I wrote to ask why a hug was so important, and Kendall's reply forced me to question my sincerity at the beginning, four years ago, when I told him he was more than a monster. "I'm not sure where I stand in your eyes," he'd written, "but I think I'm more than just the subject of a book. I know it is hard for you to think of me as a normal man, but I really am. I think there is a barrier of doubt from you. I can feel it when we talk, you visit. I really think that a simple hug would at least crack that barrier, if not knock it down."

It was hard enough for me to envision shaking Kendall's hand, reaching across the table and feeling for myself whether he possessed the superhuman force Detective Alston claimed, or whether I'd been chasing a phantom all along. For years, I'd considered touching Kendall merely a personal hurdle, something I needed to do to bridge the distance between a monster and me; to prove, really, that there were no monsters. But now I kept seeing those skulls jumbled in his kiddie pool.

There had been a certain nobility to the quest as I'd narrated it to myself at first. The idea of peering into cruelty, dissecting it to study the components, sounded almost respectable, and I had approached Kendall as an intellectual equal, a man who could discuss himself rationally. But if he'd had the presence of mind to understand why he did such things, Kendall often observed, he probably wouldn't have done them in the first place. Anyway, I'd grown tired of our games, fed up with him and impatient with myself for running an obstacle course out of pure stubbornness. Give me something, I prayed as I passed fast-food rest stops and muddy farms. Give me something.

I had even less money than the year before, so I booked a cheaper motel, outside the fence encircling the Rochester airport, where floodlights buzzed over the blacktop all night long. The front-desk girls turned toward me with bovine eyes as I opened the office door. Yes, you could hear the airplanes from the guest rooms, and would I like nonsmoking? They sat behind a beige countertop through empty hours, listening to jets whisk people away. I lay on my bed in room 304, staring at the wall above my TV. Kendall would have been lying in bed, too, gazing at the ceiling in his cell and imagining how I'd look, what I'd wear, what I'd ask.

I must wash my face. I must try to do something normal. I must not arrive at Attica looking as though I'd fallen asleep with my clothes on. The Motel 6 bathroom had a tiny sink, a stainless steel shelf, and a slab of grimy mirror above. Even now as an adult, every time I bent to wash my face I flashed back to the beveled glass mirror on Central Park West and the endurance test I used to run as a girl, with my eyes closed against the sting of soapy water, imagining a monster behind me. I'd still whirl around sometimes, my eyes smarting, to play red-light-green-light with a phantom I could not name. *You must do the thing you think you cannot do,* Eleanor Roosevelt was reported to have said. I'd recited her words to myself from the moment I received Kendall's first letter. And now, as I rubbed soap over my skin and bent over the sink to rinse, the old dread welled up, the demon poised behind me. But this time I did not turn. I stared straight into the mirror. The most frightening thing about Kendall was not merely what he'd done. I couldn't see him in his horrid attic. It was how he acted, what he said, the relentless browbeating that crammed me into categories and forced me to question every thought. *You are selfish. You are a liar.* I'd heard those words for decades. I heard them in my head every time I sat down to write. What frightened me about Kendall was how familiar he felt.

I looked at myself under the fluorescent light. I was thirty-six, but so tired. I wondered if Kendall would notice. I knew he wouldn't care. He said he wanted me to be his friend. But he would never want to know what he'd meant to my life. He would understand that at some level, he was a symbol, unimportant in himself. He would see that when I no longer feared the monster behind me,

I would leave him. And Kendall killed women when they needed to leave. So I would never try to explain. But I knew he would sense it anyway, like an animal smelling change in the wind.

AT ATTICA I sat on the old steel benches, waiting to be processed, a particle of matter tumbling through a cold and Byzantine system. Yet everything that had struck me as ominous the year before seemed to have shrunk. The prison was still a Victorian dungeon, but its doorways were shorter, its hallways narrower, the visiting room less cavernous, the guard station not so far away. I bought some microwave popcorn and a can of grapefruit juice, setting them on the table to show Kendall that I remembered his favorite snacks. He walked toward me, heavier than I'd ever seen him, his goatee streaked with gray.

I'd spent decades trying to convince people that I was a loner who never got lonely. But I'd grown so tired of presenting myself as brave and in control that I no longer bothered. Fear was the first thing we talked about. It was the trait in me that upset Kendall most—far more than my prying questions, which he found easy to deflect. Fear was proof. It meant I believed he was only what he'd done. But Kendall considered himself a thinker, a poet, and he wanted me to see that, too. He looked constantly for evidence that I understood him as something more.

"You say that, but you show me so little of yourself," I began. "You say you're more than what you did, but you won't tell me anything that might help me to see you."

Silence, as the other inmates jabbered. Ten feet from us sat David Gilbert, once a revolutionary in the Weather Underground, now a middle-aged man speaking earnestly at his visitor. She nodded, her white hair barely moving, her eyes looking as if she'd heard his speech a hundred times before. Behind them, a prisoner was hosting parents so wizened I expected to hear their joints pop as they shuffled to the juice machines. What had happened in this family to land a father here in his golf visor on a Sunday afternoon, sipping sugared juice from a can? The inmate was about fifty and mild looking in a white button-down shirt. He could have been a banker, or a pedophile, or a political activist, too. We were grouped in a tight little clump of tables, the back of my chair within an inch of my neighbor's. If Kendall was ever going to tell me about his family or Michelle Eason, it wouldn't be within earshot of a dozen other prisoners, though I took comfort from the knowledge that if his hand shot forward to clutch my throat there were people close enough to help.

"Maybe I don't want to see myself," he blurted. "There are a lot of things I still don't understand. Maybe I'm afraid of what I'll find."

"Everyone I talk to describes you as a teddy bear—is that really you?"

"I know they say that. It depresses me."

"Why is a teddy bear depressing?"

"It reminds me of who I was and everything that's gone. What could have been and now won't ever be."

Incredibly, Kendall still wanted to be seen as good. Each December, his New Year's resolutions focused on "writing more" and "becoming the person I could have been, should have been." There were broken shards of this other person tucked within his heaving brutality—the man who valued stories and recognized beauty, who understood humor and loyalty and the concept, at least, of love. In my relationship with Kendall, simplicity was the first thing to die.

I took a deep breath.

"The police in Poughkeepsie say you've got plans for me."

This was the quality Derrick always hated most about me, my way of laying things out, bare and real, just to see what came back.

"What kind of plans?" Kendall asked, looking at his hands.

"You know, murderous."

"You have absolutely nothing to fear from me."

I must have looked skeptical.

"Are you a prostitute?" he said. "Have you done anything to me?"

"No."

"Then you have no reason to fear."

All around us, people were embracing. There was more love on display in the visitors room at Attica than I saw at most family gatherings. A Latina on my right gave her husband such an intimate hug that I had to look away, mostly out of envy. I'd never had a connection like that with anyone. Kendall feigned obliviousness, though he surely noticed the pretty blonde to my left, French-kissing an inmate with angry eyes. He offered some popcorn, and I pulled an oily kernel from the bag, wondering what had changed in him since our last visit. Clearly, he had warmed a bit, though I was still leery of touching him, even accidentally. I wished he would help me.

"So when are you going to marry your boyfriend?"

"We broke up," I said. My voice sounded very thin.

"What's wrong with that guy!" Kendall slapped the table in hilarity. "Give me his address! It's because of the thing with me—you know, what you're writing."

He didn't mean it. He was shaking with laughter at his own joke. But Kendall recognized the pain tightening my silence, and he grew quiet. Puzzlement flittered across his face.

"I'm sorry," he said, averting his gaze. "Wrong question, I guess."

I knew Kendall couldn't feel for me. Every book on psychopaths addressed the issue of conscience and empathy, affirming that a killer like Kendall had none. But at the sight of my hurt, he had shown mercy.

"The cops keep telling me to watch out for you," I said. "They think you killed more than eight."

"The police in Poughkeepsie are morons. It's not like I was trying real hard not to get caught. I let them into my house. I took a lie detector test."

"I know that's true, but—"

"I don't lie to you," Kendall said, locking my gaze. "If I don't want to answer something, I don't answer. But I don't lie. I care about you."

"What?"

"I care about you," he said very softly.

I tried to ignore the sensation of prickles on my skin.

"So what about Michelle Eason?"

"What about her?"

"The police think you killed her, too."

Kendall looked at me, jumpy and pop-eyed.

"I never even knew Michelle Eason."

Not precisely a denial, nor an outright lie. He'd passed his polygraph the same way. An investigator had ticked off the names, one by one, asking about each of the disappeared women and whether Kendall was responsible for their deaths. It was a question of interpretation with him, always.

"Why do you think you passed that first polygraph?" I asked.

"Maybe I thought it was true, at least true as I saw it."

"You thought it was the women's fault? That you had nothing to do with killing them?"

"No, I'm not saying that. I know I deserve to be dead."

On the night he confessed, the police had asked Kendall to hook himself to their machine once again. But this time he refused. Perhaps he feared questions about his family. Or all that he'd done up in that attic. Or whether there were other victims no one had ever asked about.

We stared at each other like grade-school kids, Kendall daring me with a half smile and me gazing back, wishing my eyes could bore into his brain.

I was interested in his dreams, what he imagined from the safety of Attica, whether he pined for home or had fantasized a world into which he might fit.

"If you ever got out of here, where would you go?"

"If I ever escaped, I'd want to live on a tropical island or on top of some mountain—somewhere with no people."

"Do you wish you were out of here?"

"Yes," he said slowly. "And no."

It was precisely this conflict that made me think a trace of humanity still lay twisted in the wreckage of Kendall's heart. He was the guilty one. But he had not developed in isolation, and the question of blame became more complicated the longer one looked.

"You know they were going to book me for assault the night I confessed, right?" Kendall blurted. "It would have been just like before—a couple of nights in jail, and I'd have been out in a few days. I confessed because I thought I was going to get the death penalty, and it would all be over. I'd be gone."

"Is that what you wanted?"

Kendall looked at the table again, then lifted his head and smiled weakly.

What is it to walk the earth knowing you are deformed inside?

Kendall missed the world and its people. He pined for bookstores and educational television, the independence of a long drive and the right to order take-out Chinese. But the idea of freedom was complicated for him, and his anger terrifying. He was a beast who understood he had permanently left our shores, but he looked back wistfully.

"You are not only the things you did," I said. "There is more to you than your crimes."

"Thank you." He sighed like one released from an enchantment. "Thank you for finally saying that."

"If you talked about some of this, it might put things to rest."

How blithely I urged Kendall to open his diseased soul, while I was loath to do the same. My own secrets remained bandaged-over fever blisters, so reluctant was I to confront the shames cross-hatching my past. And there was nothing on earth, Kendall knew, that could heal shame like his. He gazed at me for a few long seconds, as if weighing a decision, then shook his head.

"Look, it's nothing against you—I just can't," he said.

We sat quietly, Kendall shuffling the same deck of cards I'd brought to our last visit, dealing out hands for gin rummy. This provided a breather for both of us. I was too distracted to play well, and it was a relief to allow Kendall this easy superiority. I wondered what would happen if I won.

"That's what you should be doing," he said, nodding at a girl in white shorts walking across the room toward a man with a large camera, her ponytail swinging.

"What?"

"Getting your picture taken for me."

It was what all the prison girlfriends did, handing over ten dollars for a print their boyfriends could study later.

"I'm not your girlfriend. I'm trying to understand why you did what you did."

"I know, I know," Kendall chuckled. "A guy can dream, can't he?"

Most of Kendall's life had been taken up with dreams—fantasy literature, fantasy girlfriends. Reality was next to impossible for him. But I was no longer throwing myself against stone walls. I was trying to stay within the possible.

"I'll need to be going soon," I said.

"What time?" he demanded, suddenly cold. "And what else are you going to buy me before you go?"

"Forget it," I said. "I'll leave now."

"No, no! Wait! Forget the food—I won't get anything! You don't have to go!"

About his family, Kendall would remain sealed. About his crimes, alternately bashful and coy. But on the subject of my presence, Kendall was rabid. I sat for another twenty minutes, playing cards poorly, plotting my exit. Finally, I sucked in a breath of prison air.

"I really do have to leave. It's a long drive back." I stood up slowly. I knew what was coming.

"Will you give me a hug before you go?" he asked, expectant as a puppy hoping for table scraps.

"No. But I will shake your hand."

I extended my arm, and Kendall grabbed me, spreading my fingers wide. He hooked his between them, slammed his other hand on top, and I was caught. His skin was cool, dry. But his clasp was iron. It was need, raw need—nothing polite, professional, or mutual about it. Electricity crackled up my elbow. Kendall gazed into my eyes. He was beaming.

Through all the years when I balked at the idea of touching him,

I'd never considered this moment anything more than an exercise. Symbolic, but without inherent meaning. How wrong I'd been. I looked down at him and saw something infantile, undeveloped, purely reactive. People told me that with Kendall all was a game. But that was not entirely accurate, either. This was a man of reptilian impulses, with only intermittent control. I drew my hand back and he did not resist. Nor did he exactly release me. He forced me to be honest. To state who I was and what I would no longer accept. Still mocking, half imploring, he kept smiling into my eyes as I reclaimed myself and finally pulled away.

CHAPTER 17

Discharged

I walked into the sunshine and dialed my mother from a pay phone. She asked what had drawn me to this strange quest and held me for so long. I told her that I'd wanted to be the girl who could unlock Kendall's secrets, trace the contours of his mind, and explain him to the world. I did not tell her why I needed to understand rage like his. I said that in chasing answers, I'd crossed a barren field inside myself to hold a monster's hand. I did not explain that he had become the silhouette of all my nightmares. I said only that the girl who'd written to him five years before was gone now. She'd died inside the walls of Attica.

Shame had banished me to the woods of upstate New York and kept me quiet about my reasons for corresponding with a killer. But writing about it brought me back. When I'd staggered away from the wreckage of my years with Derrick, I couldn't look at myself long enough to keep an honest journal. I alluded to my failures in code, without using proper names. But now I saw a self taking shape, pushed onto the page by a man with vise-grip hands who had forced me to speak. Into the unknown I sent more pages about our psychological wrestling match and found myself invited to write in Wyoming and Washington, places I'd only wondered at when Derrick and I drove across the west.

Still, the decision to leave my old life, which also meant leaving Kendall, took shape slowly. At first, I could hardly picture it without shaking. In many ways I was doing just as he had predicted, abandoning him when he was no longer of use—though not for the reasons either of us had anticipated. The idea of wounding him this way both terrified and tantalized me. But I was done explaining myself. I needed to act. I planned well, filing a last story for the *Times* and shaking the hands of many editors who promised to keep me in mind for work down the road, despite the fact that I had no idea what I would do when I got there. I gave away old paintings and clothes, childhood books and family treasures from the desperate years in Connecticut. Any usable furniture I left to fate by the side of a country road. That was all it took. I recovered my rent security, scrubbed the toilet bowl, and I was severed.

My idea was to head for Seattle, driving the same car I'd used to visit Kendall in prison. But now a five-hour hunk of highway was just a morning's progress. I plunged across miles, scanning the artifacts of my past piled in the backseat—a hundred pounds of notes and files on Kendall's case, literature that had acted like a life raft, photographs of friends who hadn't called since the 1980s. By the time I crossed the Pennsylvania border, I was cackling with joy. My first stop would be Pittsburgh, where a college friend researching AIDS was suffering through marriage to a man who hated humanity. I tore through Ohio and Indiana aided by phone calls from an old boyfriend who wanted to know what I was seeing: eighteen-wheelers with slatted sides, through which I locked eyes with calves on the way to slaughter, so mangy and forlorn that I opted to describe the sunsets for him instead. In Chicago, I slept in the sleek loft of an art historian friend whose marble bathroom was littered with hundred-dollar skin creams. She corralled me at the breakfast table after her husband had left for work. "All of us are living through you," she said.

On my way out of the Hudson Valley, I'd made a quick detour to check the mail, and found a letter from Kendall waiting in the Pleasant Valley post office. But I did not open it. I shoved the envelope into a suitcase and tried to forget it was there. Nor did I leave a forwarding address. I thought of Kendall ranting in his cell, scrawling blistering screeds at his entreaties unanswered. But I could not waver. I wanted nothing pulling me back. I needed velocity.

It took ten days to drive across America because I kept stopping at oddities along the way. In Wisconsin, I found a monument to obsession built by a self-trained architect fixated on Frank Lloyd Wright. Alex Jordan's sprawling House on the Rock was a maze of interconnected caverns jammed full of swords and rotary telephones; antique cash registers and vacant-eyed china dolls. Life-sized model elephants mounted each other in a pyramid. An orchestra of mannequins stood poised to play. Serpents and satyrs spun round on an enormous carousel beneath naked women hanging from the ceiling. It was like running through a child's nightmare.

"All by yourself?" breathed a guard in the darkness as I hurried along, outracing the phantoms.

"You're doing very well," smiled a toothless attendant stationed on the cobblestone streets of a fake European village.

At night, I wheeled into gas stations lit up like operating rooms and slept in motels that smelled of the past. "Just you, is it?" said a narrow-eyed boy appraising me from behind the front desk at one in Minnesota. I slept poorly most nights, memories thronging my dreams. Everyone I'd ever known came at me in the dark—teachers who'd exacted petty humiliations, former friends who'd seen my stumbles as an invitation to scorn. But the road washes away every indignity. I was untouchable, out of time. I sped forward into endless horizon, and years faded behind me. By the time I hit the yellow fields of South Dakota, I was free. Doing ninety across Montana, I took off my shirt and drove half-naked.

At breakfast buffets, where fat families squawked over unlimited waffles and political candidates yammered from ceaseless television, I'd sometimes doodle good-bye notes to Kendall. I never sent any of them. On the Oregon coast, I made straight for the wide windswept beach and there, settling my back against a low dune, I finally read his letter. I had never mentioned leaving. My last communication had been filled with all the usual questions about his past and his ghosts and his dreams. But he must have sensed the need to keep me close with something more.

> *Hey Elf,*
>
> *How I "deal" with the awful things I've done is personal. Even if I wanted to pour my heart out to you, I couldn't. . . . It is far more complicated than you know. Rage was the vehicle, but not the cause or the trigger. I no longer believe "anger management" would have helped me. I may have prevented the deaths of those women, but I think I would've needed much more involved therapy. People will never get what they want from me, because I died many years ago and several times.*

Melodramatic and self-aggrandizing as ever, but among the most revealing letters Kendall had ever sent. A pang in my chest. Had I cut off too soon, abandoned a ruined man at the point of revelation? The old Kendall was still there, of course, asking me to do him favors, send messages, run down those he'd abused. This time the quest was finding a girl named Heather. Kendall said he owed her an apology. "I should've helped her, but I realize now that I wasn't in a place to help myself. . . . Maybe if I apologize, I can regain something lost, repair a part that is broken. . . ."

I'd wanted something from him—knowledge, connection, and strangely, forgiveness, as if a moral leper held the keys to absolution. But the closer I got, the more clearly I saw that Kendall did not have any of the answers I sought. All he could do was show me more ways to see myself. I put his letter away and gazed at the ocean. He had tried, in his fashion, to point me in the right direction. But I'd been so blind, inventing a game that said if I was "real" with Kendall he would be "real" with me, though I could never abide by my own terms. I dodged and lied and redrew the boundaries again and again: I was the journalist; I made the rules. He was the subject who should be grateful for the chance to tell his story, when I could hardly face my own.

I FOUND A newspaper job in Seattle with editors who were happy to have me run down the marginal and despised. I wrote about alcoholics who let their babies starve, and teenage boys who killed teenage girls. I knocked on the door of a defrocked priest living in a trailer park, who opened it wearing the same velvet bedroom slippers his victims had described. I interviewed senior-citizen pimps and middle school gangsters and mothers who let their toddlers wander four-lane highways. Through every story, Kendall was with me, a tape measure I compared against people whose stories I tried to tell. He cast them all in a different light. He made the reviled redeemable.

His victims remained with me too, their names listed on Dr. Stone's chart; I propped it in a corner of every apartment I rented, still looking for patterns, unable to let go. I thought of Kendall when I got married, and had a child, and learned to love. Online, I kept track of the Francoises, watching as Kendall's brother built a family, his little sister earned a college degree, his mother continued working as a nurse. They posted pictures on social media, no longer afraid to show themselves. Now and then I typed his name into search engines to see what came up—a tawdry paperback, a college research paper, a grainy video. Kendall was no Hollywood killer, and he had been forgotten, left to languish in a fast-fading century.

IN AUGUST 2014, eleven years after leaving Dutchess County, I bought a plane ticket back to New York, intending to confront the past. I'd written hundreds of pages about my conversations with Kendall Francois but had been unable to finish the book because I couldn't figure out how to resolve what I'd done. At least I could measure myself against the person I had been. I would drive upstate and wend south, through the town where Derrick and I once lived, the streets where Kendall wandered, to the home where my parents still read the papers every morning. I pondered a visit to Attica. It would mean arriving unannounced, and Kendall hated that, but I knew he'd be curious to see me. Still weighing the idea, I typed his name into New York's Inmate Look-Up website several hours before my departure. I'd been doing so for years as a kind of penance or ceremony of remembrance. There was never any variation, nothing beyond the words *ATTICA* and *MURDER* and *LIFE SENTENCE*.

TRANSFERRED, the screen said this time. And then a name, Wende. Wendy?

A shiver burned through me. I sat at my desk in the *Seattle Times* newsroom, assigned to write about education but poring through documents on Wende Correctional Facility. It was a maximum-security prison with a special section for inmates in need of medical or mental health treatment. After fourteen years of stasis, Kendall had been admitted the very day I was coming back. I found a picture of him, haggard and gray, an old man in his forties.

I kissed my family good-bye at the Seattle airport, and the next morning staggered off a redeye into JFK, then boarded a bus for Grand Central Station and a train to Poughkeepsie. I wondered if Kendall could feel me now, circling close. In the old days, months sometimes passed without communication between us until someone broke down and sent a note. More than once, our letters crossed in the mail, postmarked with identical dates. I drove the Hudson Valley, remembering secret shortcuts and unmarked turnoffs until I found myself back at the hideaway shack in the woods where Derrick and I had lived. The landlord who'd hoarded rusty tools and broken appliances in the garage was dead, and someone who loved the place lived there. The grounds were tidy, Derrick's old trashed office was fringed with a balcony of potted plants, and affixed to a pine tree high above the driveway was one of those pithy signs so beloved by country dwellers: THINGS TURN OUT BEST FOR THOSE WHO MAKE THE BEST OF HOW THINGS TURN OUT.

I pulled over and called Wende. Kendall's new caseworker, a woman, said she'd just met him for the first time that morning. "He was tired. Able to communicate, but tired—very polite, though."

She sounded pleasantly surprised.

"Will he be there for just a short while, or is this more of an open-ended stay?"

She paused, treading carefully. "He'll be with us for the foreseeable."

I could take one more swing and offer Kendall a final chance get his licks in. Or I could show mercy to us both. I drove into Poughkeepsie, where a new generation of women lingered on Main Street, to Fulton Avenue, where another family had moved into Kendall's old home, so much layering-over that there was no longer any requirement to notify tenants of the atrocities that had taken place within those walls. But someone who knew had been making regular visits. On the sidewalk out front, a tree stump had been sculpted into a fairy house with a pond made of eight moonstones and a sign on its four-inch door. IN LOVING MEMORY, it said. Kendall's real-life home towered above, and it too bore a sign bravely facing the street, which spelled in thorny wicker letters the word LOVE.

I'd thought, once, that Kendall choosing me to correspond with signified something; all it meant was that I was as lost and desperate as his other victims. He had indeed killed that part of me, that vain and fragile girl. He'd forced me to confront the weakest parts of myself. But I'd built a life of which I was no longer ashamed, and ghosts from the past did not frighten me anymore. I thought of Kendall Francois and felt a disquieting gratitude. I didn't need to see him. But I did want this force from my nightmares to know what had happened when I left it behind. I wanted to tell him good-bye.

Adams Fairacre Farms, the market where I'd spent so many afternoons searching for cards to send Kendall, was three minutes' drive from his home. A song about broken families keened from the speakers. I chose a note bearing a picture of a dark sunset and sat down, once more, to write.

September 1, 2014

Dear Kendall,

I've thought for eleven years about this letter, about what I should say and what you deserve to hear about why I vanished without apology. People told me that I owed a serial murderer no explanation. But I never believed that. So here is my answer.

After our last visit at Attica, I drove three thousand miles and did not look back. I needed to make a new life. I needed to see if I could learn how to live in a family. And I think the journey began long before I turned onto I-84. I think it began with you.

In your letters, you often signed off by saying you hoped I was healthy and happy. I was neither. When I first wrote you, and in all the letters afterward, I was searching for proof that redemption was possible. No wonder you found me so exasperating.

Often you accused me of failing to listen. You were right. There were so many voices in my head that it was hard to hear. Voices shouting about what I wanted from you. Voices of judgment. Voices of my family and friends. But in all this, my own voice was silent.

You were the start of a very long road. To reach its end, I had to walk away. So I got into my car and drove alone for more than a week. I knew no one on the other side and I was terrified, but fear was normal for me then. I know you wanted to get away too, once. I know you tried. But I wish you had tried harder. I wish you had been stronger. I wish you had been able to build a new life for yourself instead of destroying everything that reminded you of the past. None of those women were your problem. I hope you figured that out. They were just symbols and body doubles, reminding you of ghosts.

You never wanted to tell me your secret life, and it is still yours. What I have written, the book you were so frightened of, is my secret life.

> *Thank you for showing me who I needed to be,*
> *Claudia*

Kendall died ten days later. He had no special knowledge or preternatural charm. He was what I'd made him.

After his death, the experts chimed in, pointing out how little "insight" Kendall had shown during his sixteen years in prison, how he'd minimized his crimes and neutralized culpability by maintaining his insistence that the women were not "innocent." I had to laugh. A serial killer who was grandiose and refused to look honestly at himself—wasn't that true by definition? The most meaningful thing about Kendall was not his avoidance of apology, nor his flouting our rules of confession and grace. It was that he'd started out like any of us, drawing pictures, playing with his siblings, even as the deficits in his home grew to a murderous thicket in his mind; even as they choked the oxygen of reason from his fantasies and left him to rail at the world with bruises that would not heal. That thicket inside Kendall concealed acts I did not want to imagine. But through it he watched me, peering curiously between the thorns. He'd once wanted the same things I did: someone to love, a career, a place in the fabric of life. He was a version of me, a comment on us. He was humanity emaciated and twisted by vast lack. It was not a mythic darkness that drove Kendall Francois. But rather, frailty.

I AM WALKING in the Pacific Northwest, on a country lane where there are no cars and no moonlight. A wet winter night without shimmer. I move through the velvet black, a darkness so deep it becomes possible to imagine I exist only as a consciousness floating through the world.

Without a body.

Without a story.

Darkness like this used to freeze me senseless. Secrets lived there, hands that could grab from unlit hallways I crossed without breathing. In my pocket, I fiddle with two talismans that return me to the present: a pen from the Motel 6 outside Attica, New York, and a deck of cards I once used to play gin rummy with a killer. It is late December, and I am headed to a holiday party where I know no one, in a country town where I have never been, on a road with no signs. But I like the sound of my footsteps echoing, crisp and solitary in the night. After a quarter mile I turn onto a narrow path and wonder if I have the right house. I knock, still unsure. Anyone could answer. Anything could happen. My life might change right here. I hear a voice coming toward me and brace as the door opens onto a warm room bursting with music and laughter and light.

Epilogue

I t took me more than a decade to make sense of my correspondence with Kendall Francois.

In my attempts to run down the riddle of this cypher, I'd behaved like an addict. I could not stop. Kendall knew the type, and like any dealer he kept me hanging on, promising that he needed only six months, a year, maybe two, to "put things in order" before he could give me the kind of accounting I craved. Often, he claimed his silence was driven by fear that I would use his words against him. A laughable concern, I scoffed to myself—what could he possibly have to lose?

But now, thirteen years after receiving Kendall's last letter, Horton's theories float back to me, and Alston's worried face, and I wonder if Kendall had something more specific in mind. I wonder if he was referring to Michelle Eason. Such a disclosure could have voided his deal with New York State and reopened the case. Kendall surely knew this. But I think back to his pop-eyed discomfort at my questions about Michelle, the way his manner changed from coy to quiet, the way he would not meet my gaze.

As years passed, police expected to see pieces of Michelle wash up on the shores of the Hudson, which sometimes happens with missing persons from the area. But no. To this day, no one has ever found a trace.

Lieutenant Bill Siegrist believes she is somewhere in the Dutchess County woods, the only one of Kendall's victims to receive a burial. He is retired now, a doting grandfather who spends mornings hunting, afternoons helping with homework. For forty years, he thrilled whenever his phone rang at night, and by the time he quit in 2009, Siegrist discovered that he no longer knew how to how to be home. He is learning. But he misses policing. Nothing since has felt quite as real.

Margie Smith rarely looks back. She retired in 2014, bought an enormous kiln, and now makes glass art. "My life is good," she said recently, before a long camping trip. "No dead people."

Walt Horton, too, has moved on. He left the Poughkeepsie detective squad after forty-three years with the department and turned toward a career in real estate. Nowadays, when he and Siegrist get together for lunch, Horton tries to convince his old boss not to reminisce too much. But the past lives inside all of us. Regret lingers. I contacted Horton recently to go over his memories of that time, and he used the phrase *in hindsight* more than once.

Skip Mannain ended his police career under investigation. He'd rushed to the scene of an outdoor shooting—a suicidal man had just murdered his girlfriend in broad daylight near the railroad tracks—and as another officer moved in, Mannain watched. He saw the gunman grab his colleague around the neck. He saw the man pull his colleague's service revolver from its holster, shoot the officer, and then himself. All the while, Mannain held his fire. The district attorney found no official wrongdoing, but Mannain never worked another day on the job. "As a cop, you walk a tightrope," said Siegrist, defending his ersatz son. "Skip made a judgment call. Everything you do as a police officer is judgment calls."

Like journalism.

So often reporters believe what I did initially, that if only we ask the right question all doors will open. But that is magical thinking. The key is always in the hands of the source, who has decided long before the first conversation how much he wants to tell, Janet Malcolm suggests in *The Journalist and the Murderer,* her meditation on the duel between a writer and source. "At bottom, no subject is naïve," she adds. "Every subject of writing knows on some level what is in store for him, and remains in the relationship anyway, impelled by something stronger than his reason."

Hunger for recognition compelled Kendall. Simultaneously, he believed I saw him only as a vein to be mined and exploited. If he revealed everything, Kendall once said, I'd disappear and never speak to him again. Malcolm believes a subject lives in dread of this moment.

For years I wondered what Kendall thought when I stopped writing and vanished without explanation. Did he rage in his cell? Curse my name to anyone who would listen? Send solicitous notes to my old post office box, trying to tempt me back? I imagine that he told himself I'd betrayed him, just as he'd predicted I would. But Kendall always meant more to me than he understood. And I believe part of him truly wanted me to be the friend we both pretended I was.

Acknowledgments

This book took eighteen years, all told, from the day I first wrote to Kendall Francois to final publication. That includes nearly a decade when I walked away from it, telling myself I would never be able to get on top of this material. Such a long gestation necessarily means many people have touched this project at different times. For early faith in my story, thanks goes first to the Eastern Frontier Society and the Hedgebrook Retreat for women writers. Journalists Mike Lewis, M. L. Lyke, and Carol Smith provided years of literary counsel and razor insights. Novelist Jennie Shortridge showed me life-changing generosity. For her pluck, grit, and incisive reading, my agent Stephanie Rostan deserves a medal. We all encounter people who see us faster, perhaps, than we are prepared to be seen. Carrie Thornton, my editor at Dey Street, is one of those. She perceived what this book could be five minutes into our first phone conversation and pushed me to make it better. Greg Villepique peppered me with the kind of eagle-eyed questions that warm a reporter's heart. And at HarperCollins, Michael Barrs, Heidi Richter, Kaitlyn Kennedy, and Sean Newcott showed an enthusiasm for this project that went far beyond their official duties. Artist Trust in Washington State, Jack Straw Foundation, and the Sustainable Arts Foundation provided important financial and moral support. Judith Lessinger, M.S.W., Dr. Stuart Kleinman, and Dr. Ken Muscatel provided incisive counsel on mental illness.

The Kendall Francois story was painful for many people, and I honor those who shared their experience of it with me. In particular, Pat Barone, Marguerite Marsh, Tammy Coppola, Heidi Cramer, James DeSalvo, and Assistant District Attorney Margie Smith. The police in this case came under bitter criticism, and for their willingness to share moments of struggle and question I wish to thank retired Detective Lieutenant William Siegrist, as well as Detectives Walter Horton, Theodore Alston, and Karl Mannain, and police investigators Arthur Boyko and Tommy Martin. I must also acknowledge my mother, father, and sister, who knew this book would expose difficult points in our family's past, and at some personal cost allowed me to take us all on a journey of memory and reconciliation. Their love through many storms is a testament to the possibility of growth and change in a family. Finally, to my family of today, Dan, Maiselle, and Gabriel, who broke the spell.

Author's Note

This is a work of nonfiction based on interviews, original reporting, police records, and letters. In sections of personal narrative where I relied on childhood memories, I have made every effort to fact-check these stories with those who were present. All characters are referred to by their real names, except for Donte Turner and Derrick, which are pseudonyms.

About the Author

CLAUDIA ROWE is an award-winning journalist who has been twice nominated for the Pulitzer Prize. Her work has been published in numerous newspapers and magazines, including the *New York Times, Mother Jones,* Huffington Post, *Woman's Day, Yes!* and Seattle's alternative weekly, *The Stranger.* Currently, Claudia is a staff writer at the *Seattle Times.* Her coverage of social issues, race, and violence has been honored by the Society of Professional Journalists, the Nieman Foundation for Journalism at Harvard University, and the Journalism Center on Children & Families, which awarded her a Casey Medal for Meritorious Journalism.